Nelson Glueck

BIBLICAL ARCHAEOLOGIST AND PRESIDENT OF
HEBREW UNION COLLEGE - JEWISH INSTITUTE OF RELIGION

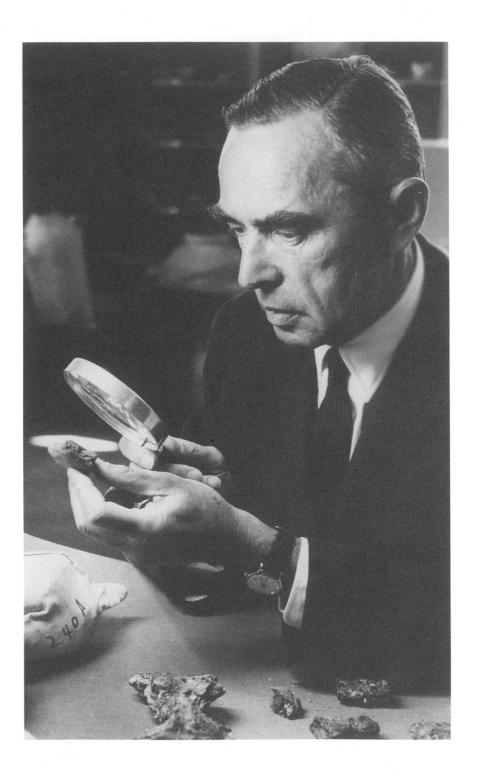

Nelson Glueck

BIBLICAL ARCHAEOLOGIST AND PRESIDENT OF
HEBREW UNION COLLEGE - JEWISH INSTITUTE OF RELIGION

Jonathan M. Brown
Laurence Kutler

ALUMNI SERIES OF THE
HEBREW UNION COLLEGE PRESS

Jonathan Brown and Laurence Kutler
*Nelson Glueck: Biblical Archaeologist and President of the
Hebrew Union College-Jewish Institute of Religion*

Solomon B. Freehof
Reform Responsa
Recent Reform Responsa
Current Reform Responsa
Modern Reform Responsa
Contemporary Reform Responsa
Reform Responsa for our Time
New Reform Responsa
Today's Reform Responsa

Walter Jacob
Christianity Through Jewish Eyes

Samuel Karff
Agada: The Language of Jewish Faith

Hayim Goren Perelmuter
David Darshan's Song of the Steps and In Defense of Preachers

Sanford Ragins
Jewish Responses to Anti-Semitism in Germany, 1870–1914

Joseph R. Rosenbloom
Conversion to Judaism: From the Biblical Period to the Present

In memory of my parents,
Abraham W. Brown and Sally Glueck Brown,
who taught me the importance of family.

To my wife and beloved friend Gracie,
who helped me create and raise one.

To Laura, Andy, Debbie, and Sharon,
whose support and love are beyond measuring.

Jonathan Brown

In memory of my parents,
Gerald and Florence Kutler,
who taught me to think.

To my wife Caren,
who taught me to love.

To my children, Noam and Yona,
who continue to teach me humility.

Laurence Kutler

Library of Congress Cataloging-in-Publication Data

Brown, Jonathan M.

Nelson Glueck: Biblical Archaeologist and President of Hebrew
Union College-Jewish Institute of Religion/Jonathan M. Brown,
Laurence Kutler.

p. cm.
Includes bibliographical references and index.

ISBN 0-87820-119-x (alk. paper)

1. Glueck Nelson, 1900–. 2. Jewish scholars — United States —
Biography. 3. Rabbis — United States — Biography. 4. Archaeol-
ogists — United States — Biography. 5. Jewish college presidents
— United States — Biography. I. Kutler, Laurence. II. Title.

BM755.G56B76 2005
296.8'341'092–dc22 [B] 2005050308

Printed on acid-free paper in the United States of America
Design and composition by Kelby & Teresa Bowers
Distribution by Wayne State University Press
4809 Woodward Avenue, Detroit, Michigan 48201

Contents

Foreword

This book is about a unique human being whose many gifts of mind and heart enabled him to make an indelible imprint on the contours of Jewish life in both America and Israel. Born at the turn of the last century, Nelson Glueck was a native son of Cincinnati who liked to call himself a spiritual son of Jerusalem. He lived an extraordinary life in tumultuous times.

He grew up in the West End neighborhood of Cincinnati, in the most modest of circumstances. His family was Yiddish-speaking, although he feigned in later life not to understand that language. Glueck came out of his home environment always sensitive to the economic privations of his youth. Once, in a confessional mode, he revealed that he had been a "change boy" in an automat in downtown Cincinnati. The tip was usually a penny or two for having run to the cashier for a diner who wanted to use a particular automat window. Having experienced privation, he was austere and frugal in his lifestyle throughout his life. Like the Bedouin with whom he traveled in his surveys of Transjordan and the Negev, Glueck could survive on a handful of figs, if necessary, on his journey through the most arid of deserts in and surrounding the Holy Land.

Glueck was reared in an Orthodox Jewish environment and developed a mystical approach to faith and a fervent attachment to the people and Land of Israel. While in his latter years he would often make sport of those who liked to wear piety on their sleeves, he was in his own way a pious person whose sense of being at one with the "God of his fathers" was a constant energizing force in his life.

Growing up in Cincinnati, he realized that if he was to break out of the immigrant milieu that was so prevalent there after World War I, he had to excel as a scholar. Accomplishing this task came easily to him, for he was a brilliant student, a quick study, and thorough in the preparation of all his academic endeavors. Glueck realized that through the funnel of the Hebrew Union College, located in Cincinnati, a first-class education was obtainable, both on the undergraduate and graduate theological levels.

His closest friend on the faculty, just a few years older than Glueck himself, was Jacob Rader Marcus, the senior in a cadre of young scholars who went to Germany for their Ph.D. studies. Marcus was one of the first to sense that Glueck had a predisposition towards Bible and classical

Near Eastern Studies. I had the privilege of translating from the German the doctoral dissertation Glueck wrote for the University of Jena. *Ḥesed in the Bible* was and still is considered a classic. It explores the biblical concept of *ḥesed* as "mutual aid and responsibility," values that remained part of Glueck's personal ethos all his life.

Glueck's love of the Bible and the Holy Land led him in the 1920s to participate in excavations of ancient Israel with William Foxwell Albright, famed already as a pioneer in the field of biblical archaeology. In a conversation with the late Professor Albright, I learned of Glueck's extraordinary memory for the artifacts he had seen and touched and his uncanny ability to arrive at the proper dating and categorization of the potsherds they had unearthed.

Glueck's years of literally wandering in the desert transformed him into a bold and fearless person. In crises, Glueck came forward and assumed command, but in the presence of politicians and manipulators, he often found himself at a disadvantage. Perhaps that was to his credit. Not always subtle, he remained steadfast in the pursuit of his goals and in his devotion to genuine scholarship. As president of the Hebrew Union College-Jewish Institute of Religion, he was more of an enthusiast than an administrator. Glueck's vision and his capacity to "light up" the eyes and kindle the hearts of others served him well. He was a superb fund-raiser and under his presidency — and because of his vision — the College-Institute flourished. He expanded the campuses of the College from one Cincinnati location to include schools in New York, Los Angeles, and Jerusalem. In California he encouraged the creation of the Schools of Jewish Communal Service and Jewish Education. And in Israel he founded and nurtured the School of Biblical and Archaeological Studies in Jerusalem.

My own relationship with Nelson Glueck began when I was a rabbinical student at the New York School of HUC. Like my classmates, I was embroiled in a contest over whether that branch of the College would continue with a full five-year program, and I was transferred to Cincinnati against my will. Although Glueck eventually lost this political struggle, some of his rabbinical colleagues continued to view him with suspicion and anger years after the events involved and the program in New York had been restored.

Nelson Glueck appointed me in 1957, the year of my ordination, as the director of the campus in Los Angeles and as instructor in Jewish history. Throughout my long association with him, I grew to love him for the great strengths that animated him. I also understood his failings, realizing that he was constantly under enormous pressure to balance the geographical interests of all the campuses of the College-Institute. Samuel Sandmel, provost of the College-Institute, Jacob Marcus, and I functioned as an advisory council to President Glueck. In the end, however, it was Glueck's instinct, his intuition, and his understanding that shaped the major decisions of the College-Institute during the long course of his tenure.

Intimations of mortality — the title of the last chapter of this book — came upon Glueck after the Six Day War (1967), when he became quite ill with viral pneumonia. He never fully recovered his strength. It was then that he would often speak to me about the future and what he wanted to see accomplished. I was honored when he expressed the hope that I would lend myself to these aims and purposes. I have rarely regretted the decision to succeed a man whose shoes could not readily be filled and which always had on them the dust of Jerusalem.

Over the years of my presidency (1971–1995), I often looked at the portrait of Glueck that hung in my office. He was a scholar, an archaeologist, and an intimate friend of David Ben-Gurion, Golda Meir, and so many others; he also opened the doors to Progressive Judaism in Israel. Jonathan Brown and Laurence Kutler have sketched the life, thought, and career of this extraordinary man with eloquence and as much objectivity as can be mustered by authors who love their subject and cherish his memory. As they aptly show, although his name means "luck," Nelson Glueck was never one to leave the future to mere chance.

— Alfred Gottschalk, Chancellor Emeritus
Hebrew Union College-Jewish Institute of Religion

Preface

It is 1936. Palestine, populated mainly by Arabs but with a Jewish minority rapidly increasing as Jewish refugees arrive from Hitler's Germany, is heading for anarchy. Riots and unrest are every day's news. Arabs are attacking Jews randomly and at will, and the British Mandatory authorities are trying to maintain order. Eventually it will take one hundred thousand British troops to keep Jews and Arabs apart. The mandate, established through the League of Nations in 1922, is in serious jeopardy.

Arabs, for their part, are denouncing the changes they see as the number of Jews living in Palestine increases by tens of thousands, changes that threaten their established way of life. Jews, on the other hand, are prepared to struggle and sacrifice in their ancient homeland, eager to renew and restore it to former glory. They are also deeply invested in providing the desperate refugees from Germany a place to live as they flee from a Europe soon to erupt into flames. For the Jewish community in Mandatory Palestine (the *yishuv*), the volatile mixture of religious orthodoxy, socialist ideology, British colonial attitudes, and Arab intransigence can lead any day to conflict — or danger.

In 1936 biblical archaeology is seen by many Palestinian Jews as part of the struggle to establish a legitimate claim to a Jewish homeland. It is thought that the Balfour Declaration of November 2, 1917, declaring British support for such a homeland, will prove meaningless if the claim cannot be built upon archaeological evidence and some indication that the stories about Abraham, Isaac, and Jacob and about the exodus from Egypt are more than mere stories. They are viewed as part of a living link with the aspirations of the present, an indispensable part of every Jew's identity.

That is why a thirty-six year old American Jew, Nelson Glueck, opens first a Bible and then a field handbook, and with a scholarly mien, suggests that the route of the exodus from Egypt, dated to the mid-thirteenth century B.C.E., ran along ancient sites bordering Trajan's highway in Transjordan. And that is why, two years later, Glueck stands at the shore of the Red Sea at a site called Tell el-Kheleifeh and proclaims it King Solomon's copper refinery and port. How extraordinary that this American-born Reform rabbi, the son of Orthodox Jewish parents from Lithuania, should find himself at this crucial moment in the Jewish homeland, standing at the juncture of geography and history.

In fact, Glueck's entire life — from his childhood explorations of fossil remains, through his training by the Classics Department of the University of Cincinnati and his pursuit of a doctorate in German universities, and finally his experience in Palestine as the protégé of the eminent archaeologist William Foxwell Albright — led him directly to these moments of discovery.

Glueck revealed the occupational secrets of the plains of Edom and Moab in Transjordan, described in detail the copper-mining industry of the western Negev, and showed how that southern desert portion of modern Israel could actually support a large population if proper irrigation techniques were used. He investigated the successful efforts of the Nabataeans to irrigate that precise area despite scanty rainfall. He published four widely-read books about his discoveries and four thick volumes of scientific research, along with hundreds of articles and monographs. And this was only the first of two careers that he would undertake — and master.

In America, the field of inquiry known as biblical archaeology arose in the 1880s and reached a high point with people like Albright and Glueck (among others) in the twenties and thirties of the new century. Biblical archaeology had emerged from the womb of Protestant theology; Glueck's presence helped add a Jewish perspective. His work brought other Jewish scholars and researchers into the field and eventually created a model for a non-sectarian archaeology.

In 1947 Glueck was invited to become the fourth president of the Hebrew Union College in Cincinnati (preceded by Isaac Mayer Wise, Kaufmann Kohler, and Julian Morgenstern), where he himself had trained for the Reform rabbinate. The institution had been founded in 1875 to prepare liberal rabbis for the American Jewish community, then numbering about two hundred and fifty thousand souls. No one could yet foresee the massive immigration that would spill forth from Russia and Eastern Europe between 1881 and 1924, bringing millions of Jews to Castle Garden, Ellis Island, Galveston, and other ports of entry.

During his twenty-four years as the president of the seminary, Glueck created or assumed responsibility for three additional campuses — in New York, California, and Jerusalem. He supervised the training of hundreds of rabbis, invited scores of Christian seminarians and clergy to obtain advanced degrees and then teach thousands of their own students about Judaism. He built substantial intellectual, emotional, and financial bridges between American Jews and the State of Israel. He was acquainted with America's leaders; he was a personal friend of all of Israel's presidents, prime ministers, ambassadors to the United States, and many other leading political, scholarly, and literary personalities all over the world.

Glueck's prominence was reflected in an invitation he received in the fall of 1960 to deliver the benediction at President John F. Kennedy's inaugural, and by his appearance on the cover of TIME Magazine in December, 1963 as part of a long article proclaiming the magnificent results of biblical archaeology. Wearing Arab head-dress (the *keffiyeh*), sunburnished and gloriously handsome, he epitomized the romantic and exotic nature of archaeology in the first half of the twentieth century.

Glueck played a series of interconnected roles: first as a scholar and archaeologist, then as an operative with the OSS (Office of Strategic Services — the forerunner of the CIA), finally as a leader of American Reform Jewry. His contribution to the field of archaeology, as well as his advancement to pre-eminence in American Reform Jewry, gained him national renown and a significant place in the history of twentieth-century American Jewry.

The scope of Glueck's life and the conundrums that define it have never been portrayed in a full-length biography. This book sets out to pose the questions, to probe the motivations, and to appreciate the complexities of an extraordinary human being. We see Glueck as the product of his time, a man grappling with immense historical realities and complex contemporary circumstances, constantly refining his theories and his relationship to Reform Judaism, Zionism, and the Jewish state. We also see, on occasion, a man struggling to control his anger and his impulses.

How did this rabbi come to suggest and defend a radically new basis for understanding the Bible? How did he achieve the success in two careers that few men or women achieve in one? If we look carefully at Glueck's efforts to attain social status through his rabbinical education and his marriage, his heritage of dissent, his ability to be comfortable in widely disparate settings, and his fascination with the character of T. E. Lawrence (Lawrence of Arabia), the strands come together.

In creating a detailed portrait of this intrepid adventurer and acknowledged leader, we have examined Glueck's correspondence from 1923 to 1971, his field notes, and other files available at the Jacob Rader Marcus Center of the American Jewish Archives in Cincinnati and at archival resources in Boston, New York, London, and Jerusalem. We have conducted scores of interviews, read unpublished studies dealing with Glueck's presidency at the Hebrew Union College, perused hundreds of articles and off-prints written by and about him, and carefully reviewed Glueck's own published works. Other sources are duly noted in the notes and bibliography.

Irony and ambivalence accompanied Glueck throughout his life. Sometimes he seemed like a naif (in Weimar), sometimes like a prophet (speaking with David Ben-Gurion). He was entranced by the biblical personalities who trod the same paths he did in the highlands of Moab or the hills of Judea. More than any other twentieth-century archaeologist, Glueck transformed the way people viewed the biblical heritage. More than any other American Reform Jew, Glueck built a solid bridge between American and Israeli Jewry. The time is ripe, as we enter the twenty-first century, for a richer and fuller portrait of this wandering Jew, who in his mature years found a way to sustain his desire for individual exploits while leading and enlarging the influence of an academic institution of great spiritual significance.

*

Many individuals and several institutions have helped us with the research for this book, and scores of people discussed with us various aspects of Nelson Glueck's life and work. We hope that each and every one of them will accept our sincere gratitude for their contributions.

Among Glueck's family members, his wife Helen and her sister Josephine Joseph were particularly helpful. Her daughter-in-law, Barbara Weinberger Glueck, provided photos and access to hundreds of Glueck's letters to the family and has graciously clarified situations about which she had first-hand knowledge. Several of the cousins on Helen's side of the family, notably Bill and Regine Ransohoff, took substantial interest in the project. Of Glueck's family of origin, his brothers Harry and Hill, along with Harry's wife Lillian, contributed their recollections of the early years. Glueck's older brother Nathan (1897–1982) edited a family newsletter in the 1940s that served as a useful source. Several of Glueck's nieces and nephews were also of assistance. Alan Shapiro, who served on the HUC Board of Governors for the New York School, provided helpful information, as did Tasia (Revel) Melvin, who provided copies of her father's family newsletter, photographs, and much encouragement.

The input of Glueck's mentor and life-long friend Jacob R. Marcus was invaluable in the early stages of the project. His recollections were especially significant inasmuch as he served as acting president in Glueck's absence during much of Glueck's twenty-four year tenure at HUC. Marcus's papers and insights (which we were able to glean during the last year of his life) gave us much insight into the ways in which Glueck operated. Other vital sources of information were Alfred Gottschalk, Glueck's successor as president of the College-Institute, and the following long-time faculty members: Eugene Borowitz, Edward Goldman, Samuel Greengus, Robert L. Katz, Eugene Mihaly, Ellis Rivkin, Richard Sarason, and Ezra Spicehandler. The late Paul Steinberg, dean of the New York School for forty years, not only recalled the early days of the Jewish Institute of Religion, but also worked closely with Glueck in establishing the Jerusalem school's first major initiative, the Summer Institutes in Near Eastern Civilizations.

We are grateful for the information provided in two unpublished works: Daniel Syme wrote his rabbinical thesis on HUC's first four presidents, and Ariel Stone wrote a detailed commissioned piece about the history of HUC-JIR in Jerusalem. Michael A. Meyer's essay on Glueck, "With Vision and Boldness," which appeared in Samuel Karff's centennial history of the HUC-JIR, was a constant reference point for this work, as was his *Response to Modernity: A History of the Reform Movement in Judaism*. Further, his willingness to translate correspondence from German to English helped ensure that vital information was available to us. Ellen Norman Stern, author of *Dreamer in the Desert: A Profile of Nelson Glueck,* also offered encouragement and advice.

Many alumni of the Hebrew Union College-Jewish Institute of Religion responded to requests for information and anecdotes; they are identified in the footnotes, and we are grateful for their assistance. Hayyim Goren Perelmutter deserves special thanks for supplying a sheaf of correspondence relating to the proposed name change for HUC-JIR in 1957. Our gratitude also to Wolli Kaelter and Gunther Plaut for recalling their arrival in Cincinnati in 1935 and their initial encounters with Helen and

Nelson Glueck. We are also grateful to Rabbi Kaelter for his perceptive reading of some of the chapters and his constant encouragement. Roger Herst is to be thanked for his submission of "A Roman Incident," which serves as an important footnote to Chapter Twelve. A number of active and honorary members of HUC-JIR's Board of Governors responded to our inquiries about their involvement with Glueck, including Norma U. Levitt, Claire Miller, and S. L. Kopald, Jr., who served as chair of the College-Institute's Board of Governors in the mid-1960s.

Extensive interviews with some of the archaeologists and semiticists who were either students of Glueck or who knew him in the 1930s and 1940s, including Avraham Biran, Cyrus Gordon, Avraham Malamat, Binyamin Mazar, Trude and Moshe Dothan, and Ruth Amiran, helped create a realistic sense of the nature of Glueck's accomplishments. Omar, who served as cook at ASOR for thirty years and was still alive as this project was undertaken, also provided some "color" to the narrative.

Others who had worked with Glueck in administrative capacities — Kenneth Roseman, as dean of the Cincinnati School in the 1960s, Eugene Mihaly as executive vice-president, and Esther Lee, Inna Pomerantz, and Gad Granach, who worked at the Jerusalem School during the same decade, provided interesting anecdotes and insights into Glueck's behavior and priorities. Ginny Ben Ari, a current employee of HUC in Jerusalem, and the late Michael Klein, the former dean, were also helpful.

Thanks also to William Dever, currently serving on the faculty of the University of Arizona, to Eric Meyers, Professor at Duke University, who kindly offered to read the entire manuscript, and to Seymour Gitin, director of the Albright Institute, for generously giving of their time and for helpful critiques of the archaeological information provided in this book. Emily Wright, widow of G. Ernest Wright, was also contacted, and gladly offered what assistance she could. Cyrus Gordon and Marvin Pope also contributed some material.

With respect to institutions, the Jacob R. Marcus Center at the American Jewish Archives in Cincinnati, initially led by Abraham Peck and then by his very able successor Gary Zola, and the staff of the AJA, especially chief archivist Kevin Proffitt, was a critically important arena for our research. Dehvra Bennett-Jones, a graduate student recommended by the AJA, researched publications and catalogs of the University of Cincinnati during Glueck's days as a student there. We are also grateful to the AJA for awarding several research fellowships to Jonathan Brown for work on the Glueck project. We are grateful for the photos of Glueck supplied by the Archives. They were expertly scanned by Phil Reekers.

The archives of the Pittsburgh Theological Seminary were mined for Glueck-related material, inasmuch as Paul Lapp of the PTS had been connected with the Gezer project, and Eleanor Vogel, who served as Glueck's administrative secretary for many years, had deposited her papers there as well.

The director and staff of the Harvard Semitic Museum in Cambridge, Massachusetts were also most helpful in locating Glueck-related materials in their archives and supplying photographs to enhance the manuscript.

The Central Archive for the History of the Jewish People in Jerusalem provided significant folders full of correspondence between Glueck and Judah Leon Magnes.

We acknowledge the valuable assistance of the directors of the joint Tel Aviv University/Pennsylvania State University excavations at Megiddo in the Jezreel Valley. Israel Finkelstein and David Usshishkin of Tel Aviv University and Baruch Halpern of the Pennsylvania State University, along with their staff, provided Jonathan Brown with "below-ground-level" experience.

As the project made its way from research notes and interviews into chapters, very significant assistance was provided by Annie Rose, Associate Professor of Religion and History at the Pennsylvania State University, whose dedication to research and scholarship provided a paradigm for us, as well as by Alex Joffe, formerly an Associate Professor of Archaeology at PSU. Fred Matson, Professor Emeritus of Archaeology at the Pennsylvania State University, offered encouragement early on, and Stanley Weintraub, Evan Pugh Professor of the Arts and Humanities at PSU and a loyal friend, also read and critiqued several chapters. Weintraub also pointed us in the direction of Charles Montagu Doughty's *Arabia Deserta*, which Glueck referred to as "the companion of my youth" and whose romantic aura and description of Doughty's travels with the Arab *hajji* on the way to Mecca inflamed Glueck's imagination.

Other readers who gave helpful advice along the way include Lance Sussman, then on the faculty of the State University of New York at Binghamton and now senior rabbi at Knesseth Israel in Philadelphia, and Dr. Saul Friedman of Kent State and Youngstown State Universities. We are profoundly grateful to our first editor, Gordon Cohn of Long Beach, California, who gave dozens of valuable hours to correcting spelling, grammar, and syntax, and suggesting revisions. Sheila Panitz of Norfolk also helped us work through many difficult passages.

We also acknowledge the work of Patricia Kelvin of Youngstown, who did additional editing, and that of Jonathan Sarna of Brandeis University, who put the finishing touches on the manuscript prior to our submitting it for publication to the HUC press.

During the course of the research, two graduate students were engaged to glean material from Glueck's voluminous correspondence during the 1930s and 1940s. Mary Miles identified key paragraphs in that correspondence and examined dozens of books for references to Nelson Glueck in the Pattee Library at PSU. Jonathan Roos worked in the Jacob R. Marcus Center on Glueck's correspondence as HUC-JIR president.

When Jonathan Brown initiated this project in December 1994, he knew he would need assistance from someone with a background in Semitics and Archaeology. Laurence Kutler, then working as head of the Hebrew Day School in Youngstown, had such a background and agreed to collaborate on the project. He has kept the biography "on track," challenged unfounded conclusions, and provided the material for all the chapters that focus on archaeology.

The research and travel necessary for the completion of this project would never have been possible without the generous support of two people who were close to Nelson Glueck for many years. To Audrey Skirball Kenis, widow of Jack Skirball and wife of Charles Kenis, and to Richard Scheuer, former chairman of the HUC-JIR Board of Governors, following in his father Sy's footsteps, our profoundest gratitude. Richard Scheuer has provided not only funding at a significant level, but suggestions and critiques that have been unfailingly helpful. During the one year that remained in Helen Glueck's own vital and fascinating life after we began the project, she provided financial support as well.

To our spouses and families who had to put up with late nights, early mornings, innumerable trips to the post office, and occasional absences while one or the other of us was away doing research in Cincinnati, Boston, Los Angeles, New York, London, or Israel, we offer our profoundest thanks.

— Jonathan M. Brown & Laurence Kutler
September 2005

1

From Ponovezh to Cincinnati

Like most of the Jews who arrived in Cincinnati in the last decades of the nineteenth century, Nelson Glueck's parents came from Eastern Europe. His father, Morris Glueck (Moshe Yitzchak Revel), was born in Ponovezh, Lithuania in 1869 and emigrated in 1887 at age eighteen. Glueck's mother, Anna Ethel Rubin, was born near Kovno, Lithuania in 1874 and came to Cincinnati in 1888 with her parents and siblings when she was fourteen. Both were products of the traditional Jewish upbringing that was seriously challenged during the nineteenth century by the forces of change making their presence known in Europe at the time.

Lithuania, part of Russia since the 1795 partition of Poland, was the home of tens of thousands of Jews who, on the whole, lived comfortably with their non-Jewish neighbors. Ponovezh, a district capital in the Vilna region, had seen its first Jews in the fourteenth century — Karaite prisoners of war brought back from the Crimea.[1] By the seventeenth century there were enough Jews in Ponovezh to build a tall wooden synagogue on the left bank of the Neviazha River. They lived in the Jewish quarter, Slobodka, and developed the trade, crafts, and small industries of the city, which later served as a center for followers of the Haskalah (enlightenment) movement and earned a reputation as the "little Vilna." Vilna, the Lithuanian capital, had become a great center of both traditional learning and modern studies and achieved its own fame as *yerushalayim shel lita* (the Jerusalem of Lithuania).

By 1847 there were nearly 1,500 Jews in Ponovezh, a number that increased to 6,627 in 1897, representing half of the total population of the town at the time.[2] Ponovezh's Jewish students studied at Russian elementary and high schools; the famous poet Yehuda Leib Gordon served as a teacher in one of the government schools. A modern Hebrew school in which Bible and secular subjects were taught was founded in the 1870s. A small Zionist group was organized in the 1880s.

While the Haskalah movement was definitely a presence in Ponovezh, its emphasis on science and secular studies did not disturb the Revel family's commitment to traditional Judaism. Rabbi Nahum Shraga Revel, Morris's father, had named his son Moshe after his maternal grandfather, Rabbi Moshe Yitzchak Revel, a scholar of great renown, descended from generations of rabbis. A son of Nahum's by his second wife, Leah Gittelevitch, Bernard (Dov) Revel, was destined to become the head of Yeshiva University, the pre-eminent Orthodox university and rabbinical seminary in America.

When Moshe Yitzchak Revel turned eighteen, he faced the daunting prospect of becoming a Russian soldier. For much of the nineteenth century, Jews serving in the Russian army were "encouraged" to convert to the Russian Orthodox faith. Separated from their families and communities, they often did so. Although seeking converts was no longer the avowed goal of the Russian army, Jews hardly felt welcome in its ranks and, in any event, were precluded from assuming authority over non-Jewish soldiers. Indeed, since the 1881 assassination of Czar Alexander II, conditions for Jews everywhere in Russia had become increasingly difficult, and tens of thousands left in pursuit of a better life elsewhere; a significant number of those immigrants headed for America, as did some members of the Revel family.

Because he feared that the Revel name on his passport might cause him to be arrested at the Russian border for evading conscription, Moshe changed it to *Glueck*, the Yiddish word for "luck." The Anglicization of his first name from Moshe to Morris may have been the suggestion of an immigration official at Castle Garden, where immigrants arriving in New York harbor were processed before the opening of Ellis Island.

Moshe's ultimate destination was Cincinnati — on the Ohio River just north of Kentucky, already known as the "Queen City of the West"— where he hoped to find a place to live and some kind of gainful employment. Cincinnati's growing Jewish population (in 1870 around 8,000 and by 1900 15,000[3]) included a number of Orthodox congregations that were being strengthened by the arrival of Jews from Eastern Europe like the Rubins and Morris Glueck. Within that greater community one could readily find *landsmanschaften*, organized groups of people from the same general geographical area in the Old Country. These *landsmanschaften* provided supportive services, social opportunities, and burial rights for their members. They formed synagogues of their own and fostered the establishment of all the necessities of a traditional Jewish life: kosher butcher shops, matzah bakeries, and *mikva'ot* (ritual baths), as well as rabbinical courts and scribes to write *gittin* (divorce decrees).

But the essential character of the Jewish community in which Morris Glueck and Anna Rubin found themselves in the late 1880s was not Orthodox. Most of the earlier Jewish immigrants had come from German-speaking lands. They came for the same reason that thousands of non-Jewish Germans arrived in Cincinnati prior to and after the Civil War: to escape political unrest and in search of economic betterment. For more than half a century, Germans had been the largest group of immigrants settling in Cincinnati; more than 40,000 entered the city after the American Civil War.

Among the German immigrants were many Jews who had been influenced by German-Jewish religious ferment and became involved with the Reform movement in Judaism. By the mid-1870s, with the founding of the Union of American Hebrew Congregations in 1873 and of the Hebrew Union College in 1875, Cincinnati had become the heart of American Reform Judaism. This reality was to have a profound effect on Nelson Glueck.

At the time, most of Cincinnati Jewry lived in the city's West End, not far from the downtown area bordering the Ohio River. The downtown's northern edge was the Miami River canal (today's Central Parkway), which enabled goods to be transported from the Ohio River into the interior of the state. That canal divided the downtown area from a section that came to be known as "Over the Rhine," where many of the non-Jewish Germans settled.

Having established himself in his adopted city as a peddler, Morris Glueck met and courted Anna Ethel Rubin, the teenage daughter and second of four children of David Moses Rubin and Chana Rivka Katz. Anna's siblings included Harry, Fanny, and John. Morris and Anna were married on May 28, 1893 and settled in a modest home on West Court Street, where they lived for twenty-four years and where all of their nine children were born. Nelson, who arrived on June 4, 1900, was their third child and second son, following his older sister Rachel (Rae), born in 1894, and his older brother Nathan, born in 1896, to whom Nelson bore a remarkable resemblance. Morris and Anna gave their second son the Hebrew name of Nisan, the first month of the Hebrew calendar.

Six more Glueck children arrived after Nelson: Samuel in 1902, Benjamin in 1904, Harry in 1906, Esther in 1909, Sarah (Sally) in 1912,

Morris and Anna Glueck on their wedding day, May 28, 1893. (Courtesy of Susan Cook)

and Hillel (Hill) in 1915. Anna was forty-one when her youngest child was born.

According to family lore, as a youngster Nelson displayed an unusual curiosity about the past, and his father often took him to museums where fossils were displayed. A favorite outing was to the earthworks created by the Mound Indians some thirty-five miles northwest of Cincinnati, where Nelson loved to scratch the surface looking for artifacts of a lost civilization. On one such excursion, he reputedly dug into the earth with a small stick, loosening the soil and uncovering a pink quartz arrowhead with a few grains of sand embedded in its crevices.[4] Perhaps he wondered about the people who had created and used that arrowhead long ago.

In 1913, his Bar Mitzvah year, Glueck entered Woodward High School, which was then located between Twelfth and Thirteenth Streets on Sycamore, within easy walking distance from his West Court Street home. Also close to his home was the Alms and Doepke department store on Central Parkway from which his father obtained the dry goods that he

Benjamin, Harry, Nelson, and Nathan Glueck, ca. 1909. (Courtesy of Barbara Glueck)

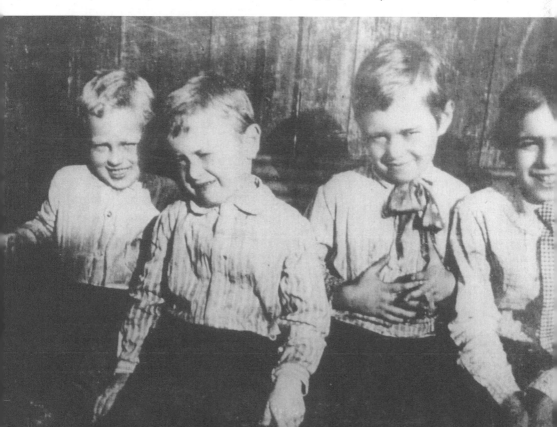

peddled in the surrounding neighborhoods. At Woodward, Glueck, whose nickname was "Nelly," joined an oratorical group, where he honed his speaking skills, and the Art League, whose purpose was beautifying the campus with works of art. With those of his classmates intending to go on for more education, he took the General Course, "designed especially for the student who wishes to have a broad, general foundation which will admit of subsequent specification, either in business or in college."[5]

Glueck completed his high school education in three years, but by the late spring of 1914 he had made an important decision: to enroll in the Hebrew Union College, the only Reform Jewish seminary in America. HUC had recently moved from its downtown location in Cincinnati to a lovely suburban campus in Clifton, one of Cincinnati's seven hills. The Glueck family made a similar move in June 1917, when Morris and Anna bought a home in Avondale at 859 Hutchins Avenue. The new house featured amenities that the house on West Court Street lacked: a cast-iron stove and a pull-chain toilet.[6] It remained in the family until Anna's death in 1954.

Why would the son of Orthodox parents and the nephew of a prominent Orthodox rabbi decide to enroll in a Reform Jewish seminary? According to one source, Morris assumed that his son would become a traditional rabbi. Nelson, however, had a curious and inquiring mind and reportedly told his father that he would not reject the study of a subject that interested him simply because it "wasn't proper" for an Orthodox rabbi to know about it. Morris Glueck is said to have recognized his son's proclivity for science and non-Orthodox Judaism and actually encouraged him to enroll at HUC, knowing that with such interests, Nelson would not be accepted at an Orthodox yeshivah.[7]

A more likely explanation: although Glueck was still young, he was also intelligent and self-aware, and he understood that achieving success in American terms called for embracing a way of life that was not readily compatible with Orthodox Judaism. Eventually he would come to view the Hebrew Union College as a "finishing school," and rabbinical ordination as a means of entering into polite society. Ever the pragmatist, Glueck chose the path that he had every reason to believe would enable him to make his mark in the world. For him, and perhaps for others of his cohort of young students, the rabbinate was not a calling, but rather a career with built-in honor and ascribed status.

2

Education for the Reform Rabbinate

Experiences gained, lessons learned *

The University of Cincinnati in 1916 was an institution that served its student constituency much as the City College at that time served its students in New York: providing a quality education at minimal cost. Most of the Cincinnati students, including Nelson Glueck, rode a trolley-car to their classes. Conscientious and bright, Glueck enrolled in courses in the departments of History and Classics; he fulfilled his curricular requirements in four years. A handwritten example of his work still exists. It was a paper submitted on January 12, 1920, entitled "The Legend of King Arthur, Treated Historically." The instructor marked it with an "A" and the comment "an admirable treatment — full, thoughtful, and scholarly."[1]

Concurrently, Glueck attended classes at the Hebrew Union College. The College's nine-year course for candidates for the rabbinate was divided into a preparatory as well as a collegiate department. Glueck was enrolled in the latter. According to Rabbi David Philipson, author of a fiftieth anniversary history of HUC, its curriculum at the time included Bible, Hebrew, Aramaic grammar, Mishnah, Talmud, Philosophy, Theology, History, Homiletics, Midrash, and Codes. In addition, Liturgy, Pedagogy, Jewish Social Studies, Jewish Ethics, and Jewish music had been added just prior to Glueck's matriculation.[2]

The president of the College during Glueck's first student years was Kaufmann Kohler, whose tenure began in 1903 and extended until 1921. When Kohler was welcomed to his new post, Bernhard Bettmann observed that "With Dr. Wise and Dr. [Moses] Mielziner of blessed memory, the era of construction has passed, and now the period of development begins."[3] It could be said that if Wise was the grand architect of Reform Judaism in America, then Kohler was its chief interpreter.[4] He accepted the presidency on the condition that the College would continue to be the exponent of American Reform Judaism as taught and expounded by Wise. He then proceeded to intensify academic work at

---

* Quotations at the beginnings of chapters are the words of Nelson Glueck unless otherwise noted

the College — making HUC independent of the University and raising it to the standard of a post-graduate institution. In the end, he contented himself with adding a fifth year to the collegiate department, by which time the students would, in any event, have completed their university studies. He introduced courses in biblical criticism, Apocryphal and Hellenistic literature, and historical and systematic theology. Though he stressed scientific thoroughness, he also placed a high premium on spirituality, sincerity, and moral integrity.[5]

Julian Morgenstern was appointed to the HUC faculty in 1907 and assumed the presidency when Kohler died in 1921. Morgenstern sought to build a faculty "primarily composed of its own alumni, thoroughly versed in Jewish knowledge and trained in the techniques of scholarship and teaching."[6] He wanted graduates "to have a sound understanding of the American Jewish scene, its trends, its needs and its proper goals." He sought to build an institution that would "steadily expand its service to enlarge its influence in American and World Israel, and which would become one of the outstanding seminaries and centers of Jewish research and creative scholarship in all the world."[7]

Morgenstern took a direct personal interest in Nelson Glueck, perhaps because a friend of his had taught the young man at Woodward High School and had spoken enthusiastically of his potential. During the ensuing years Morgenstern and Glueck would maintain a correspondence that continued well beyond Glueck's accession to the presidency of the College. Glueck's other teachers included Abraham Cronbach, Solomon Freehof, Louis Grossman, Jacob Z. Lauterbach, Jacob Rader Marcus, David Neumark, Henry Slonimsky and Louis Wolfenson. From this group of scholars, Marcus would emerge as Glueck's life-long friend and mentor.

Glueck's high school and college years encompassed those of the Great War. When it began, in August 1914, some of Cincinnati's German-Americans united to form relief organizations and collect money for the Kaiser and for the Austro-Hungarian Empire. But when America entered the war, on April 6, 1917, the declaration unleashed a flood of anti-German sentiments across the nation, and within three days, German street names in Cincinnati were changed and German books and periodicals removed from library shelves. A prominent HUC faculty member, Gotthard Deutsch, came close to being dismissed from the College for refusing to testify in court that he would prefer an American victory to a German one.[8]

Demonstrating a love of his country that would not abate throughout his life, Nelson Glueck immediately stepped forward during the week of his eighteenth birthday (June 1918) and signed up for military training. His cohort of university students was assigned to barracks on the outskirts of Cincinnati. Training began in the late summer but before it was completed the war ended.

*

Glueck's published writings during his years in the collegiate department at HUC reveal a thoughtful young man who possessed a solid grounding in the classics, definite opinions and tastes, and an often florid style of expression. His essays appeared with some frequency in the *Hebrew Union College Monthly*, a journal edited by the students.[9] It included travel and personal notes, speeches by members of the faculty and Board of Governors, and student articles and book reviews. In 1920, for example, Glueck published a passionately enthusiastic review of a book by historian Gotthard Deutsch, *Jew and Gentile: Essays on Jewish Apologetics and Kindred Historical Subjects*.[10] Glueck called his review "An Ebullition about a Book," stating that "like Diogenes of old in search of a wise man, we (students) persist in our search for a sensible book; unlike his labors, ours are blessed with success." He continued:

> For out of the murky fog of miserable passions which envelops us, out of the dreary depths of dull ignorance and the fathomless chasm of colossal prejudice in which so many lie in a . . . self-induced intellectual stupor, there has issued forth a quiet voice, which is to us as a cool hand is to a fevered brow.
>
> We feel as if, suddenly, we had been transported from the fetid heat of a glaring street, from all its small ways and petty practices to the rambling path in a green forest, through whose tracery of boughs and limbs, of twigs and leaves, there flows a flood of joyous sunlight.
>
> A new book has been written, based neither on prejudice or passion, nor on chauvinism or mere cant. It is founded on real scholarship — as rare a jewel as is intellectual honesty — on a

thorough understanding of the material presented, on a desire to inform. It is the result of a lifetime of learning. It is the *Jew and Gentile*, by Dr. Gotthard Deutsch.[11]

A year later Glueck wrote a review of Israel Zangwill's *The Voice of Jerusalem*[12] for the *Monthly*. Zangwill, one of the most important and widely read Jewish writers at the turn of the century, raised concerns that continued to resonate long after his books were published.[13] "Indeed," Glueck wrote,

> viewing the world as it is, Mr. Zangwill has at last become reconciled to his religion, and considers it far better to be an ostentatious, persecuted Jew, than a powerful Gentile dispensing justice and love. As a Jew who has felt the ancient crime of his people, I was not comfortable to hear that it could not be shaken off, that it was stamped into our very visage![14]

Glueck's reference to the "ancient crime of his people" could only mean that he had accepted the Christian interpretation that Christ's crucifixion was the responsibility of the Jews of Jesus' generation. His next paragraph makes that abundantly clear:

> In vain I told myself that the crucifixion was a Roman and not a Jewish punishment . . . in vain I protested that the death of Socrates was not visited upon the Greeks, nor that of Savonarola on the Italians, nor that of Jean d'Arc on the English; there remained nonetheless weighing upon me the long odious tradition of the centuries, the changeless Christian hate, which has turned the *Judengassen* [Jew-alleys] into shambles, and which is chronicling itself in fresh lines of blood in forlorn ghettos of Galicia and the Ukraine, lost in the pursuit of peace. Perhaps, I thought, recalling the greatness of this martyred son of the Jews, it was a righteous historic Nemesis that has nailed his people on the cross for two thousand years.[15]

Even in these early writings, it is possible to detect the beginnings of Glueck's profound interest in generally mending fences between Christians and Jews, a goal he would specifically seek to actualize in one way by providing Christian seminarians with an opportunity to study at the Hebrew Union College.[16]

                        *

Like many of his HUC classmates then and now, Glueck tried his hand at teaching Sunday school in a local congregation.[17] And like every other rabbinical student, he was expected to obtain some experience at a "real" pulpit. That usually meant accepting responsibility for a small congregation that the student would visit regularly, either on a bi-weekly or monthly basis, depending on the size of the congregation and available funding. Glueck's first assignment was a High Holy Day pulpit in Henderson, Kentucky, in the fall of 1920. Describing her childhood experiences in Henderson in a newspaper article in New York, a Mrs. Clarence K. Whitehall recalled:

> Into this somber patch of darkness came a white knight — a circuit-riding rabbi from the Hebrew Union College in Cincinnati. He was an Adonis, a stunning apparition, a man who enjoyed the printed word, who encouraged us to read, who showed us there was a world beyond Henderson. He was a completely novel experience and he changed our lives.[18]

During 1921–1922 and 1922–1923, Glueck's last two years at the College, he assumed a bi-weekly pulpit in Saginaw, Michigan: Congregation Beth El. He established a regular correspondence there with Lillie Lenhoff, who served as the Sunday school supervisor for the Jewish community in the town.[19] At the conclusion of his first year there, Glueck wrote to Ms. Lenhoff:

> I left Saginaw feeling very happy indeed. The kindness and courtesy, the helpfulness that was constantly extended to me by everybody — alone enabled me to do whatever little I may have [done]. I fully realize my many shortcomings, and am greatly indebted to all of you.
>
>   I look back and shall continue to look back upon my year in Saginaw as one of the most formative years of my life. The experiences gained, the lessons learned, the stimulation and encouragement received, enable me to go on happily in a life's task that is not always without its troubles and difficulties and disappointments.[20]

Glueck indicated that he was looking forward to the coming year, "when it will be again my privilege to conduct services in Saginaw."

*

During those years Glueck was also deeply engaged in writing his rabbinical thesis, "The Story of the Ten Martyrs," which dealt with the legends surrounding the ten rabbis killed by the Romans during the period prior to the Bar Kochba rebellion of 132–135 C.E.[21] In the thesis Glueck sought to establish two propositions: that neither the Roman decree prohibiting circumcision nor the intent of the Emperor Hadrian to erect a pagan city on the ruins of Jerusalem (*Aelia Capitolina*) were designed to aggravate and humiliate the Jews. Rather, he argued, the prohibition of circumcision applied to the whole empire and was enacted because it was considered a mutilation of the body, in the same category as castration. The decision to build a city on the ruins of Jerusalem was, in Glueck's opinion, Hadrian's response to seeing that a place once inhabited could be inhabited again; the project would also provide ample opportunity to display his fondness and talent for architecture and building.

Given the extreme cruelty of the persecution of the Jews under Hadrian and the Roman emperor's clear intention of humiliating the rebellious population as much as possible, it is difficult to defend Glueck's conclusions. In the foreword to his essay, Glueck spoke of legends as the common possession of all peoples:

> In legends are expressed desires unrealized, hopes unfulfilled, loves and hates grown inordinately strong. In legends, heroes are idolized and enemies are conquered and punished; the people's verdict on history is given. In legends are sorrow and disappointments and misfortunes magnified. In legends do masochistic impulses find an outlet.

Glueck then identified the ten martyrs as one of the Jews' significant legends:

> It is the historical development of this legend which this thesis proposes to trace. More specifically, it is to reveal the elements of truth

upon which this legend is based, to depict the condition which brought about the martyrdom of certain teachers, to indicate how legend wove in tapestries of brilliant colors the stories of actual and imagined martyrs, to show how the natural desires of the Jewish people to commemorate a period of their history, to glorify their heroes, and to vilify their enemies, occasioned certain legendary developments, that this thesis has been written.

He wrote that the story of the ten martyrs is interesting not only for itself but also because it contains certain theological elements that had been discarded by official Judaism:

> For instance, the doctrine of lasting sin as revealed in the state-ment that because of the crime committed by Joseph's brothers in selling him into slavery, ten prominent men from each generation were to lose their lives; and the doctrine of metempsychosis, as revealed in the statement that the souls of Adam and Joseph became in turn the soul of Rabbi Ishmael.

After a thorough analysis of the development of the legends connecting the martyrs, Glueck concluded:

> The legend of the ten martyrs became of important liturgical interest. The various poets who wrote of them were not interested in adding to the martyr legend, but rather in making use of it as a suitable theme for poetry. It would seem that in developing as the martyr legend did, from isolated facts to a rounded out, completely detailed legendary whole, and finally being made the theme of po-etical composition, it followed a natural course of development.[22]

What is striking about Glueck's thesis is the manner in which he delved through the layers of material that had been built up over many centuries around a scattered set of circumstances. In reconstructing the history of the legend, he facilitated a process whereby the past could speak to the present. That skill would be honed in later years when he embarked on his career as an archaeologist.

*

On June 2, 1923, a Shabbat afternoon, Glueck was ordained at services held in the HUC Chapel. After the invocation by Rabbi Samuel Schwartz of Chicago, Mr. Alfred M. Cohen, president of the board of directors, offered a review of the year. The Baccalaureate sermon was given by Rabbi William Fineshriber of Memphis, after which Morgenstern placed his hands on each candidate in turn, thereby ordaining Glueck along with his classmates Michael Aaronsohn, Solomon Bazell, Louis Binstock, Sheldon Blank, Max Bretton, Benjamin Frankel, Mayer Lipman, David Nathan, Walter Rothman, and Samuel Wolk.

Some months prior to his ordination Glueck had approached Morgenstern and told him of his desire to carry out graduate studies abroad, preferably in Germany. Morgenstern paid careful attention to this request, for Glueck would then be following the same path he himself had traveled years before, a path that would lead to an appointment on the HUC faculty. He agreed to help Glueck obtain a Morgenthau traveling fellowship.[23] In the event, classmates Blank and Rothman, Glueck's close friends, would accompany him on his voyage to Germany, where, like Glueck, each would seek and obtain a Ph.D.[24] Jacob Rader Marcus, ordained in 1920 and already on the faculty, had been granted a leave of absence in 1923 to pursue his own studies in Germany and would be able to assist Glueck and his newly ordained colleagues when they arrived.

Glueck graduated from HUC with a thorough grounding in and a personal preference for the classical Reform Judaism whose approach to God, Torah, and Israel was spelled out in the Pittsburgh Platform of 1885. Classical Reform placed only marginal value on ritual and a great deal of emphasis on ethical behavior. Thus Jewish dietary laws, ritual garb, and distinctions between priest, Levite, and Israelite were no longer observed, while concern for the poor and the underprivileged was emphasized. The traditional thrice-daily services were essentially replaced by one weekly service, held late Friday evening, well after sundown.

Classical Reform declared that the traditional second day of many holidays no longer needed to be celebrated, and some congregations even went so far as to observe harvest festivals like Sukkot, Pesaḥ, and Shavuot on Friday evenings, no matter when they actually occurred. Classical Reform rejected the belief in the coming of the Messiah and called on Reform Jews to live in such a way as to bring about a messianic age through morality and social justice.

Finally, in place of the age-old hopes for a restoration of a Jewish commonwealth under a descendant of King David, Reform affirmed as its mission the building of synagogues and strengthening Jewish life in the Diaspora, which was no longer even to be thought of as any form of exile (*golus* or *galut*).

Glueck knew what it meant to be living as a Jew in America. He did not yet have any idea of what life as a Jew in Berlin would be like in the 1920s. He would soon be immersed in the cultural and political excitement of the Weimar Republic, with its undercurrents of strife, violence, and antisemitism.

3

The Lure of a German Doctorate

*'I have — because of deepening understanding and
increasing knowledge — become a better Jew.*

The path to German universities in search of a higher degree had been
followed for more than a quarter century by quite a few Hebrew Union
College graduates, as well as by many other American Jewish leaders.
For the HUC men, this was a sort of pilgrimage-in-reverse, inasmuch
as a large segment of the HUC faculty since the College's earliest days —
and through the time of Glueck's tenure as a student — had been born in
Germany and earned their doctorates in the land of Schiller and Goethe.
Thus, in 1900 the newly ordained Judah L. Magnes, who would later emi-
grate to Palestine and help found the Hebrew University in 1925, had
been encouraged to go to Germany to drink deeper of the wells of Jewish learning. Perhaps the deepest well of such learning was the Berlin
Lehranstalt (Hochshule) für die Wissenschaft des Judentums (Advanced
Institute for the Scientific Study of Judaism), founded in 1872. It was designed to provide for the preservation, advancement, and dissemination
of knowledge about Judaism.[1]

There were, however, reasons other than faculty experience and the
examples of Magnes and Morgenstern that impelled Glueck to do his
post-graduate work in Germany rather than elsewhere in Europe. Glueck
was interested in all subjects theological, and Germany had twice as
many theological students in one city as England did in all its universities. Moreover, Germany offered a Protestant theological approach that
was far more creative than anything England or France could provide.
Internationally recognized German scholars such as Hugo Gressmann
and Willi Staerk were willing to reinterpret theology in radical ways.
German universities also engaged in more progressive Old Testament
scholarship than did comparable institutions in other European cities.[2]
Discoveries regarding the chronology of the history of Israel in relationship to other Near Eastern civilizations, the topography of ancient Israel,
and the religions of Israel's neighbors were quickly absorbed into German
scholarship. Combining archaeological discoveries with careful biblical

criticism, Gressmann and Hermann Gunkel were in the forefront of those researching the comparative study of literary genres to establish the historicity of the pre-monarchic period of Israelite history (before 1,000 B.C.E.). All of these efforts were a critical part of the intellectual climate that nourished Glueck in his graduate days.

Glueck arrived in Germany in the summer of 1923 aboard the SS *Manchuria,* along with his HUC classmates Sheldon Blank and Walther Rothman. Jacob Rader Marcus met the ship in Hamburg and treated the newcomers to their first German beer.[3] Glueck then continued on to Heidelberg for the summer sessions and moved to Berlin in the fall. In a letter he wrote to Morgenstern in December he recorded his initial impressions of the city:

> I like Berlin, although I have not been around very much. It has a distinct personality of its own, which expresses itself in different tones of voice, as it were, as one has occasion to pass through the various thoroughfares, to visit the unending number of interesting places, to come into contact with the native Berliner.[4]

Berlin of the Weimar years earned an international reputation for its artistic and cultural life, its ready availability of pleasures of the flesh and the senses, and its high and low forms of entertainment. Josephine Baker, the "toast of the twenties," was performing there. Moral scruples were loose, promiscuity was *comme il faut,* the sniffing of cocaine routine.[5] Years later Sheldon Blank recalled those heady days:

> Everywhere one looked one saw the *Schutz Polizei,* the *Schupo*; on the public squares were armored cars and tanks, and on the street corners, the sirens. Everywhere you heard sirens.... But don't misunderstand me. I don't mean the klaxon sirens that blast your eardrums. I mean the sirens immortalized by Heinrich Heine, the flaxen Saxon sirens that go: "Psst. Schatzie. Come with me!" Yes, the streets of Berlin were filled with these sirens.[6]

If the *Kurfürstendamm* offered diverse pleasures, the rest of the city, and indeed all of Germany, was in chaos, with inflation spiraling out of control and violent political demonstrations commonplace. France and Belgium had sent troops to occupy the Ruhr in January, and many Germans, protesting this act with passive resistance, began to bring production and transportation in the Ruhr to a standstill.[7] In support of the passive resistance, the government spent forty million gold marks a day, sums that could not be made up in taxes and consequently resulted in the printing of money at an astonishing rate. In June of the previous year, following the assassination of the Jewish foreign minister Walther Rathenau,[8] the tempo of inflation had accelerated until by the end of the year the exchange rate was 7,000 marks to the dollar. That, however, was nothing compared to what would happen in 1923, when by November the exchange rate was 4.2 billion to the dollar.[9]

Opponents of the government blamed the Jews for fostering the inflation. But although some Jewish merchants and industrialists did benefit from the situation, the vast majority of Germany's half-million Jews suffered along with the rest of the population. On October 23, 1923, a World War I corporal named Adolf Hitler attempted to seize control of the Bavarian government in Munich with the intention of continuing on to Berlin. His small cadre of followers invaded a political meeting in the Bürgerbrau cellar in the heart of Munich. "The national revolution has begun," cried Hitler. When he marched his men into Munich the next day, however, the police opened fire. Sixteen of his followers lost their lives, and Hitler himself was arrested.[10]

Glueck was very aware of and yet somewhat disengaged from the events and incidents swirling around him in Berlin. While he may not have fully understood the implications of the times in which he was living, he took note of both the chaos prevailing at the time of his arrival and the positive change effected by the appearance of the new currency. At the same time, he tended to minimize the significance of violent attacks against the Jews of Germany. As he noted to Morgenstern in December 1923:

> You probably read the angry headlines about the Berlin pogroms. The papers outside of Germany have tremendously over-exaggerated the affair. The mobs did attack the Jews, but merely undressed a number of money-changers, who unfortunately, for the most part, are Jews, Germans, and Russians. One man died of wounds the

next day. It was a very serious affair, but not as bad as some of the real pogroms in Russia and Poland must have been.[11]

The reference to "money-changers" reflects a certain disdain that cultured American Jews like Glueck had developed towards a class of Jews from which they felt quite distant and distinct, a disdain often tinged with a touch of embarrassment that he might be thought of as "one of those people."

In the same letter to Morgenstern, Glueck took note of the response of one of Germany's largest political parties to the "Berlin pogroms": "A few days later, the Social Democrats held mass meetings in which they officially protested against the anti-Semitic agitation. The bursting of the Hitler bubble has also helped to quiet the dangerous anti-Semitic agitation. One still sees *hackenkreuzes* [sic] [swastikas] everywhere." The appearance of the new currency, he noted, had a calming effect on the situation:

> The mobs, vicious and plundering, the long lines of people before stores where food of any kind was sold, are no longer to be seen. The appearance of the new money has had the astounding effect of making Germany possibly the most expensive country in the world to live in. . . . Undoubtedly, the poorer classes are starving, and were it not for the Quakers and the help received from other countries, conditions would have become anarchic here. . . . Every now and then, troops with fixed bayonets are seen rushing through the streets. America has to help, or there must inevitably come a smashup.

Studying under such conditions must have been difficult, and Glueck acknowledged that he was only able to do so by taking in "all of the cheerful sights" that helped to balance the larger picture. Moreover, it was always possible to read quietly in the magnificent Prussian State Library as well as in the library at the University of Berlin.

Glueck spent most of his time with his American friends — Rothman, Blank, and Marcus — and did not enter into coffee-house debates on the *Kurfürstendamm*. Unlike Judah Magnes, whose student days involved endless discussions with Jewish students from Germany and Eastern Europe,[12] Glueck had little interest in arguing with the Zionists, Socialists, and Communists among the Jews of Berlin. Not only did he hold himself aloof from such debates; he preferred not to be recognized as anything other than a graduate student from America. As he wrote to Adolph Oko, the HUC librarian, "I am not a rabbi here."[13]

It was in this atmosphere of indulgence, uncertainty, creativity, and violence that Glueck passed his first few months in Berlin. He was not, however, in good health. Recurrent stomach pains caused him to seek out a specialist, who determined that he had an ulcer. He was put on a strict diet and told to curtail his activities.

A major cause of Glueck's anxiety was his inability to understand German well enough. To be accepted for study at a German university, he had been required to pass a language exam, but he still found German very difficult. He wrote, in German, to Morgenstern, "Although I have arrived at a stage where I can understand the lectures fairly well, still I have a tremendous distance to go before I know the language, and learning the language well I consider one of my prime tasks."[14] His illness made matters worse, but Sheldon Blank visited him every day and read to him from German texts. Glueck felt he had crossed a major threshold when he began to correspond with Morgenstern in German. He promised his friend, "What I don't say now I will say later when I am stronger in the language." He asked Morgenstern's forbearance for any errors that might appear and hoped to make further progress. With characteristic determination, Glueck applied himself assiduously, and inside of a year he did become fluent.

His newly acquired language skills enabled him to meet his other academic goals: to take courses in as many Semitic languages as he could, to learn the Bible well, to write a doctoral dissertation suitable for publication, and to consider the course of his future career. During his early months in Germany, Glueck was unsure whether he should pursue a degree in Semitics or in history:

Shall I, next year, go over to Semitics and work for my doctorate in that field, or shall I continue along the lines I am now pursuing and try to get my doctorate in modern history? And again, is it better for me in regard to my future work to have a knowledge of Arabic, Syriac, and Aramaic, or is it better to specialize in history and philosophy and economics? And one thing more: it will be easier for me to get a degree in Semitics than in history.[15]

As time went on, however, he decided he would be better prepared for a rabbinical career if he took a degree in history, "especially in its relation to the Jews, and economics and philosophy, rather than just Oriental languages."[16]

Partly for health reasons, and partly because he was fed up with the tumult of Berlin, Glueck decided in the winter of 1923–1924 that he would move to a different city. He wrote to Morgenstern:

> Perhaps sooner than you expected, I have accepted your advice and am leaving Berlin to attend a smaller university. Berlin is too large for me and too noisy and new. Probably I will go to Heidelberg. According to a comparison of the various university bulletins, I have reached the conclusion that there is no bad university, but that in various branches, smaller universities are better than Berlin.[17]

Glueck had other reasons for moving: Berlin was a significantly more expensive place to live than any of the small university towns he was considering. Moreover the cosmopolitan city presented cultural and social distractions to the serious student — and with so many Americans in Berlin, one could hardly immerse oneself in the German language.[18] Arriving at his chosen destination, he described Heidelberg's romantic environment:

> When one sits under the *Schloss* [castle] walls in Heidelberg at the close of the day, watching the quietly flowing Neckar, turned gold by the rays of the setting sun, and looks over the old, old city, alive with history, so to speak, into the valley beyond, one indeed can join in whole-heartedly and passionately and sing "*Alt Heidelberg, die feine.*"[19]

But the move to Heidelberg did not cure his medical problems: "I am in failing health," he wrote to Morgenstern. "The ulcer seems to be healed, but an inexplicable something makes it practically impossible for me to walk. The doctors have advised me to wait and see if time will bring its own cure."[20]

Glueck's assessment of the general situation in Germany during the spring of 1924 was upbeat. He told his family that things were much calmer, even though the people were still significantly burdened and many were still lining up in front of soup kitchens. The currency was more stable, and there was a general sense of relief from the recent economic whirlwind.[21]

He mentioned that the American General Charles Gates Dawes had visited Paris and that French newspapers were incredulous about Dawes' proposal to extend the amount of time the Germans would have to pay back their war debt. Glueck wrote that Dawes' "outspokenness, his utter disregard of the diplomatic amenities, are confounding his European associates on the Reparation Committee." While Glueck expressed his hope that something good would come of the Dawes proposal, he feared that "France and her satellite Belgium will block all efforts to come to any sane economic conclusions."[22]

In Heidelberg he enrolled in courses and read works of Wellhausen, Kittel, and Staerk. But after completing only a single semester there, he decided to move on to the University of Jena. In November, he wrote to his parents: "You ask me why I left Heidelberg — for the simple reason that the Ph.D. requirements there are twice as many and four times as hard as the requirements here. I shall save at least a year by studying at this university."[23] He looked forward not only to being with his friends again — Rothman and Blank were already in Jena — but also to be studying personally with Willi Staerk and with Professor Heinrich Hilgenfeld.[24]

Toward the end of the summer Glueck received a letter from his cousin Jacob Finkel, who had come to Berlin from Kovno to become a locksmith. The letter sparked some thoughts on Jewish solidarity, which he shared with his parents:

> It seemed a little funny, hearing all of a sudden from a close relative who is not an American, but a Lithuanian Jew living in Berlin. It makes one realize anew the international character of the Jew; it makes me feel as much European as American. I shall be happy to become acquainted with him, and I hope someday to take a trip to Lithuania and pay a visit to the relatives on your side, Papa, and on Mama's side.[25]

Finkel's ultimate intention was to go to Palestine as a *ḥalutz* (pioneer). Pehaps his cousin's plans influenced Glueck to entertain first thoughts about doing likewise.

As the High Holy Days of 1924 approached, Glueck received word from Morgenstern that he had been awarded the Morgenthau traveling fellowship for a second year. Expecting to matriculate at the University of Jena in the next few weeks, Glueck wrote home that he was enjoying his stay in the attractive little university town with lovely botanical gardens on the Jenergasse. He still had fond feelings for Heidelberg, however, and returned there for Rosh Hashanah services before he traveled to Wurzburg to be with Blank and his aunts for Yom Kippur.

At the conclusion of the winter term (1925) in Jena, Glueck turned in the proposal for his doctoral thesis, and then took time off to visit Paris. "My trip to Paris" he wrote to his brother Harry, "made me lazier than ever. So there has to be a battle royale going on between my lazy self and my energetic self. My energetic self is gradually winning out, but yesterday my energetic self gave my lazy self such a swift kick in the *tuches* [rear end] that I couldn't sit down."[26]

By 1926 he had settled down to complete his thesis, entitled *Das Wort "Ḥesed" im alttestamentlichen Sprachgebrauche als menschliche und göttliche gemeinschaftsgemässe Verhaltungsweise* (The word "Ḥesed" in Old Testament Linguistic Usage as Human and Divine Reciprocal Conduct).[27] Glueck's choice of topic may be traced to research currents in German religious studies at the time, which exhibited general interest in the exploration of theologically bound terminology. Solidly grounded in philology, Glueck sought, through form-critical and traditional-historical methods, to understand the religious statements of the Hebrew Bible as they applied to the covenantal term *ḥesed*, which he ultimately rendered into English as "loyalty," "mutual aid," or "reciprocal love," in addition to "grace."[28] His work shows that the *ḥesed* idea did not spring into existence full-blown with its definitive meaning precisely shaped. Instead, he followed what he believed to be the idea's dynamic development as it paralleled the biblical writer's growing insight into the divinely based relationships of man to man and man to God.

Glueck divided his thesis into three sections: the first depicts and defines acts of *ḥesed* by humans in a secular setting; the second speaks of it in a religious setting; and the third describes *ḥesed* as an integral part of Divine conduct. To exemplify the third definition, Glueck referred to the passage in Genesis in which Abraham's steward Eliezer traveled to the town in Mesopotamia where Abraham's brother Nahor lived. Once there the servant entreated God to help him fulfill the task that Abraham had set out for him: "O Lord, the God of my master Abraham, grant me good luck today, and show *hesed* to my master Abraham" (Genesis 24:12). He then established a specific set of circumstances designed to let him know whether God would show *hesed*:

> So I will stand by the spring while the daughters of the townsmen come out to draw water. Let it be, that the maiden, to whom I will say, "Please, lower your jar, that I may drink," and who says, "Drink, and I will also water your camels," she will be the one that you have appointed for your servant Isaac. By this I shall know that you have shown *hesed* to my master [Genesis 24:13–14].

The matter worked out just as he had hoped; when Eliezer learned the name of the gracious young woman, he thanked God for having led Rebecca, Abraham's niece, to him, to be affianced to Isaac: "Blessed be Adonai, the God of my master Abraham, who has not withheld his *hesed* and his faithfulness from my master. For God has led me on the right road to the house of my master's kinsmen" [Gen. 24:27]. In these passages, Glueck demonstrated that *hesed* is a divine favor due Abraham because of the special relationship that existed between the patriarch and his God.

Copies of the thesis were presented to Staerk in Jena and forwarded to Morgenstern in Cincinnati for their review and comments. After spending the winter holidays of 1926 in Jena, Glueck returned to Berlin early the following year to see to its publication. Although he and the publisher disagreed about whether the thesis should appear as part of a series or be published on its own, in the end it was published independently, and Glueck was required to purchase five copies at 150 marks apiece.

Having achieved his major objectives in Germany, Glueck was free to attend some of the classes for which he had not found time in the past. He wrote Morgenstern: "The winter semester is over. Never before does a semester seem to have gone by so quickly. I devoted the greatest part of the time to Assyrian, with the result that I expect to be able to skip the second level entirely, and enter the third level course under Meissner next semester.["29] That semester completed, Glueck wrote his family on June 5, 1927 and summarized his experiences in Germany: "Aside from that first awful year, my stay in Germany has been wonderful. I feel that I have used my time advantageously, I have grown much, and I have — because of deepening understanding and increasing knowledge — become a better Jew."[30]

Now Glueck had time to think about his future: his immediate plan was to spend a year in Palestine. He would venture back to his Jewish roots in the ancient and sacred soil of Palestine and adjacent lands so central to the biblical experience. Palestine beckoned to him both for the historical terrain it offered and for the theology nourished by it. Where would he stay? Morgenstern advised him that the Johns Hopkins based archaeologist William Foxwell Albright was back in Palestine excavating at Tel Beit Mirsim.[31] Perhaps he might try to connect with him.

Glueck wrote to Albright, asking him whether he could stay at the American Schools of Oriental Research as Sheldon Blank had done two years earlier. Albright's affirmative reply sealed the arrangement. Stimulated by reports of archaeological discoveries in the Near East and looking forward to spending a year or so in a part of the world saturated with Jewish history, Glueck prepared to leave Germany. He spent a farewell week at Jena, a few days with Walter Rothman and his wife in Switzerland, and a happy time in Italy, where he initiated a life-long love for the Italian countryside. On September 7, 1927 he sailed on the *Suwa Maru*, which conveyed him from Naples to Port Said. From there Glueck planned to take the ten-hour train trip to Jerusalem, where he would celebrate the High Holy Days in Palestine for the first time.[32]

4

The Nascent Archaeologist

Archaeology is the handmaiden of history.

Palestine in 1927, when Glueck arrived, was a country administered by the British government under a mandate of the League of Nations affirmed at San Remo in 1920. The mandate would last from 1922 to 1948 and provide the crucible in which the Zionist enterprise could learn how to govern a country. Jerusalem served the British as their administrative capital, and the American Colony Hotel on Salaḥ ed-Din street provided them with their premier social "watering-hole."[1] Glueck later discovered the unique ambience of the hotel and eventually spent a considerable amount of time there, becoming a friend and confidant of the British officials and Arab leaders who also enjoyed its charms. But that was all in the future.

At the time, Glueck was influenced by the enthusiasm of his friend and mentor Jacob Marcus, who had spent the summer of 1926 at the recently founded Hebrew University of Jerusalem. Marcus had seen at first hand the opportunities that such a university could provide to American scholars. He believed that the new school could produce graduates who would be conscious of their cultural traditions and of the possible ways they could improve the world. In fact, he saw the Hebrew University as a place that would "revolutionize world Jewry and start the blood pounding through its veins."[2] Marcus had shared his visionary optimism with his younger colleague, and that, coupled with Glueck's yearnings for archaeological adventure, had no doubt convinced him to come to Palestine.[3]

Twenty-seven years old, fresh from his sojourn in Germany and fortified with a Ph.D. from the well-regarded University of Jena, Glueck inaugurated his connection with Palestine in Jerusalem, the historic city of David. Jerusalem had been conquered by many different armies throughout the millennia. The latest general to enter the city in triumph had been the British General Edmund Allenby, who liberated Jerusalem from four centuries of Turkish domination in December, 1917. Jerusalem in those days was a city of modest size, a bit "backward" because of centuries of Ottoman neglect. Of all the great designs of Suleiman the Magnificent (1520–1566), only the city wall that he built remained. At the beginning of the century, when it was still one of the furthest outposts of the Ottoman Empire, Jerusalem had a population of 70,000, of whom the majority (45,000) were Jews, and most of the rest Muslim Arabs.[4] Followers of a pastiche of Christian denominations comprised the remainder of the population. In addition to its permanent residents, the city was host to many pilgrims who came to view and pray at its shrines from all corners of the world. The largest number of visitors to Jerusalem in the first decades of the twentieth century came from Russia. As so many had before him, Glueck found Jerusalem fascinating:

> This city grows on one more and more. One sees all kinds of people and hears all kinds of languages. I guess every type of Jew in the world is represented here, from smartly dressed American businessmen to the Polish Jews with their *peyyot*[5] and *kaftans*[6] and fur-trimmed hats. Automobiles, carriages, diminutive donkeys carrying two big men, camel trains, goat herds pass one promiscuously on the street. It is the orient, a fairly modern orient, but nevertheless the orient. I have just been over in the old part of the city, passing through some of the narrow, quaint bazaars.[7]

While the initial years of British rule in Palestine were relatively peaceful, the anti-Jewish riots of 1929 resulted in the deaths of scores of Jews and the destruction of the historical Jewish community of Hebron. Thus was inaugurated a period of palpable tension and bloody conflict, which lasted until the British relinquished the mandate in May of 1948.

What was Glueck looking for when he arrived in Jerusalem? The training he had received at the Hebrew Union College scarcely conditioned him to take a favorable view of the Zionist aspirations of Palestinian Jewry. He was, however, conscious that he was following in the footsteps of his rabbinical colleague Judah L. Magnes, who had settled permanently in Palestine some years earlier. Having completed his dissertation on biblical theology, Glueck longed for an experience with the land itself and an encounter with the geographical locations that framed the sacred story of his people.

The man who would be of inestimable assistance to Glueck was waiting for him at the American Schools of Oriental Research on Salah ed-Din Street. William Foxwell Albright had arrived in Jerusalem eight years earlier to become the acting director of the American Schools. Albright had developed an insatiable curiosity about the ancient Near East when he was still a precocious adolescent. As Philip King, the historian of the American Schools, described it, "The classic [book] at that time, *History of Babylonia and Assyria* by R.W. Rogers, fired Albright with such youthful enthusiasm that he could hardly wait to get to Jerusalem before . . . all the tells [archaeological sites] had been dug."[8] Having written an outstanding essay on the ancient Akkadian language while still in high school, Albright had been awarded a fellowship to study Semitics at Johns Hopkins University, where he earned a doctorate and wrote a dissertation on the Assyrian Deluge Epic. In Palestine, Albright soon became Glueck's mentor. All of the initial steps in Glueck's career were accomplished under Albright's tutelage, most notably at Tell Beit Mirsim, whose excavations marked a watershed in the techniques employed by archaeologists to stratify what was found at a dig.

Before Glueck could enter seriously into any archaeological endeavors, however, he needed to acquire the language of Palestinian Jewry. He wrote to his family and explained: "Till I have mastered at least Hebrew well, I shall not have time to do much sightseeing."[9] By reputation, the very best teacher of Hebrew for foreigners like Glueck was Dr. Yitzchak Epstein. Just two weeks after he arrived, Glueck reported, "I have begun to take my noon and evening meals at Dr. Epstein's house. So far I am very well satisfied, especially because I hear nothing but Hebrew and beautiful Hebrew there. I even think that I shall move over there entirely." Indeed, for some weeks Glueck boarded with the Epsteins to give himself a "leg up" on the learning process.[10] Glueck soon became an "enthusiastic Hebraist," and spoke English only to Christians. His zealousness for Hebrew reached such a pitch that one day his teacher said to him: "From now on I am referring to you not as Nelson Glueck, but rather by your Hebrew name, Nissan Mazal."[11]

Some of the neighbors noticed Dr. Epstein's long-term guest. One Jewish Jerusalemite entered Dr. Epstein's home and said to him, in Yiddish: "I see that there is an American Jew coming in and out of your house to study with you. What is his profession?" (in Yiddish: "*Az vos tut er?*"). The visitor was astounded at Epstein's response: "*Er liegt in drerd*" ("he lies in the earth"), conveying a truth about Glueck's vocation but implying that Glueck was dead.[12] Glueck was not present at the time, but he surely would have understood the Yiddish (it was spoken in his childhood home) — and appreciated the humor.

*

The first archaeologist of note to recognize the importance of dating the layers of a tell by means of ceramic remains was an Englishman, Sir Flinders Petrie.[13] Before Petrie's pioneering work in the 1890s, archaeologists had very few clues to the dating of any stratum of a site. Digging at Tell el-Hesi, the "mound of many cities," Petrie demonstrated by his careful excavation the value of the humble potsherd for dating ancient remains. He claimed that he could ride over the ruins of ancient civilizations and determine their age without even dismounting from his horse![14] Thirty years were to pass before Albright came along to make much more systematic use of this new technique. During those years, excavations at Gezer and Samaria had greatly enlarged the corpus of knowledge of pottery forms and the major periods in Palestinian history to which each belonged.

As devout Christians, both Petrie and Albright brought to their work a passion for the discovery and positive identification of biblical antiquities that could connect the faithful with the places and people described in their sacred texts. Such efforts could anticipate support from their native lands and their denominational headquarters.[15] Indeed, in the 1920s archaeology in Palestine was undertaken by four nations — the Americans, the British, the French, and the Germans — each of whom had established an independent institution to further its work and to coordinate local efforts. Three of the schools were located near Ethiopia Street in new Jerusalem: the American Schools of Oriental Research (ASOR), the British-sponsored Palestine Exploration Fund, and the German Deutscher Palästina Verein. The French did their work through the École Biblique, not far from the Jaffa Gate of the Old City. The staff and students of these institutions would assist the field archaeologists in the identification and publication of their findings; they also managed the funds sent to them from abroad.

Archaeological activities in Palestine had gained momentum with the completion in 1924–1925 of the new building of the Jerusalem branch of

ASOR, which served as the social center for American archaeologists in Palestine, a place where they could network with their colleagues and further their knowledge. In his role as director of ASOR, Albright helped foster cooperation among the various expeditions as they conducted their surveys and excavated their allotted sites. Albright himself surveyed the region adjacent to the Dead Sea in 1924. The expedition, organized under the auspices of ASOR and the Xenia Theological Seminary (based in Pittsburgh), surveyed the Jordan Rift Valley. One of the sites they excavated there, Bab edh Dhra, dating from the Bronze Age, yielded a cemetery and stone pillars.

Perhaps the first Jewish Palestinian archaeologist was Lipa (Eliezer) Sukenik, a mathematics and geology teacher in a Jerusalem high school who roamed the neighboring hills and sought to identify the antiquities he stumbled across there. His most famous early discovery was a fourth-century synagogue in the Jezreel Valley, part of Kibbutz Beit Alpha, which contained an exquisitely preserved mosaic with signs of the zodiac and images of Abraham and Isaac at Mt. Moriah. Sukenik was joined in his excavation of Jerusalem's Third Wall by Leo Ary Mayer (1895–1959), who in 1925 was appointed as lecturer in the Institute of Oriental Studies of the newly established Hebrew University.

Whereas the search for buried treasure had motivated almost all of the nineteenth-century archaeologists who dug in the Middle East, by the time Albright did his pioneering work in the 1920s, the goal of excavating had become primarily the proper identification of biblical sites and, somewhat later, their proper stratification. More specifically, this work was conceived as a search for knowledge about the places frequented by the Hebrew patriarchs and Israelite kings, by the Maccabees, and by the early Christians. It is not surprising, therefore, that many of these early and mid-twentieth-century archaeologists were clergymen, as were Albright and Glueck, or the sons of clergymen.

Working with Albright, Glueck encountered a personality and a dedication to archaeological research that resonated completely with his own emerging awareness of what biblical archaeology and the biblical archaeologist were all about. If archaeology could be used to undermine the methodology of Julius Wellhausen[16] and prove the historical truth of the Bible, then Albright and Glueck were all for it. Both sought to construct a history of Israel based on the critical assessment and synthesis of biblical, archaeological, and Near Eastern studies. Glueck accepted Albright's theory that the patriarchal and Mosaic periods were histori-cal and could be dated to the Middle and Late Bronze Ages. In short, all that Glueck had hoped to study in ancient languages and history was already in the mind and grasp of the erudite scholar from Johns Hop-kins. A master/disciple relationship ensued, and a tremendous loyalty between the two men emerged that would last throughout their lives.

How did Glueck react to Albright's Protestantism? Albright took his Methodism seriously. He proclaimed his religious principles in the face of a secular, sometimes skeptical scholarly world:

[Albright] grappled with the problem of showing that a transcendent God could be found in human history. He believed simultaneously in the principles of higher criticism and in eschatology. But it was not clear how the natural could translate into the supernatural, how the human story could have a non-human significance.[17]

Albright spent his career recovering chapters of the ancient story of bib-lical Israel while ensuring that his own faith would remain intact.[18] These religious issues were reflected on, if but briefly, in a letter Albright wrote to Glueck in December of 1929. Glueck was back in Cincinnati then, teaching at his alma mater and planning to return to Palestine the fol-lowing summer. Albright wrote:

It will be a pleasure to have you with us this summer. I think that we can provide you with tent quarters at the excavation. Until I have raised a certain sum, it will be impossible to say just how well provided with funds our expedition will be. I should warn you in advance that the expedition will have a decidedly religious tone, though it will be very mixed in composition. But in our Dead Sea expedition of 1924 we had men of every faith, including Mr. Sukenik, to whom it was a novel, and at first, disconcerting experience.[19]

Glueck's academic life in Germany was dominated by a culture of learning influenced by the Enlightenment. Graduate schools like the ones Glueck attended grew more and more secular. While Glueck was no fundamen-talist, he too would struggle with those who thought it inappropriate to use Holy Scriptures to assist in a scientific endeavor. Indeed, neither Methodism nor Reform Judaism particularly encouraged digging up the past. Each saw itself as a religion of reason, a cool and deliberate detachment from the biblical account of the violent and tumultuous history of the Israelites in Canaan. Yet neither Albright nor Glueck was immune to the increasing public interest in archaeological discoveries in both the nineteenth and early twentieth centuries. Priam's Troy had been unearthed by Heinrich Schliemann in the late nineteenth century, causing a tremendous stir as thousands came to recognize that there was actually a Troy, just as Homer had described it, and a King Priam with his fabulous treasures. Subsequent archaeological work failed to confirm Schliemann's identification of the site with King Priam's reign, but the excitement generated by his discoveries never abated.

*

The 1920s, as already noted, was a seminal decade for archaeology and prehistory, and publications such as the *Sunday Illustrated News* of London were full of reports of amazing discoveries. Even before Glueck had completed his rabbinical studies in Cincinnati, the world's attention was focused on Egypt when, on November 29, 1922, the "gold-clad" King Tutankhamen's chamber was officially opened by the Earl of Carnarvon and Howard Carter, and boatloads of American and English visitors were arriving in the Middle East to view the newly found treasures.

During the years that Glueck studied in Germany, other discoveries in the fields of archaeology and prehistory were stirring enormous interest in both the world of academia and in the public imagination. The prehistoric wall paintings at Lascaux in France were discovered in 1925, and the wonders of Minoan Crete and the Indus Valley were being touted. But of greatest potential interest to Glueck were the excavations at Ur, the traditional birthplace of Abraham, being conducted by C. Leonard Woolley.[20] These excavations produced a plethora of magnificent artifacts recovered from the distant past. Two ancient cemeteries, for example, revealed masterpieces of the goldsmith's art. Discovered among the royal graves was a spectacular gold wig of one of the Akkadian kings, an artifact two thousand years older than the gold mask of Tutankhamen.[21] The public response to Woolley's pioneering work made it clear that there would also be significant interest in discoveries made in Palestine and in its geographical neighbors prominent in the biblical account. Toward that end, Glueck and Albright focused their attention on the dozens of Palestinian and Transjordanian sites not yet excavated.

Among the many important excavations in Palestine in the 1920s and 1930s were those done by the British in Jericho. From 1930–1936 John Garstang resumed the dig previously undertaken by Sellin and Watzinger in the early 1900s. Garstang's stratification of Jericho was later revised by Kathleen M. Kenyon, director of the British School of Archaeology in Jerusalem, when she re-dated the so-called "Joshua Walls" to the early Bronze Age, a full thousand years before the Israelite conquest under Joshua. There was no trace of a city wall in the late Bronze Age (1550–1200 B.C.E.), which was the generally accepted date of the Israelite incursion. Like Kenyon, Glueck was also critical of Garstang's fieldwork and called it "an example of how not to proceed."[22]

An excavation of Samaria in 1931 brought together a joint British-American-Hebrew University team. The Germans, not to be left out, participated in field archaeology at Shechem (Tell Balatah) between 1926 and 1934. The Danes worked from 1926 to 1937 at Shiloh, a biblical site that was destroyed in the Iron I period (1200 B.C.E. to 900 B.C.E.), probably by Philistines.

The excavations at Lachish (Tell ed Duweir), thirty miles southwest of Jerusalem, produced important documents. The Lachish letters, actually *ostraca* (ceramic material with names, words, or numbers written on it), were ink messages from the military governor of Lachish to a subordinate officer. The cache was uncovered in the guardhouse at the city gate in 1935 by the British archaeologist James Starkey, who was later murdered by armed bandits in 1938 during the Arab uprising.

Clarence Fisher, trained originally as an architect at the University of Pennsylvania, also played a significant role in Near Eastern archaeology during the 1920s, 1930s, and early 1940s. ASOR was his base of operations, and Nelson Glueck admired him greatly, not only because of his archaeological skill and methodology, but also for his personal qualities. Fisher undertook a major dig at Tell el Husn, situated fifteen miles south of the Sea of Galilee in modern-day Beit She'an. He and subsequent archaeologists excavating from 1921 to 1933 distinguished eighteen levels of occupation dating from 3500 B.C.E. to the early Arab period (636 C.E. to 750 C.E.). They also noted that Egyptian temples from the late Bronze Age were reused by the Philistines.

In 1925, John Breasted of the Oriental Institute of Chicago commenced excavations at Tell el Mutesellim, the site of Megiddo (Armageddon in the New Testament — where the climactic battle between Gog and Magog is to take place at the end of time). Fisher served as director of the project from 1925 to 1927, and Philip L. O. Guy, who would later become director of the British School of Archaeology in Jerusalem, succeeded Fisher from 1927 to 1935. A strong advocate of aerial photography, Guy had suspended a camera from a hydrogen balloon and managed to take superb photos of his site. Gordon Loud, who would later play a role in Glueck's life during World War II, directed the project from 1935 to 1939, when the outbreak of the war brought the project to a halt.

William Bade, a professor at the Pacific School of Religion, commenced a dig at Tell en Nasbeh, eight miles north of Jerusalem and identified with the biblical Mizpah. During excavations between 1926 and 1935, he uncovered massive fortifications from circa 900 B.C.E. Albright's work at Tell Beit Mirsim (1926–1932) and his refining of the ceramic index for Palestinian pottery helped Bade establish dates that could not be determined through stratigraphy alone.

There is no indication that either Glueck or Albright felt impelled to do any archaeological work in Jerusalem during the early years of their relationship. Perhaps because other archaeologists had already staked their claim to some of the most interesting sites,[23] or because of the political complexities, or because of the sensitivity to competing religious interests in Jerusalem's sites, Glueck and Albright looked elsewhere for the tells they proposed to examine. During his first year in Palestine Glueck made substantial progress, both in mastering spoken Hebrew and in acquiring the techniques he needed to proceed further in his archaeological endeavors. Wishing to further develop those skills, he wrote to Morgenstern asking if he might stay away another year before returning to serve on the faculty of HUC. Morgenstern replied that while he appreciated Glueck's desire to do a thorough job in these branches of knowledge and to come back to Cincinnati for his future work with the most complete and adequate preparation that it would be possible for a young scholar to acquire, he thought it was time for Glueck to leave Palestine:

> A number of considerations prompt me to this [conclusion]. In the first place, there is no pressing necessity that you should master thoroughly Modern Hebrew and Modern Hebrew Literature, and

also Arabic in the same manner that you mastered German. After all, you are to be a Biblical scholar, not a modern Hebraist nor Arabist. There could be no end to your preparation for Biblical scholarship. No man can hope to master all of this preparation.[24]

*

Glueck accepted Morgenstern's advice. As 1928 began, he wrote his family, "In all probability I shall return to Cincinnati sometime next fall, probably at the beginning of September."[25] He continued: "I may say that I hope to be connected in some manner or other with the Hebrew Union College. However, until I hear definitely what's what, it would perhaps be well for you not to speak about it." By the end of May, he was able to write home that he had received a telegram from the College informing him of his appointment to the faculty at a salary of $4,000 for the first year.[26]

In the interim, Glueck's passion became Tell Beit Mirsim, the archaeological site located fifteen miles west of Hebron that Albright had begun to dig in the spring of 1926. Working extremely hard during that first season, Albright was able to report in the *Bulletin of the American Schools'* October issue: "Nowhere in Palestine has the writer seen such ideal conditions for precise stratigraphical results. The site is free from encumbrance and exhibits three very strongly marked burnt levels, belonging to three complete destructions of the city by fire."[27]

Albright carefully studied the pottery from the successive strata and substrata. He was able to piece together the history of the site, develop the town's plan and organization, and through the burned sections to explain the catastrophes that overtook the community. This approach allowed him to identify the site as biblical Debir or Kiryat Sepher, a city captured by Joshua (15:38) and mentioned in the Book of Judges (1:11–12). It was, at the time of the conquest, a royal Canaanite city in the southwestern part of the *shefelah* (lowland), near where the Negev begins. When Albright first encountered the tell, he was impressed with its size, occupying three hectares (about seven and a half acres). It rose nearly five hundred meters above sea level. Surface exploration revealed that the mound had not been occupied since the sixth century B.C.E.[28] Further excavation indicated that it was first settled in the twenty-third century B.C.E. during the Early Bronze IIIB era. Albright had noticed that the pottery resembled that which had been imported into Egypt during the Sixth Dynasty (twenty-fourth to twenty-second centuries B.C.E.). Thus the site, in its totality, revealed a clear ceramic chronology of Palestine between the twenty-third and the seventh centuries B.C.E. As a result, part of an historical picture emerged that helped to explain the origins of the patriarchal traditions recorded in the Bible. Tell Beit Mirsim, after its conquest by Joshua, typified a town in pre-exilic Judah, that is, prior to 586 B.C.E.

Glueck arrived at Tell Beit Mirsim in the spring of 1928 accompanied by fourteen other students. The whole group attended lectures and went on trips with Albright. He took them to the eastern Galilee where, Albright recalled, a "beautiful week in December was devoted to a study of the ancient sites."

> We made the German hospice at Tabghah our base, and for nearly a week we enjoyed the charm of one of the most delightful spots in Palestine, where nature and man vie with one another to make the stay agreeable. From this base we made trips on foot, by car, or by boat to most of the interesting points on the Sea of Galilee as well as from Beth-shean in the south to Hazor in the north. While the weather was too dry for the suffering ground, it was ideal for our purposes, and the wind subsided for a whole day in order to make our trip on the lake feasible.[29]

Glueck visited other sites of interest in Palestine and Jordan on his own. A letter home in February of 1928 described his journey to and across the Dead Sea, heading up the Arnon River gorge, arriving eventually at some hot springs adjacent to the river. He went to Tel Aviv to celebrate Purim in early March, and in April he was one of several thousand witnesses to the Samaritan observance of the Passover sacrifice on Mt. Gerizim, near Nablus.[30]

He was delighted to be in Palestine: "I am very pleased that I was privileged to be here in the land of my forefathers, to walk in their footsteps, to feel their spirit, and to see with my own eyes the fulfillment of the Jewish dream to resuscitate and revive this land."[31] Celebrating the Jewish holidays in Palestine also was especially meaningful:

It is good to be in Palestine and to sense the Jewish special seasons and holidays; these times are full of life and value. I celebrated the first Seder with Dr. Epstein, of whom you have heard. In Palestine there are not two Seders like in the Diaspora.[32] The next morning, I ventured out with a group of friends for a wonderful hike to Aza and other cities in that part of the country. I returned today sunburned, tired, and happy.

　　　　　*

The letter ended: "What a shame to have to leave. This place captures my heart." He was so busy with his travels and his work with Albright that he wrote home in late May apologizing for not having written for several months: "I was a traveler, in the full spirit of the phrase 'from Dan to Beersheva,' to Moab and Edom as far as Petra, and in the Sinai."[33]

Glueck learned much from his meanderings, but Tell Beit Mirsim was his primary classroom. Rising at four o'clock in the morning, he dug for hours and spent additional hours cataloguing the baskets of sherds that were placed on the ground for his inspection. Allowing them to tell their story, Glueck quickly became an expert, able at a glance to determine the age, origin, and value of a piece. Years later his Israeli colleague Avraham Malamat confided that Glueck's reputation of being able to "read" pottery from the back of a camel both amazed and infuriated his fellow archaeologists.[34]

Learning about the organizational aspects of the expedition was also an important lesson for Glueck. He observed that a capable administrator arranged the schedule and work assignments, negotiated the leases, and sought funding for the project. But even the most capable administrator was not able to prevent the voracious fleas from landing on Nelson Glueck at night. Somehow Albright was never bothered by the insects, attributing his immunity to his Chilean birth.[35]

Glueck learned that the role of the architect in an archaeological excavation was also crucial. It was the architect who conducted the surveying and drew up the plans necessary for the excavation to begin. No less important was the photographer who depicted each level and stage of the process as the site was being excavated. Since the upper levels had to be removed to obtain access to the lower ones, the recording of the levels to be removed had to be very precise: they could never be reconstructed *in situ*. Other specialists (such as metallurgists, geologists, and hydrologists) had to be consulted as needed.[36]

Beyond the logistics of excavating a site, beyond the thrill of knowing that his ancestors had lived there, Glueck learned first-hand how to relate archaeological evidence to biblical texts. If surface pottery could give dates that so closely approximated the results from systematic excavation, Glueck thought, why not apply this decidedly easier technique to the virtually unknown lands east of the Jordan River and fill in the many blanks on the map that made the borders of Moab and Edom nearly impossible to trace? How useful could or should the Bible be as "a spade to dig with?"[37] Glueck could not have had a better guide for answering this crucial question than Albright, who had created the discipline of biblical archaeology.

*

After a five-year absence, Glueck returned to Cincinnati in September 1928 to take up his teaching responsibilities at the Hebrew Union College. He had been hired as an instructor in Hebrew and Bible, two years after Sheldon Blank had accepted a similar position. Glueck, Blank, and Marcus would now play seminal roles in preparing several generations of students for the Reform rabbinate.

Since the founding of HUC in 1875, its several presidents had brought to the position very specific and diverse attitudes toward the Bible and the meaning of revelation. Under the leadership of Isaac Mayer Wise, the school had staunchly maintained the view that the Torah was a divine document, a communication from the mouth of God to the people of Israel. A major challenge to that view, gaining increased attention at the time of Wise's tenure, was higher biblical criticism, a new science emerging from acute textual analysis.[38]

But if Isaac Mayer Wise saw higher biblical criticism as the enemy, Gotthard Deutsch, who joined the HUC faculty in 1891, was heard to say that the evidence presented by the "modern criticism" made it impossible to accept the statement that the Pentateuch existed in its entirety at the time of Moses. An even more radical viewpoint was promulgated by one of the most prominent of American Reform rabbis, Emil G. Hirsch, of Chicago, who announced that "not one single line of the Pentateuch was written by Moses in its present form."[39]

Both Deutsch and Moses Mielziner, another HUC faculty member, wholly approved the methods of higher biblical criticism. So did

Kaufmann Kohler, who became HUC's second president in 1903. Kohler's statement in a volume published by the students in 1904 is characteristic:

> Once the insights are attained the whole Bible presents to the inquirer a gradual evolution of the God idea . . . and what geology did for us in laying bare the different strata of the earth telling of the various epochs of creation, Higher Criticism does in disclosing the various stages of growth of the truth of the divine revelation.[40]

Rabbi Stephen S. Wise, who would enjoy a long and illustrious career as a rabbi, teacher, seminary president,[41] social activist, and Zionist, gave a lecture at the College in March of 1907, entitled "Is the Bible in Danger?" in which he stated:

> Yes, the Bible is in danger, not by reason of the searching of the critics, but at the hands of its friends. For my part I believe that the higher criticism was not only timely but saving. It has brought men now to focus their attention on the authority of the content of the Bible, rather than being diverted by theorizing as to its external sanctions. The Bible of the twentieth chapter of Exodus or the nineteenth chapter of Leviticus or the sixth chapter of Micah or the twenty-third and fifty-first Psalms can never be lost or endangered.[42]

Perhaps the man who most directly influenced Glueck's approach to the biblical text was Morgenstern, who as a scholar paid the highest homage to the documentary hypothesis. Not only did he accept the rubrics J(ahwistic), E(lohistic), D(euteronomic), and P(riestly); he added a fifth source, K (for Kenite) and distinguished within the major sources a goodly number of strata and substrata. Other scholars, including Blank, applied the higher critical theories to the books of the Prophets and the Writings. Glueck believed he was free to utilize their data with regard to source or date for his archaeological explorations.[43]

*

It is difficult to recreate Glueck's teaching strategies or assess their effectiveness. The general impression is that Glueck did not have the requisite patience to deal with students who were not as diligent in preparing their assignments as he thought they should be. Further, he drilled them unmercifully and "occasionally threw chalk at those who had difficulty with Hebrew grammar."[44] Students did not always know how to respond to him. On the first day of an introductory course on grammar, for example, Glueck called the roll. When he came across the names of Malcolm Stern and Dudley Weinberg, he stopped and asked: "What kind of names are these for Jewish boys who want to become rabbis?" Needless to say, Glueck had been asked the same question by one of his professors, and had been waiting for an opportunity to "turn the tables."[45]

Of course teaching Hebrew grammar was hardly Glueck's forte. Later, when he spoke about Albright's excavations or about his own explorations in eastern Palestine (Edom, Moab, and Ammon), he could be absolutely eloquent, and all who heard him were inspired by his enthusiasm and by the excitement he conveyed in recovering the story of the Jewish people in their migration from Egypt to Canaan.

Glueck advanced quickly towards tenure at HUC. By 1932, he was an assistant professor; two years later he was promoted to associate professor and began teaching the courses formerly taught by Moses Buttenwieser, who had become emeritus in 1934. In 1936 Glueck's title became Professor of Bible and Biblical Archaeology. Equally important, as Glueck moved up the academic ladder towards a full professorship, the College recognized his need to continue his active involvement with archaeological fieldwork in Palestine; he was granted leaves of absence, sometimes for prolonged periods, so he could complete his surveys.

When he returned to Palestine in 1930, Glueck continued his archaeological apprenticeship under Ovid R. Sellers at Beth Zur, a Maccabean fortress.[46] At the time, Sellers was Professor of Old Testament Language and Literature at the Presbyterian Theological Seminary in Chicago. After two more seasons at Tell Beit Mirsim (1929 and 1931), Glueck and Albright began exploring sites in eastern Palestine (Transjordan). In a letter written in May 1931, Glueck described his excitement at being able to travel with Albright, whom he described as a "mine of information," and with whom he would walk at least daily for an hour or more talking "shop." He noted, "We are planning all sorts of trips and expeditions for the future, in Palestine, Syria, Sinai, and Arabia."[47]

Glueck learned from Albright more than the discipline of a scientific expedition and the significance of reading pottery for dating the strata uncovered at a dig. Many of Glueck's teachers in Cincinnati and in the German universities he had attended were scholars whose aim was to establish the grounds of religious belief in accord with what could be scientifically determined. At Tell Beit Mirsim, working with Albright and with Melvin Kyle, Glueck was in the company of men whose lives were not bifurcated into science on the one hand and faith on the other. They were perfectly comfortable pursuing their faith with the implements and methodology of science.

*

The excavations at Tell Beit Mirsim were not without their lighter moments. John Bright, a shining star in the constellation of biblical scholars and author of *The History of Israel*,[48] recalled an incident that occurred there in 1932:

> News had been received that important visitors, including the American Vice-Council [*sic*] and others, were coming to view the digs and would remain for dinner. This seemed to Albright the ideal time to have some fun. Plans were laid. Albright paid some of the Arab potsherd "boys" to catch a couple of lizards that swarmed all over the place. Nelson Glueck's job was to conceal one of the (recently deceased) lizards on his person, and during the soup course surreptitiously place it in his soup, and then with the next spoonful, fish it out for all to see, crying: "How did this lizard get into my soup?"
>
> Others of us were coached to feign illness, while still others, exhibiting disgust, were to pretend to carry on with a stiff upper lip as if nothing had happened.
>
> All went as planned. Glueck played his part masterfully, pulling out the lizard with a roar of shocked surprise and looking as if he were going to be ill. Albright shouted with feigned anger, "I told the cook never to make that lizard soup again!" He then called to the cook and spoke to him sternly in Arabic (actually, he made casual conversation about the meal, but since none of the visitors understood Arabic, the effect was the same), and as might be predicted, pale faces were everywhere, some of the guests looked ill (and it

unfeigned), and one may even have stepped outside. Albright, seeing that matters had gone far enough, explained that it was all a joke, and everybody laughed.[49]

*

Glueck was fresh from two seasons of digging with Albright at Tell Beit Mirsim and had completed his first year as an instructor on the faculty of HUC when he spoke at the annual meeting of the Central Conference of American Rabbis in June, 1929. Entitled "Recent Archaeological Work in Palestine," his address began with the assertion that "archaeological finds in Palestine and surrounding countries have added enormously to our knowledge of the Hebrews whose history has been and is still most incomplete. . . . Much light has been cast upon life in Palestine from discoveries made outside of it."[50]

He took his listeners back to 1865, the year that the Palestine Exploration Fund was organized under British auspices. Its mission was to encourage topographical and geographical research and to study prevalent plant and animal life as well as the inhabitants and their culture. No actual excavations, he noted, had been undertaken until 1890, when Flinders Petrie conducted his systematic excavation at Tell el-Hesi. In quick succession, a number of important excavations followed.[51] Glueck concluded:

> The entire range of history is now the concern of scientific Palestinian archaeology, including even its prehistoric times. The discovery in the Galilee of the skull of the Neanderthal type sets the beginning of paleolithic culture in Palestine probably before 10,000 B.C.E. Thus do the mists, which shroud the history of earliest man in Palestine, begin to be blown away.[52]

Glueck's report stirred much interest. At its conclusion, Sheldon Blank stood up and stated:

> The emphasis up to the present time has been upon those sites which illustrate the culture of Palestine previous to the entrance of the Hebrews. They are important as giving the cultural background which Israel largely adopted. But for the Assyrian, Babylonian, Persian, Greek and Roman periods, very little evidence has been

uncovered. And these are precisely the periods in which we as Jews are particularly interested. In addition, some sites, such as the site of Bittur [Beitar],[53] have unique Jewish interest, and will never be dug except by Jews."[54]

Thus Blank proposed the following resolution:

> The Central Conference of American Rabbis favors the excavation of an historical Jewish site in Palestine under its auspices and in conjunction with the Hebrew University in the established manner in which that institution cooperates with organizations in such work; and further that the CCAR instructs its Executive Board to devise means whereby sufficient funds may be made available for the proper conduct of such an excavation.[55]

The resolution passed by a substantial majority. Morgenstern shared Glueck's sense of the significance of archaeological discoveries in Palestine for Judaism, and in particular for Reform Judaism:

> You have heard Dr. Glueck say that the Oriental Institute of the University of Chicago is undertaking very extensive archaeological investigations in the country ranging from Egypt on the southwest to Asia Minor and Mesopotamia on the north and east. They are undertaking this under the supervision of the eminent Egyptologist, Professor Breasted, because of their general interest in the evolution of human culture and human civilization.
>
> Now that indeed is a sufficient reason for undertaking such an enterprise, yet we Jews have a far more significant interest in this work. We have gotten to that place where most of us realize that the actual history of our religion, the actual history of the unfolding of Judaism, is by no means that which the Bible — literally interpreted — presents. That source presents information from a theological perspective, and represents the point of view of Jewish thought in the eighth, seventh, sixth, and fifth centuries, and so on, B.C.E.
>
> It is highly important that we come to know what the actual history of the unfolding of Judaism was, and this we can only know by reinterpreting the Bible from a scientific standpoint; only by

reconstructing for ourselves as completely as our sources will permit, the entire picture of the life of Israel in Palestine, from the earliest times.[56]

It was this consonance between Reform Judaism and scientific historical study that had been the hallmark of Reform Judaism ever since the days of the *Wissenschaft des Judentums* movement of the early nineteenth century.[57] Morgenstern concluded his remarks by expressing the hope that "the day would soon come" when the Hebrew Union College would have a chair of Jewish Archaeology.

Glueck, in his report, had sounded his own cautionary note about the efficacy of the Bible for reconstructing Jewish history:

> The chief source of information [about Palestinian sites], the Bible, is deficient in complete, objective, historical fact. It is not a book of history, as we understand the term today. It is essentially a theological document presenting a specific religious point of view. The facts that serve this purpose have been retained, often in barest outline, or reinterpreted. Others have been omitted entirely. A king is great or small, good or bad, depending upon whether he conforms to that which was proper in the eyes of the Lord or not.[58]

On the other hand, Glueck referred to archaeology as the "handmaiden of history." He said: "The ground shall be made to reveal its secrets. Every tell must be excavated, for the sake of the cultural records stored in it."[59] Glueck had amply demonstrated to Albright that he possessed two of the absolutely necessary attributes of an archaeologist: stamina and painstaking persistence.[60] Now he was demonstrating to his Reform colleagues his unique ability to combine information gleaned from the Bible with "facts" on and under the ground.

*

Awaiting Glueck in Cincinnati when the archaeological season had ended in 1929 were not only his position at HUC and opportunities to share his discoveries with students, colleagues, and a fascinated public, but his future helpmate, the woman who would share his life for more than forty years. Helen Iglauer was born into a family of well established, comfortable, assimilated German Jews who typified Cincinnati's Jewish elite in the early twentieth century. Her father and maternal grandfather were physicians, and early in her own life she determined that she too wanted to be a doctor. Helen was born on February 4, 1907, the eldest of three children[61] of Samuel and Helen (Ransohoff) Iglauer.[62] She was raised until her teenage years in Avondale and attended Walnut Hills High School, from which she graduated in 1925 in the first class to complete the six-year college preparatory program for which the school later achieved regional renown.

After receiving her undergraduate degree at the University of Wisconsin in Madison, Helen returned to Cincinnati, where she was introduced to the young instructor at HUC by its librarian, Adolph Oko.[63] He said to her in his best Teutonic English: "Helen, I vant you to meet someone. He's the handsomest man I ever saw, but he's a son of a beech." Being the kind of person she was, Helen wasn't put off in the least by this unusual description of a potential husband, and soon Glueck and the aspiring doctor fell in love.[64]

Helen's announcement that she would marry a rabbi came as a distinct shock to her parents. In their circles, religion was usually a peripheral matter, and while her mother had served as vice-president of the oldest Reform congregation in Cincinnati and chair of its music committee, her father never attended services and was described as a confirmed agnostic.[65]

Nonetheless, Glueck found a way to win her parents' approval. One evening the couple, now engaged, was sitting in the family living room on Glenmary Avenue discussing their plans while Dr. Iglauer lay dozing on the couch nearby. Helen abruptly said to Nelson: "Promise me you won't ever take a congregation!" She was concerned about the responsibilities she would have as a rabbi's wife and the effect it would have on her budding medical career. "I'll promise no such thing," Nelson replied. With that, Dr. Iglauer sat bolt upright and said, "I like that young man!"[66]

Their relationship was built on love, but also on a deep appreciation of their mutual needs to establish their respective careers. It would never be easy. When Helen applied for an internship, it was her marriage to Nelson Glueck that posed a problem. The chief of staff at the University of Cincinnati Medical School, Marion Blankenhorn, wanted to turn her down, not because of any flaw in her academic record, and not even (so he said) because she was a woman, but because, in his view, her husband was going to be a famous man, and she would have to sacrifice her professional goals in order to help him.

> *Blankenhorn:* "You'll just never have time for your medicine."
>
> *Helen replied:* "I just don't think that's true."
>
> *Blankenhorn paused and then said:* "I'm going against my better judgment, but I guess I'll admit you anyway on account of your father."[67]

After a relatively brief courtship, Helen and Nelson were married on March 26, 1931 in her parents' living room. Only the family and a few friends were invited. The guest list had been shortened because of the death of Helen's brother Charles a few weeks before the wedding. Both sets of parents were present, along with Helen's sister and at least some of Glueck's seven surviving siblings.[68] The newlyweds spent their honeymoon at the Don Ce-Sar Hotel in Florida, located on St. Petersburg beach, twelve miles from the city.

The unique nature of the couple's relationship was quickly revealed when Nelson, married slightly more than a month, left in early May via train to New York, where he would board a ship that would take him back to Palestine. At breakfast aboard the Southwestern Limited, traveling along the Hudson River, he wrote to Helen: "It was rotten waking up this morning. Gee, but I felt lonely. I haven't really noticed I was away till now. I felt pretty low last night, but this morning it was terrible."[69]

From New York: "How I love you. I'm in a complete daze here. I don't know whether I'm coming or going. All I know is that I miss you terribly, and that there is an ache because I am going away without you. But we'll see each other soon; then it will be grand!"[70] Then from his ship, the RMS *Lancastria*, he wrote again: "Helen dear, received your telegram and was awfully happy to have word from you. You are the object of all my thinking. I miss you even more than I thought I might. It will be Saturday before we land in Le Havre, and I am very lonely without you. Funny how attached one can become to another person."[71] On May 2, he wrote:

Just saw some porpoises leaping out of the water, and thought of our stay in Passe-Grille [*sic*].[72] I swear — at the moment I don't know whether we've been married for a long time or a short time, or indeed whether we are married at all. All I know is that I love you, and that my entire "me" is completely yours. I do know that I belong to you, and want to remain bound to you, and that this separation hurts. And I know that I want you to belong to me, to love me. Indeed I feel, I know you do, but I'll never take you for granted. I'm going to treat you as if you had always to be won. And you do, and I do.

He continued:

Personalities grow or decay. They are no more static than bodies, and emotions either deepen or dull. Therefore each of us will have constantly to win the other, that is to win more of the other. You are rich and we shall grow in stature as we let the roots of our being strike ever more deeply in the soil of our love. In this sense I feel married to you, that before me lies the happy future and possibility of the achievement of an ever closer union with you. I love you.

Despite these lofty declarations, Glueck's frequent absences, extending for months at a time and sometimes for much longer, would put a strain on their marriage.

5

Head of the American Schools

Out of the dust and sands piled up by
three millennia of time, a slender young man has unearthed
secrets hitherto little known and hardly realized.

— Irving A. Mandel

William Foxwell Albright's tenure as head of the American Schools of Oriental Research was interrupted in 1928–1929 when he returned to Baltimore, but he was back in Jerusalem by the summer of 1929. In 1931 he and ASOR joined forces with the McCormick Theological Seminary in Chicago in a project at Beth Zur, a Maccabean fortress located four miles north of Hebron.[1] When in the spring of 1932 Albright decided to return full-time to teaching at Johns Hopkins University, the American Schools sought an appropriate replacement for him as head of the institution in Jerusalem.

There were few candidates. Those archaeologists who failed to appreciate Albright's pioneering technique of reading ceramic remains were not given serious consideration.[2] Instead, Albright turned to his student Nelson Glueck, whose dedication to his work and passion for discovering the roots of his Hebrew ancestors all commended him for the position. Although he was an unusual choice for a school supported primarily by American Protestant seminaries, perhaps Albright reasoned that Glueck could make good use of his knowledge of the Hebrew Bible to help locate sites to be excavated, and that the archaeologists working under his guidance would benefit from his energy and enthusiasm for the tasks at hand. Albright obviously also minimized the fact that Glueck's administrative skills were untested. Dating pottery might be an admirable attribute, but it didn't translate into the requisite experience for planning, funding, and running a major archaeological excavation. Nonetheless, after working with Glueck for three years at Tel Beit Mirsim and observing his work at Beit Zur, Albright had confidence in his young protégé.

Glueck took over when Albright returned to Baltimore in 1932, and the next year he also accepted an appointment as Annual Professor of the

School in Baghdad; he was well on his way to becoming an independent and innovative archaeologist. In December 1932, the newly appointed head of ASOR began his first exploration of eastern Palestine, intending to locate as many biblical sites as possible east of the Jordan River, to define the boundaries of the ancient kingdoms of Edom and Moab, and to gather information on other strata of settlement. He set out for Mafraq in northern Transjordan accompanied by his wife Helen, by Mrs. George Horsfield, wife of the director of the Transjordanian Department of Antiquities, and by six soldiers and an officer of the Arab Legion. Mafraq was a quiet, undistinguished town at the time. Before World War I, a railway line — the Hejaz — had been constructed and ran through the town, serving Muslim pilgrims participating in the *haj*, the annual pilgrimage to Mecca. During that war, T. E. Lawrence and his Arab auxiliaries succeeded in blowing up long stretches of the railway and thus rendering it useless to the Turks.

Mafraq's strategic importance as a crossroads convinced Glueck that the town had been inhabited during the Iron Age — the time of the Israelite kings. On this expedition Glueck honed his knowledge of the use of cisterns, reservoirs, and rainfall in the arid desert of Transjordan. Riding at the head of the group as they passed a reservoir some thirty-five kilometers from Mafraq, he explained to his companions that the water supply allowed the settlement to thrive in the desert. One strong rain at the beginning of the rainy season could fill the reservoir and supply the needs of an entire village.[3] This kind of knowledge would serve Glueck well in his later work in the Negev and make him a valuable advisor to the British Eighth Army during World War II.

At the southern end of Transjordan was the town of Kilwa, which Glueck may have known about from the letters of Gertrude Bell, the first European traveler to take note of the town.[4] Between Mafraq and Kilwa lay the settlements and remnants of the ancient Moabite and Edomite civilizations. The young archaeologist studied the water situation in each village he encountered in order to identify the *wadis*, river beds that were dry during most of the year, but bursting with water during the occasional desert rainstorms. While the *wadis* could provide water only infrequently, the cisterns, when filled, provided a reliable water source for the Bedouin and their goats and camels. In Kilwa, Glueck found small buildings constructed of basalt blocks. When he came across a

Maltese cross carrying the inscription: "In the name of God . . . made this cell," he presumed that the site was the seat of a Christian monastic community.[5]

As significant as the cisterns and settlements were, the roads and caravan routes held even greater fascination. Glueck was excited about the prospect of mapping out the King's Highway, known in various historical periods as either Trajan's or Sultan's Road. He hypothesized that the highway was the same one Moses had used to lead the Israelites northward, and, given the topography of the area, the road was still being used in modern times — leading from Aqabah in the south as far as Syria in the north.[6]

In this first expedition, Glueck explored the regions from the Yarmuk River bordering Syria to the Gulf of Aqaba at the southern extremity of the Negev. The gulf forms part of the great Rift Valley, which reaches from Turkey to East Africa and contains the Jordan River and Valley, the Dead Sea, and the Wadi Arabah. He also traversed a wide area of the highlands above the Wadi Arabah. Glueck's second expedition fixed the borders of Edom to the south. In both, he examined ancient towns, forts, and mining sites. The first trained archaeologist to visit many of these sites, Glueck was able to use his ability to date and identify pottery and to sketch in broad strokes the history of the area east of the Jordan River and the Arabah rift.

Through intense, concentrated effort Glueck sifted through thousands of pottery sherds and reached several conclusions based on his surveys: first, that Edom and Moab had known flourishing civilizations in two designated periods — the twenty-third to the eighteenth centuries B.C.E., and the thirteenth to the eighth centuries B.C.E. He was unable to definitively account for the five-hundred-year hiatus between the two, but surmised that the Hyksos invasion[7] had caused the downfall of the earlier civilization. He concluded that the "ending" in the eighth century B.C.E. might have been the result of the Assyrian monarch Tiglath Pileser III's incursions into the area, or it might be dramatic proof of the account of the Israelite king Amaziah, as it appears in II Kings 14:7: "He defeated ten thousand Edomites in the Valley of Salt, and he captured Sela in battle and renamed it Joktheel, as is still the case."

Glueck's endeavors established an archaeological record of Edom and formed the basis for a history of the region. His work also generated a number of other hypotheses: that Edom and Moab were occupied simultaneously and that their histories ran two parallel courses; that the history of these settlements and their abandonment could be explained by political and economic factors rather than by climatic changes; that the Hyksos may have been responsible for the destruction of both; and that an advanced civilization flourished in Edom from the twenty-third to the eighteenth centuries B.C.E. and then disappeared. Glueck saw in these events confirmation of the battles described in Genesis 14. Agreeing with Albright, Glueck identified this period, Middle Bronze I, with Abraham.

Further, Glueck hypothesized that the complete absence of settlement in Moab and Edom between the eighteenth and the thirteenth centuries B.C.E was possibly due again to the Hyksos threat, which created the impetus for the population to abandon the unwalled settlements and concentrate in fortified towns. The five-hundred-year decline in population parallels the sedentary settlement of the Negev, the Wadi Arabah, and the Sinai. Glueck hypothesized that the explanation for this phenomenon lay with the heavy use of coastal routes between Canaan and Egypt, while the collapse of the Middle Bronze I civilization made it too difficult or dangerous for sedentary people to live in the interior.

From the eighth century B.C.E on, Edom's power rapidly disintegrated — a decline that Glueck ascribed to the constant warfare with Israelite kings, including but not restricted to Amaziah. In their initial period of expansion, the Edomites had competed successfully with their neighbors and engaged in trade, agriculture, mining, and smelting. Their boundaries were well protected by a system of border fortresses, each one visible from the next. His final conclusion concerned the end of the Early Iron Age II period. In many sites, from about the eighth century B.C.E on, there was another gap in the history of settled communities in Edom. That hiatus lasted until the appearance of the Nabataeans in the fourth century B.C.E., by which time the newer inhabitants from South Arabia had gained control of the trade routes leading out of the Arabian Peninsula. The Nabataeans adopted the methods of organization and defense that the Edomites had used a thousand years earlier; they built many new settlements, fortresses, and watch towers of their own. After three

centuries of growth, unusual success in harnessing scarce rainwater
for irrigation, and the completion at Petra of a magnificent capital
carved out of red sandstone, the Nabataeans were overcome by the
forces of the Roman Emperor Trajan in 106 C.E. and quickly collapsed
into insignificance.

*

When Glueck went out into the desert he traveled with two companions:
Ali Abu Ghosh, a Muslim Arab, and Rashid Hamid, a Muslim Circassian
whose father had been the governor of the district of Jerash (north of
Amman) in the last decades of four centuries of Turkish rule (1517–1917
C.E.). In the company of these two guides, Glueck was assured of admission to the Bedouin tent-camps whose support, or at least tacit approval,
was critical to the success of his missions. Both guides had special status because of their association with the Transjordanian Department of
Antiquities; they were indispensable to Glueck, who always sought their
advice, even if he did not always follow it.

Glueck recalled a particular incident in Transjordan when Abu Ghosh
was leading the expedition up to a pleasant hilltop where the group decided to make camp. Weary after the day's journey, Glueck decided not
to visit the encampment of the local Bedouin chieftain. Abu Ghosh
remonstrated with him to no avail. In the middle of the night, a menac-
ing group of armed Bedouin approached them. Glueck described what
happened next:

> A shout stopped them, and then it took a very long explanation to
> satisfy them as to our identity. Not having visited their tents when
> we were so near, they thought that we must be up to no good busi-
> ness, which they proposed to forestall before it could be executed.
> Had we not had something to conceal, so ran their logic, we would
> have presented ourselves in the normal and polite fashion, made
> ourselves known, and given them the pleasure of extending hospi-
> tality to us.
>
> We talked ourselves out of the embarrassing situation, and finally
> were left to sleep out the rest of the night after we had assured them
> that we would appear on the morrow and have breakfast with
> them. We did not tell them that another reason for our reluctance
> to spend the night in one of their tents was a sudden but deter-

mined disinclination to be bitten by the innumerable fleas certain
to be encountered there.[8]

*

Having taken a leave of absence from her medical studies to join her
husband, Helen Glueck arrived with him in the late summer of 1932 to
take her place as the wife of the director of ASOR. Glueck was eager
to introduce her to Albright. As he had written to her from the SS *Lancastria* on his way back to Palestine just a few weeks after their wedding
in Cincinnati:

> I have been boosting your stock, telling him what a good sport, ath-
> lete, etc., you were, and how, especially with your medical education,
> you would prove to be a distinct asset to any expedition. So be pre-
> pared in several years to be dragged along to some crazy place on
> some crazy expedition. I'm wild to go to Sinai and Arabia.[9]

Helen cherished a very vivid memory of her first exposure to Jerusalem
and to ASOR. Speaking many years later about her experience, she said:

> In those days Jerusalem was a small city, something like 60,000
> inhabitants. We lived in a completely Arab neighborhood; the Amer-
> ican School was one of the few places where Jews and Arabs could
> meet. There were such exciting people around — among them fellow
> Americans like Judah Magnes, founder of the Hebrew University,
> and Henrietta Szold, founder of Hadassah. Dr. and Mrs. Magnes
> were probably our best friends.[10]

Retrospectively she described what it was like to live in the Jewish community of Jerusalem in the early 1930s:

> You never dressed up. Entertaining was different too. People had
> very few worldly goods. You would be invited out, often for Shabbat,
> but then again, not even necessarily for dinner. You'd come over for
> coffee after dinner, or if you were invited to eat, you could guess
> what would be served. If it was a Russian home, you'd get cabbage
> rolls or something similar; if it was a German place, you'd always
> get *kugel* [noodle pudding]!

Helen recalled asking Nelson, upon her arrival at ASOR, "Who does the marketing?" He replied: "I don't do it — the cook does!" Helen was determined to take matters into her own hands:

> Nelson and I took a walk in the old city. It was very different then — no souvenir shops, just basically fruit and vegetable and meat stalls — I could never get used to slabs of meat hanging up with flies in all directions. When I learned that Shukri the cook got a kickback from the vendors he used, I said: "I don't think that's right." So Nelson said: "Why don't you try it for a week?" So I did. And not knowing a word of Hebrew or Arabic, it was quite a task. I lasted one whole day, and gave the job back to Shukri!

Glueck rarely had time to spare on non-archaeological matters during the first season's excavation at Tell el-Kheleifeh, the biblical Etzion-geber, in 1936. But Helen was again in residence at ASOR as the wife of the Director. She had returned to the States in 1933 to complete her medical studies, and now, as Dr. Helen Glueck, was at her husband's side. According to family members, it would prove to be a difficult year for her. She and Nelson were hoping to have a child after five years of marriage, but their baby was still-born.[11] After recovering physically and emotionally from her loss, Helen found work as the housekeeper at the American Schools and could by then speak with the plumber in Hebrew![12] Occasionally Glueck would return from his excavating to spend time with her. In May of 1938, he wrote to the Cincinnati family:

> Helen and I went to the Toscanini[13] concert. Two days later, with a new architect, and Iliffe,[14] we returned to Aqabah in one day via Hebron and Beersheba (with a police escort). And then via Kurnub and the Arabah to our camp. In about a week we shall return to Jerusalem, and call it a season. I am nowhere near finished, and we will have to dig here again next spring if I can raise the money.
>
> I think I already told you that we have excavated the largest smelting and refining plant in the Ancient Near East. We are still working on it, because it is an exceedingly intricate structure, and has been badly destroyed, after being rebuilt in three different periods. Working it all out has been sort of fun, after the sand and heat has been forgotten a bit.

In the late summer of 1938 Helen was pregnant again; it turned out to be a difficult pregnancy, and she spent a good part of it confined to her bed. The Glueck's only child, Charles Jonathan Glueck, named after Helen's late brother, arrived on March 10, 1939. Helen was being cared for by Dr. Zondek, a member of the staff of the Hadassah-Rothschild hospital on Mt. Scopus, and a close personal friend. Despite the stress of the pregnancy, the baby boy was healthy, and Glueck seized the opportunity to inform his in-laws in his own inimitable style:

> *Dear Ma and Dad Iglauer,*
>
> My son has arrived! He weighed in at 4 and ½ kilos! Meanwhile Dr. Haim Yassky,[15] the director of the hospital and his wife had come round and were waiting outside the birthing room with me. Then the nurse brought out the brat[16] well-wrapped up in a blanket to be taken outside to the building where the maternity ward is located.[17]

Later that summer, eager to get back to Cincinnati and the support of her family and friends, as well as to get away from Palestine's unsettled and often dangerous conditions, Helen left Jerusalem with her baby; she would never again live in Palestine or Israel, though she accompanied her husband from time to time when he traveled there.

*

In the spring of 1935 an article by Glueck in *The American Israelite*, a Jewish weekly published in Cincinnati, generated enormous interest in his work.[18] Glueck claimed that "the happy destiny of the Jews — at least of many thousands of them — lies in Transjordan."[19] The bases for his astonishing conclusions were, first, that there were thousands of acres of fertile land available; second, archaeological evidence indicated that the high plateau lands of Edom and Moab had been heavily populated throughout their early history, had been later abandoned, and were currently desolate only because of political factors; third, ample water was available; fourth, the climate was healthful; and fifth, the native Arab population of all Transjordan was only about one-third of the native Arab population of Palestine. According to Glueck, settlement of Jews in Transjordan was "inevitable."

Further, Glueck said, "The Jews' future in Palestine lies not in obtaining

Western markets, but in reopening the Eastern world, and in restoring its ancient fertility and wealth. The Jews are the natural persons to do this." Given Glueck's reputation as an archaeologist, his application of ancient findings to solve modern problems might have been taken seriously by some. However, it seems that no practical programs ever emerged from his proposal.

In his wanderings in Transjordan, Glueck seemed unconcerned about the first stirrings of armed resistance to Jewish settlement in Palestine. His first three years as director of ASOR were essentially free of the kind of trouble that occurred later with persistent frequency. By 1935, however, the banditry of a group known as the Black Hand, led by Sheikh Izz el-Din el-Qassam, posed a serious threat to Zionist settlers. The Sheikh and some of his close followers were eventually killed by a British patrol in November 1935 — thereby giving Arab nationalism its first *shahid* (martyr). But before Glueck embarked on his third expedition, the troubled relationship between the native Arabs and the growing Jewish population, expanded mostly by immigrants from Germany, erupted in violence, compelling him to pay attention. Three Jews were killed by Arabs on April 15, 1936, and the Mufti of Jerusalem, Haj Amin el-Husseini, coordinated a series of strikes and violent protests in many localities.[20] Rioting spread throughout the country, and the turmoil lasted for four years, almost until the outbreak of World War II.

In response, the British sent a group of jurists, known as the Peel Commission, the first of a number of such commissions, whose appearance accentuated the difficulties Britain was having with the Mandate. The Peel Commission met with representatives of all interested parties, and their conclusions were announced on July 7, 1937. They called for a partition of Palestine between an Arab segment and a Jewish segment, with some portions to remain under the control of the mandatory authority. A Jewish state would be established from Tel Aviv to the Galilee, and the Arabs would retain the central hill country and the Negev, under the suzerainty of Emir Abdullah of Transjordan.

The recommendations of the Peel Commission were hotly debated by leaders of the Jewish community in Palestine, including Judah Magnes, Chancellor of the Hebrew University, who thought such a partition would be a recipe for disaster. Glueck agreed with his rabbinical colleague and fellow American. Unlike Magnes, however, he did not publicly proclaim his opinion and certainly made no effort to participate in any of the discussions that roiled the Jewish community. Granted, he was often many miles away, engaged in archaeological surveys, but apparently he believed the British Mandate to be a reliable source of stability in Palestine, as it was in Transjordan. As long as he could do his excavations and his friends weren't getting shot, he had no special inclination to be working on behalf of an independent Jewish state.[21] Indeed, throughout his life Glueck maintained a neutral stance when it came to Zionist politics, just as he had done in regard to the proposal for a Jewish army. Many years after he completed his terms of service with ASOR, he noted in his diary: "I think everyone connected with ASOR should stick to his scientific work and not venture into the field of politics or politicizing. During my tenure at ASOR I never engaged in public or newspaper or magazine discussion about political matters."[22]

Because of his many contacts, Glueck was well versed in the comings and goings of the two most prominent Arab families in Jerusalem, the Husseinis and the Nashashibis. Nevertheless, he never once provided information to the authorities about them and later noted, "I guess that is one of the reasons I was not rubbed out during that period, nor my wife or anyone at the School ever threatened, let alone harmed."[23] By the end of 1938, three years of rioting had taken their toll, and the British were sending in more and more soldiers. Eventually 100,000 British troops would be maintaining the security of Palestine, a burden of which the British would eventually tire. In September Glueck wrote to his family:

> Returned yesterday from a successful exploration in Transjordan. The situation has in no wise improved, but it cannot get much worse. About nine thousand more troops are coming in at the end of the month. The dormitory [at ASOR] is practically empty.[24]

Jerusalem was at the center of the storm. In late October Glueck reflected on the futility of the British efforts to control the situation:

> The old city has been recaptured [from marauding Arab bands] but most of the members of the bands escaped over the walls by ropes. Twenty-nine Arabs were reported killed by English soldiers. About half a dozen were women and children who had accidentally

gotten in the way of bullets. The other 23 Arabs died laughing, I believe, at the windmill antics of the soldiers who went through all the motions excepting capturing or annihilating the enemy. A troop of boy scouts could not have done much worse.[25]

*

During his third expedition, Glueck continued to obtain a great deal of chronological information by examining the potsherds and remains from ancient sites. He had established the main features of the sedentary kingdoms that ruled that area in the early Iron Age and paid special attention to the site of er-Rameil in the southeast corner of Moab because it preserved an example of a strongly fortified village, surrounded by an outer wall and a moat.[26] In all, Glueck found thirteen such fortresses — which he speculated were used to guard against the incursions of nomads.

Another of his accomplishments during this period was correcting the dating of the Iron Age settlements in southern Gilead and Ammon, which had previously been assigned to Middle and Early Bronze Age settings. The most prominent remains were found along the caravan route leading from Arabia and the Red Sea to Damascus. While conducting his field surveys in Transjordan, Glueck set aside three months in 1937 — March, April, and December — to conduct an excavation at Khirbet et-Tannur, to be carried out jointly by ASOR in Jerusalem and the Palestine Department of Antiquities under the guiding hand of Sir Gerald Lankester Harding.[27]

In the course of Glueck's surface explorations of Transjordan, he had found hundreds of Nabataean sites, all of which were unmistakably characterized by sophisticated Nabataean pottery. Thanks to Glueck, the concept of Nabataean culture was radically changed. He showed that they had ceased to live as a group of semi-nomads and had, between the second century B.C.E. and the second century C.E., become an advanced culture. They engaged in lucrative commerce — using caravan routes and forming political liaisons of the highest order with their neighbors, the Jewish Hasmonean dynasty and the Edomite Herodian family.

The Nabataeans worshipped their gods at shrines found in many villages and sites. Of all the sanctuaries in the entire Nabataean kingdom, that of the great high place of Zibb Atuf at Petra was probably the most sacred and most frequented, and thus the most important.[28] Khirbet et-Tannur, however, seems to have been an exception inasmuch as it was solely a religious site without an adjacent village.[29] Glueck's initial examination revealed the site to be a gem of a small Nabataean temple in utter ruin on the pinnacle of the massive and almost completely isolated hill of Jebel Tannur. Shattered by earthquakes and scarred by vandals, the aura of its initial beauty still clung to it at the time of Glueck's visit, nearly two millennia after its destruction. Strewn about were masses of distinctive Nabataean pottery, including delicately painted, plain and rouletted wares and pieces of Pergamen-type *sigallata* — ceramic objects with stamped decorations. Glueck was immediately captivated by the surface remains and decided on the spot to arrange for an excavation.

The results of his efforts confirmed his initial reaction. An entire pantheon of Nabataean deities was uncovered. Atargatis, the main one, appeared alternatively as a dolphin goddess or as a goddess of vegetation, and thunderbolt-carrying Zeus-Hadad was her consort. Even the planets known at the time were deified and played a role in the Nabataean theological system. Glueck hypothesized that the Nabataeans, though strongly influenced by Hellenistic culture, were still predominantly Semitic. This last ingredient would provide Glueck with a clue to the importance of the site as a religious center.

Caravan traffic bypassed Khirbet et-Tannur. Because the site was connected to no roads at all, Glueck reasoned that only those who made a special pilgrimage would have visited it. With two nearby Nabataean sanctuaries affording visitors access, why then go through the discomfort of traveling to remote Tannur? Why was the temple of Khirbet et-Tannur necessary? Every Nabataean community in the entire kingdom had a sanctuary, a temple or an altar of its own. Any one of them dedicated to any god could easily cater to the religious needs of the Nabataean worshipper. So why build a temple in a remote, inaccessible area? What function could it serve that the others could not?

Khirbet et-Tannur is situated 550 meters above sea level, atop Jebel Tannur, an isolated mountain between Wadi el-Hasa (Nahal Zered) and Wadi el-Aban. The site is approached from the southeast by a single path cut in the rock near the top. In its austere isolation, it is comparable to Mt. Sinai, where the freed Hebrew slaves in the Exodus narrative encountered their God. Glueck noted that both sacred sites shared the qualities of remoteness and desert locale, thus investing them with a spiritual dimension, given that the Semitic concept of holiness involves a spatial separation from everyday life.

The temple is the only structure on the east side of the Khirbet et-Tannur site. The floor of its altar slopes to the southeast, allowing rainfall to run off. The altar stood on the north side of the court, and perhaps on the east side there was a ritual pool in the unpaved area. The sanctuary of all Nabataean temples was oriented to the east. Theoretically, during the solstice this would allow sunlight into the sanctuary, which was approached by four steps leading to a gateway. Over the main doorway was a bust of Atargatis. The inner court of the sanctuary was paved but open. In its center stood a shrine also oriented toward the east. A stairway led upwards, presumably to the altar. The pilasters of the east facade were decorated with rosettes and vine patterns. They were set on Attic bases (a style of pottery developed in Athens from the late seventh to the fourth centuries B.C.E.), with the winged victory (Nike) motif. In the arches, two cult reliefs were set: one of the god Zeus-Hadad and the other of Atargatis. It is possible that these cult figures were reused in the later shrine.

The second shrine was built around a smaller, cruder one, which Glueck found to be the original shrine of the site and the nucleus of the temple complex. The sculptured objects found during the excavation included a large head of the god Zeus-Hadad, revealing Hellenistic and Parthian influence; a stone water basin, on the front of which is a lion realistically carved in high relief; and a winged victory (Nike), which was found after the excavations and belongs to the zodiac. Several fragments were found of the winged Tyche, carrying aloft a cornucopia.

Glueck distinguished three building periods at the site: the initial era of construction was dated to the first century B.C.E.; from a Nabataean inscription the second period was dated to the second year of the reign of King Aretas (7 C.E.), and the last phase to the second century C.E., not long before the destruction of the site's temple, probably caused by an earthquake.

It is normal in archaeology for the last to be first and the first to be last, particularly in places where the unfolding scene and progressive span of history remain attached to the same spot. For Glueck, then, it was exciting to see the three altars unfold their history beneath his hands. It was like reading a book backwards, but with increasing excitement along the way. He initially concluded that Tannur's appeal must have been regional or national in character. Awesome to behold, it stood apart from all the other shrines, including Petra, in its solitary splendor on top of a holy hill, a fitting abode for its deities. Its solitude could be thought of in defensive terms, though that did not seem to have been a requirement for other Nabataean temples. At one point he reasoned that it was simply an old Edomite altar that the Nabataeans took over. However, he found no evidence of Edomite occupation. Perhaps it was the ancient lure of a mountain that tempted the Nabataeans, just as Sinai had overwhelmed the Semitic Israelites.

The sanctity of Jebel Tannur may have been heightened by the volcanic nature of a nearby mountain on the far north of Wadi el-Hasa. Zeus-Hadad was an old mountain god and a powerful consort to Atargatis. The volcanic nature of the area would probably have appealed to the thousands of Nabataean worshippers, who could bow before his image and offer up their flocks and the yield of their fields in hopes of prosperity.

The fortunes of nations are vitally determined not only by the exigencies of war but by the forces of commerce as well. Economic blight resulting from exhaustion of raw materials and shifting of trade routes often adversely affected entire regions, states, and cities in ancient times, even as they do in our own day. After the incorporation of the Nabataean kingdom by the Romans into their *Provincia Arabia* at the beginning of the second century C.E., the diversion of immensely profitable caravan traffic by the Roman masters drained the economic life blood of the Nabataean body politic.

Within less than a century, the unique and magnificent civilization lost its identity and ceased to exist, and the Nabataeans were absorbed by other populations and cultures. Their far-flung trade connections, reaching from Arabia to Syria, from Petra to Alexandria, and to Ascalon, Rhodes, and Rome simply faded away. The production of their beautiful and sophisticated pottery ceased. Their stylized sculptures, Hellenistic-looking temples, and amazing accomplishments based upon extraordinary agricultural, engineering, economic, and related cultural skills were relegated to the past. The fantastic city of Petra, hidden in clefts of the Edomite hills, remains an impressive monument to the incredibly high estate they achieved.[30]

Glueck was able to make a case for considering the Nabataeans a strong territory-based kingdom rather than a nomadic caravan people. He elucidated their art, their religion, their strong political organization, and their agricultural life, as demonstrated by remains of enclosures and irrigation systems in once-cultivated fields. Decades later, in the 1960s, when he completed his major work *Deities and Dolphins*,[31] he presented answers to the questions of location and holiness that had occupied him in the 1930s during the months of tedious excavation. The noted archaeologist G. Ernest Wright, in a review published in the *Journal of the Central Conference of American Rabbis* (October 1966), characterized Glueck's book as the most complete survey ever written of the gifted Nabataeans.[32] Wright noted that *Deities and Dolphins* was not an organized presentation of Nabataean history but rather an exploration of Nabataean art and religion through the prism of Khirbet et-Tannur:

> [Glueck tells] in eloquent fashion the story of a people who originally maintained an abstemious way of life similar to the early Rechabites and the later Essenes, but whose creative genius advanced them to a highly developed stage in commerce, art, architecture, and engineering.[33]

*

Nabataea, however, with all its storied beauty and intriguing religion, was of little popular interest back in the 1930s. The excavation that truly captured the imagination of contemporary Palestinian Jewry was Glueck's work at Tell el-Kheleifeh, the biblical Etzion-geber.[34] Glueck had decided to conduct a full-scale excavation there on the heels of his first survey at Khirbet et-Tannur scarcely a year before. In contemplating the site, he was influenced by a widespread desire to establish evidence for monarchical presence in a southern area — an area that Jewish inhabitants of modern Palestine hoped would one day be part of a Jewish state. Glueck himself felt a deep emotional connection with the Solomonic past in ancient Israel, just as he had felt a similar connection with the patriarchs during his explorations of eastern Palestine.

In his *Rivers In The Desert: A History of the Negev*, published in 1959, Glueck vividly recalled the first time he saw the mound in the Arabah that Fritz Frank, the German archaeologist,[35] had recently identified as King Solomon's seaport on the Red Sea:

I shall never forget the day we came to the crest of the inconspicuous watershed near the southern end of the Wadi Arabah, and saw the deep blue tongue of the Gulf of Aqabah ahead of us. It extended southward as far as one could see between haze-shrouded hills of forbidding mien, forming a jagged barrier on either side. Our camels, sniffing the moisture in the air and anticipating the sweet water they must have sensed awaited them, quickened their pace and soon broke into a steady run.

Our weariness suddenly vanished. At this juncture of the continents of Asia and Africa, the boundaries of Arabia, Transjordan, Palestine and Sinai touch the northern end of the gulf, with parts of all of them becoming visible to us. This was the scene that had presented itself to the people of the Exodus. We were racing forward into the past. And soon we reached the water's edge, near which Etzion-geber had once stood.[36]

Glueck noted that the desert glistened with the light reflected from thousands of pieces of flint and copper ore mixed with the sand. He was hoping to find proof that a copper smelting plant stood here; its purpose would have been to prepare the copper ore from Timnah, which he had already identified as Solomonic.

On this expedition, Glueck was accompanied by the noted American semiticist Cyrus Gordon, who held a fellowship from ASOR in 1934–1935 and joined Glueck in his survey of Palestine.[37] Despite Gordon's skepticism (he thought it too far from the water's edge — five hundred meters — to be a port) Glueck returned to the site in November 1937 with another group of students and colleagues and conducted a surface survey to ascertain its suitability for a full-fledged excavation. Although, as noted in his field records, there was some uncertainty on his part,[38] Glueck became convinced that Tell el-Kheleifeh was indeed Etzion-geber, an equation that became the cornerstone of his reconstruction of its occupational history.[39]

Believing the site to be the gateway to Africa and Arabia, and that he could tell the story of the shipping industry of the Solomonic era from its excavation, he returned the next year (1938) with adequate funding from the Smithsonian Institution. The history of Etzion-geber, if confirmed by his explorations, would add a significant dimension not only to the accomplishments of one of ancient Israel's most celebrated kings;

it would also establish the Negev as a rich source of mineral deposits, even in the twentieth century — comparable to the resources of the Dead Sea, which were at that time already providing thousands of tons of high quality phosphates for a regional market.

Glueck addressed two other issues in the excavation: To what extent could his discoveries reflect the existence of the Solomonic empire's interest in shipping? To what extent were international commercial interests evidenced in the remains? The sparse nature of those remains did not provide sufficient answers to these questions, and consequently controversy flared, as we shall see below, in Chapter Eleven.

From March to May 1938 Glueck unearthed more than a third of Tell el-Kheleifeh's northern perimeter, uncovering in the process a complex of three small rooms. The walls of the building contained apertures along two rows. Glueck interpreted these perforations as flues. According to his theory, the building was a smelting plant wherein copper was processed; the flues transferred the heat between the chambers while the draft was provided by the upper course. Concluding that the complex was a large and elaborate refinery, Glueck sought to explain why Solomon would locate a refinery of major proportions in a coastal region removed from Timnah[40] to the west, where the ore was mined. Glueck had previously described Timnah as the largest and richest copper mining and smelting center in the entire Arabah. He proposed the following explanation:

> The builders of Etzion-geber had in mind the needs of the large refinery they were planning to erect and chose after careful examination the one site in the center of the south end of the Arabah where the winds blew strong, and constantly, and from an almost unvarying direction. They needed a constant draft from a known quarter to work the furnaces of the refinery.
>
> Without this draft, for the sake of which they were willing to endure frequent sandstorms, they could not have erected a large and elaborate refinery, and would have had to rely upon the primitive bellows-system in vogue before.[41]

The 1939 excavation season was conducted during April and May. The earliest remains at the site were dated to the tenth century B.C.E., allowing an interpretation of Solomonic origins for the early history. Glueck was convinced that Solomon was the only monarch with the resources and capability to carry out the construction of a highly complex and specialized site for smelting ore.[42] Coupled with the presumed status of the site as a port, Glueck presented Etzion-geber as a complex serving not only the kingdom of Israel but also Arabia and Africa. Indeed, Solomon's reign was a time of great economic prosperity and administrative initiative; the biblical tradition assigns innovations in trade routes in southern Arabia to that king. The port of Etzion-geber opened up economic opportunities for the southern portion of the kingdom, counterbalancing trade with the Phoenician cities of the north. Southern trade initiated by Solomon centered on Sheba and Ophir — the former generally believed to be located on the East African coast, and the latter near the bottom of the Arabian peninsula (I Kings 9:26–28; 10:1–13).

The second occupational level did not reveal much information after the reign of Shishak, the Egyptian pharaoh who destroyed it around 923 B.C.E. In that year, Shishak conducted a campaign against Israel that led to the destruction of great areas of the Judean kingdom. On their way to Jerusalem, Shishak's forces overwhelmed the defenders at Tell el-Kheleifeh, and the Judean king Rehoboam, Solomon's son, was required to pay a heavy tribute to the Egyptian king (I Kings 14:26) in order to save his capital.[43]

Certainly the trade routes were interrupted by this devastation, but before Shishak's incursion, Solomon was able to amass a great deal of gold from his southern routes. The later kings of Judah attempted, with little success, to re-establish this trade. If Tell el-Kheleifeh was also a royal fort at that time, then it would have played a significant role in the gold trade. Unfortunately, Glueck found no evidence to support the Arabian-Judean connection.

The site's third occupational level, assigned to an eighth-century B.C.E. date, is the most recent and best preserved. In his field diary Glueck describes a typical sherd found at the site:

> This inscriptional material is found in Phoenician-Hebrew inscriptions of a particular type denoting ownership, referred to by scholars as the "belonging to Qawsanal the servant of the king" type. The inscriptions are preserved on cheap and accessible sherds. The notes are quite common in Israel and demonstrate the widespread

evidence of writing. Names of owners, the contents of vessels, or their weight were incised or written in ink upon the sherds.[44]

Glueck and his team uncovered fragmentary architecture from the fourth and fifth levels, sufficient to extend the occupational history of Etzion-geber to the fourth century B.C.E. From the Aramaic *ostraca* (pottery sherds with inscriptions) found at Tell el-Kheleifeh in 1939, he could conclude that the site was occupied until 300 B.C.E.

*

Detailed and technical accounts of Glueck's explorations in Transjordan (1932–1934 and 1936–1940) and in the Negev (1942–1947) were published in the annual reports of the American Schools of Oriental Research in 1934, 1935, 1939, and finally in 1951.[45] Descriptions of these discoveries reached a more popular audience in his first book, *The Other Side of the Jordan*, published in 1940 by ASOR in New Haven. In it, he sketched the results of his archaeological explorations and excavations "toward the rising of the sun" (Joshua 12:1). Writing for the first time for non-scholars, Glueck presented his material "without the framework of scientific apparatus, but also without the sacrifice of scientific exactitude." He let his readers see, through the eyes of a *bedouin*, how a *frenji* (foreigner, i.e. Glueck) was perceived around an antiquity site — engaged in photographing, sketching, collecting potsherds, and asking all sorts of questions about sources of water. "I have on occasion," wrote Glueck, "been assiduously collecting sherds on a *tell*, when suddenly an Arab has appeared out of the blue, and asked whether or not it is some precious metal I am looking for, and if perchance the *frenji* possesses some magic whereby he can change the dull pottery to glittering gold."[46]

*

Civil disturbances continued to mar Palestine's political horizons. In a letter to Helen postmarked July 19, 1939, Glueck reported that a Jewish strike took place throughout the country that day, lasting from two p.m. until midnight. It was called to protest against the latest sell-out of the British government in canceling all Jewish immigration after June 30. Glueck wrote: "It is simply unbelievable, but the British Cabinet is desperately trying to gain the good will of the Arabs, and thinks to obtain it in this wise."[47] In his *ASOR Newsletter* No. 10, of August 18, 1939, Glueck wrote:

> The disturbances still continue in Palestine, if indeed considerably checked. The morning's newspaper reports that all traffic in and out of Hebron has been banned for some time, because a British military patrol had been fired on, and a British Lance-Corporal had been killed. A bomb was thrown in the main streets of Jerusalem two nights ago, and thirteen Jews were sent to the hospital. However, the conditions are quiet enough on the whole for the High Commissioner to have deemed it possible to leave for England on a lengthy vacation. Given the fact, however, that war was imminent, one could reasonably speculate that the High Commissioner was called back to London for consultations.

Two weeks later World War II began; for Glueck, as for most Palestinians, Jews as well as Arabs, its initial impact was limited. In his *ASOR Newsletter* No. 12 he wrote, "The German attack on Poland has had no immediate effect here, except to cause the prices of food to rise, aside, and of course, from filling everybody with consternation and foreboding. Several hundred Germans have already left the country, and it is taken for granted that the others will be interned." Another effect of the outbreak of war was the removal of all the British officials from the Rockefeller Museum, which was quite close to ASOR, and a place that Glueck visited frequently. They had all been assigned to wartime duties, so when Glueck visited the museum on September 1, there was not a single British official there. He was relieved that plans had been made to remove the objects on display to the basement for safekeeping.

With bookings for forty lectures[48] in the United States, Glueck arranged to leave Palestine for America on the *Excalibur*, which sailed from Haifa on September 11, and arrived in Boston on October 2. As he left Jerusalem Glueck saw a large registration center where Jewish citizens were offering their services for the war effort, from military enlistment to volunteering for hospital duty. Along the Street of the Prophets he passed the German Consulate, which was padlocked and guarded by two armed men: one British soldier and one Jewish policeman. En route to Haifa on September 10 he experienced his first air-raid blackout when all the lights in Haifa were turned off. Staying at a hotel atop Mt. Carmel, Glueck wrote Helen that it "was interesting to see the entire city below plunged into darkness. A number of destroyers anchored in the Haifa harbor and the presence of a boom there, which is closed to shipping at six p.m., are added indications of the menace of war as it affects Haifa."[49] As the *Excalibur* embarked westward laden with five cases of antiquities from the excavations at Tell el-Kheleifeh, their owner was busy making careful notes about all the ports at which the ship called. Alexandria, he noted, "seemed quite normal"; Piraeus, the port for Athens, was "dead," and "the harbor at Naples didn't seem nearly as busy as usual. Nor was there much movement of any other kind: scarcely any cars were visible on the streets of Naples because, presumably, of the scarcity of gasoline."[50] As the ship approached Boston it developed a terrific list, and Glueck observed that "it seems quite appropriate that the ship should be sailing at a crazy angle, when everything else in the world is so distinctly cockeyed."[51]

*

Even as he looked forward to being home, Glueck expressed deep concern about the school in Jerusalem. He wanted to get back there as soon as possible, and in the spring of 1940 he did return to the Middle East. Although certainly not the safest place in the world, it was still not involved as a theater in the war, and Glueck became convinced that he could proceed with the third season of excavations at Tell el-Kheleifeh. He then addressed himself to reviewing the interpretation of the main building on the site. He was puzzled because the flues that were vital, in his theory, to the production of copper, were covered over with plaster. This fact could have signified one of two things: either the flues were not flues but something else altogether, or refinery technology had changed in the Arabah in the early Iron Age.[52]

In the 1940 season Glueck also resolved the question of successive periods at Tell el-Kheleifeh. Different types of bricks and methods of bricklaying contributed to the problem of defining phases and relationships in construction. Period 1 was ascribed to Solomon and terminated with Shishak's invasion and destruction. The second level, which comprised the fortification system surrounding the industrial complex, was assigned to the period following Shishak. The third period was assigned to Uzziah in the eighth century B.C.E., when the name of the site was changed to Elath.

With all the evidence sifted and examined, Glueck was convinced that Etzion-geber was built by King Solomon. He surmised that the roasted ores from the mines were smelted into metallic copper to provide for the vessels in the Temple in Jerusalem and refined and cast into finished copper implements for commercial export. The metal would have been taken to Ophir by way of Tarshish to be exchanged for gold, ivory, and spices.[53] Jews throughout Palestine — including many leaders of the *yishuv*, were fascinated to learn about Glueck's conclusions.

On the other hand, those conclusions would eventually be challenged by several leading Israeli archaeologists. Binyamin Mazar, for example, suggested that Tell el-Kheleifeh was initially a Judean stronghold located at the end of the routes leading to the Red Sea, and that during the seventh century B.C.E. it passed into Edomite hands. An alternative supposition held that the site was founded as an Edomite fortress and was never related to the Judean kings at all. However, the Negebite pottery militates against this approach. From a strategic perspective it may be possible to argue, as did Mazar, that the "fortress" of Tell el-Kheleifeh represented a major effort of the Judeans to control the approach to the Red Sea .

*

By late spring of 1940, with the Germans marching toward Paris, Glueck remained on site at ASOR, mostly to attend to the School and its property and to work on his *Explorations in Eastern Palestine.* Conditions in Palestine had actually improved by that time. Norman Bentwich, a British Jew who played an important role in the Mandatory government, noted in his autobiography, *My Seventy Seven Years: An Account of My Life and Times, 1883–1960*:

> The few weeks which I spent in Jerusalem in 1940, just before Italy entered the war on the side of the Axis, were heartening. The contrast of mood between that spring and the last was amazing. In May, 1940, peace reigned within; the whole country was tranquil. No permits were required for movement; no barriers remained on the roads, no patrols scoured the streets and highways. The relations

between Jews and Arabs were normal; the two peoples dealt with each other and traveled with each other. External war on a world scale had brought internal peace.[54]

At the end of the summer of 1940, Glueck returned to Cincinnati. Only his associate, Clarence Fisher, remained at ASOR, and no new students would be coming or allowed to work if they did somehow arrive. No longer able to journey westward via the Mediterranean because of the war, Glueck engaged a driver, Emil Abu Dayeh, to take him to Baghdad. They began their trip heading eastward to Amman, then on to Mafraq, and after surviving a flood on the Euphrates and a dust-storm in the desert, they arrived in Baghdad, where Glueck stayed at the YMCA. The next morning he boarded a train to Basra on the Persian Gulf, and from thence a boat to Bombay. Finally, on July 17, he was able to board an American ship, the SS *President Monroe*, whose amenities and cuisine were far superior to what he had experienced in India. On August 24 he disembarked on American soil and continued his odyssey by train to his teaching responsibilities, his family, and soon a very different assignment.

Glueck's arrival in the Queen City generated significant excitement among the rabbinical students. Writing for the *HUC Monthly,* Irving A. Mandel wrote a piece called "The Return of Ulysses":

Out of the dust and sands piled up by three millennia of time, a slender young man has unearthed secrets heretofore little known and hardly realized. Slowly and methodically he has brought new light to bear upon the life and culture of the Jews of antiquity. He has been characterized as one who has unquestionably done more to recover the lost archaeological past of Transjordan than any other scholar.[55]

6

Opportunities at Home and Abroad

*'I want to offer my services to the government
under any conditions, anywhere.*

In its June 26, 1941 issue, the *American Israelite* reported that "Dr. Nelson Glueck, native Cincinnatian who won international fame through his archaeological research as director of the American School of Oriental Research at Jerusalem, has been called to the Institute for Advanced Study at Princeton University. There he will a join a distinguished company, including Dr. Albert Einstein." The plan was for Glueck to be in residence during the second semester of the 1941–1942 academic year. It was a great honor, to be sure, but in the event, Glueck did not go to Princeton.

*

In the summer of 1941, with America not yet involved in World War II, it was still business as usual for the Hebrew Union College in Clifton. But all was not well in downtown Cincinnati at the offices of the Union of American Hebrew Congregations. Its current leader, Rabbi George Zepin, had been serving as secretary of the organization since 1910 and during his tenure had overseen only marginal increments in membership and income. Assisted by a very small staff and frequently charged with incompetence and lack of initiative, Zepin announced his intention to retire.

The committee seeking his replacement was well pleased with the results of its efforts. The man who agreed to step into the vacancy was Edward Israel, an HUC graduate, class of 1919. Israel had served for many years as chair of the Social Action Commission of the Central Conference of American Rabbis and had a solid reputation as an advocate for social change. His administrative skills were highly regarded and he was in the prime of life — not yet 50. As he assumed his new responsibilities in the summer of 1941, Israel recognized immediately that the UAHC could not be an effective force in national Jewish life if it remained in Cincinnati, where it would always be in the shadow of HUC. The Union needed to create its own destiny in a "more important" city such as Washington, DC. Israel also recognized that the title of "secretary" in no way described the responsibilities of the office; "executive secretary," perhaps, even "president," would be far more suitable. Israel's vision for the Union of American Hebrew Congregations, however, was never realized; he succumbed to a heart attack on October 19, 1941, the day on which he had planned to propose these significant changes to the UAHC Board.

Shocked, the members of the UAHC administrative committee found themselves under considerable pressure to locate a qualified replacement. They were not interested in reopening a nationwide search and instead turned unanimously to fellow Cincinnatian Nelson Glueck, a full professor at HUC who had already established himself as an eminent archaeologist. Glueck no doubt attracted the committee's attention for two special qualities: not only did he initiate and carry out major archaeological surveys and excavations with confidence and decisiveness; he exuded a charisma rarely found among academics.

Because Glueck was a tenured faculty member at the Hebrew Union College, however, the committee's recommendation required the approval of the College's Board of Governors. Either because they assumed that having someone on the faculty serving as head of the UAHC could only strengthen the relationship between the two institutions, or because they felt that with Glueck as head of the UAHC, there would be no further talk of moving the organization to Washington, they approved the appointment.

Glueck began his job with the Union in early 1942. Declaring himself "fired up by the challenge [the position] presents," he told the committee:

> I consider it a happy augury for our future that you have selected a man to head the Union of American Hebrew Congregations who will continue to be a professor at the College. By that fact you have emphasized what should be and henceforth will be the essential unity of both organizations, animated by the desire to attain the same ultimate goal. They shall function as one organic whole.[1]

It is hard to envision what that "one organic whole" would look like — the two organizations had very different missions and a wide disparity in resources and influence. But even HUC's student body reacted positively to Glueck's appointment. In the February 1942 edition of the *Hebrew Union College Monthly,* student rabbi Bertram W. Korn wrote:

> For most of the students at HUC, Professor Glueck was an unknown quantity until he returned from his long stay in Palestine last year. In the few months since then, he has endeared himself to us as a teacher and as a friend. We found him to be fascinating and inspiring not only as a scholar and archaeologist, but also as a person. It is therefore with a great deal of joy that we welcome the announcement of his appointment to his new position as Executive Secretary of the Union of American Hebrew Congregations.
>
> In his dual capacity as professor at the College and as head of the Union, he symbolizes for us the actualization of the dream of Isaac Mayer Wise for an inner unity and harmony of purpose among the various institutions of Reform Judaism.

*

The Central Conference of American Rabbis was split between those who favored a Jewish state and those who opposed it on philosophical and practical grounds. In the 1930s the membership had agreed "not to fight the Zionist fight" on the Conference floor, a decision that engendered a decade of relatively congenial discussions.[2] But the split between the Zionist and the anti-Zionist factions lay just below the surface, and the gulf became more visible when Rabbi James G. Heller, a leading Zionist spokesman, was elected president of the CCAR in 1941. His election meant that he would preside over the 1942 convention, to be held at the end of February.

At that convention, thirty-three Reform rabbis introduced a resolution favoring the formation of a Jewish army in Palestine. The proposal had been initially made and strenuously promoted by Peter Bergson,[3] a Palestinian Jew associated with the Zionist Revisionists.[4] The Jews he represented were prepared to fight for an independent state, and the sponsors of the resolution wanted the Conference to proclaim its support. The resolution read:

> Be it resolved that the Central Conference of American Rabbis adds its voice to the demand that the Jewish population of Palestine be

given the privilege of establishing a military force which will fight under its own banner on the side of the democracies under Allied command, to defend its own land and the Near East, to the end that the victory of democracy may be hastened everywhere.[5]

The resolution raised a storm of controversy. Glueck told Rabbi Solomon Freehof, a leader of the non-Zionist faction, that he was "besieged" by telegrams about the Jewish army, pro and con.[6] In reply, Freehof expressed his unequivocal opinion that it was "no help to the cause of the army for the Conference to be the thirty-first or the thirty-second organization to have endorsed it, but it was of great harm to the Conference to become involved in the argument, which is largely Zionist versus anti-Zionist."[7] Glueck told Freehof that he agreed with him, but apparently he did not express this view openly in the debate. The motion to support the Jewish army was adopted by the Conference by a vote of 64 to 38.

The decision stunned those Reform Jews who remained opposed to political Zionism. One of them, the prominent New York banker Captain Lewis L. Strauss, persuaded his rabbi, Julius Mark of Temple Emanu El, to send a message to members of the British cabinet informing them that America's Jews held divergent opinions on the Jewish army issue. That letter triggered a series of events that led to the formation of the American Council for Judaism (ACJ). The nucleus of the ACJ's leadership and most of its members were the rabbis and Reform laity that maintained Reform's long-held anti-Zionist position.

In the meantime, American Zionists held a highly successful conference at the Biltmore Hotel in New York, May 9 to 11, 1942, at which they openly committed themselves to the goal of a Jewish Commonwealth — a Jewish state in Palestine. In November of that year, the Zionist Inner Actions Committee in Jerusalem approved the Biltmore Program as the official policy of the World Zionist Organization. Nelson Glueck's voice, however, was not heard; he did not so much as attend either conference. His absence reflected a stunning lack of engagement for a man who was on his way to becoming a major leader of the Reform movement in America. Because Glueck favored his scholarly pursuits over his organizational responsibilities, the UAHC would be without effective leadership for the remainder of a critical year for American Jewry, and it would play no meaningful role in the development of national Jewish policy during that period. Had Edward Israel lived a few years longer, a very different scenario might well have evolved.

Or maybe not. There had been in the American Reform movement those who believed that an American city could be "our Jerusalem, this happy land our Palestine."[8] Moreover, the idea of an independent Jewish state was anathema to some of the Union's current leadership, and they would hardly have countenanced their Executive Secretary speaking in favor of a Jewish army. Besides, Glueck himself held no brief for an independent state. His position was then — and remained until the state was established in fire and blood — that if the Mandate would ever be revoked by an international body or relinquished by the British, the only viable plan was a bi-national state with Jewish and Arab leaders working together on behalf of their constituents.

Moreover, for Glueck the urge to return to archaeological work, especially when combined with the patriotic impulses on which he had acted in 1918, militated against an active role within the Reform movement. The attack on Pearl Harbor on December 7, 1941 precipitated a major revision of Glueck's plans and priorities, inducing him to volunteer his services to the government when war was declared against Japan on December 8.[9] Within a week he had written to Dr. Walter Livingston Wright, Jr., in the Near East Section, Office of the Coordinator of Information,[10] Washington, DC:

Dear Dr. Wright,

I want to offer my services to the Government under any conditions, anywhere.[11] I should be prepared to serve at home or abroad. I should be glad to get on a freighter and go to the Near East or any other part of the world; to do anything here in Washington, or elsewhere which might be desired.

In response to Glueck's request, a memorandum was sent from the historian William J. Langer, Director of Research in the office of the Coordinator of Information, to David Bruce, chief of the London office of the Office of Strategic Services (OSS) in January of 1942: "I think Dr. Wright may already have called your attention to Nelson Glueck. I may add that Glueck seems to me like a most unusually interesting fellow whose knowledge of Arabic and extreme acquaintance with the Arabic world should make him a useful person for special confidential work."

Glueck, eager for a reply from Wright, heard instead, on January 9, 1942, from a high-ranking officer in the British Secret Service, M. Preston Goodfellow, Major General, Staff, G-2, who wrote: "It may well be that we will find use for your unusual talents at a later date."

It took two months for that "later date" to materialize, during which time Glueck continued to press his case by forwarding a memorandum on Palestine and Transjordan to the Office of the Coordinator of Information. Finally, on March 3, 1942, a note from Kenneth Mygatt, Coordinator of Information, confirmed: "We have on our list the name of Dr. Glueck, but we have not been given the date when he will be ready to leave the USA. I have asked for an air priority for him."

By the end of the month Glueck had an assignment from the Office of Strategic Services, which after the war became the Central Intelligence Agency (CIA). His pay was about that of a lieutenant colonel in the army — $400 per month, plus a $10 per diem allowance. By May of 1942 Glueck had released his already tenuous hold on the reins of the UAHC and was on his way to the Middle East, with no projected date of return. A year and a half after leaving the region on a ship heading toward India, Glueck now traveled by air via South America and Africa to Egypt — with a code name — as an operative for the OSS. His years of experience in the desert, his knowledge of water supplies and ancient roads, and his network of personal Arab contacts in the region made him a valuable military resource.

Helen was informed that Nelson had arrived safely in Cairo on May 4, 1942. At the time, the Egyptian capital, occupied by the British, was crawling with spies and deserters. Like Jerusalem then and now, Cairo was known as the "city of gold," both because of the way the dust in the air picked up the light of the sun and because many of its buildings looked like the beaten gold that thieves had plundered from the ancient tombs.

From Cairo, Glueck was sent to Transjordan. In both locations he primarily came into contact with British soldiers and civilians engaged in war-related efforts. He seemed to have a profound respect for them and in time would come to know many of them well. En route he stopped at several sites where he was supposedly doing archaeological work — his cover throughout the war. While the available documents do not indicate the true nature of Glueck's assignment between May and August of 1942, he was generally believed to be undertaking a survey of North Syria and Iraq. OSS files released in the early 1980s, however, revealed that Glueck's most significant work during his service as an OSS operative was in connection with the fighting in North Africa. That theater of the war had opened in September 1940 when Mussolini attempted to capture Egypt's most important cities, Alexandria and Cairo, as well as the Suez Canal, by advancing eastward from the Italian colony of Libya. Seeking a quick victory, Mussolini hoped to inflate his diminished prestige after his army's poor showing in southern France. His advance, however, was soon thwarted.

The front line of the war in North Africa moved back and forth after the German General Erwin Rommel had been assigned to that arena; he succeeded in recapturing the area from the British in 1941. By the summer of 1942, however, the British forces had been heavily reinforced and re-equipped. With America now in the war, Rommel knew that time was against him; he had to reach the Suez Canal soon or the prize would forever elude him. Between him and the canal lay the British Eighth Army, newly invigorated by General Bernard Law Montgomery ("Monty"). The allies held a strong line some forty miles long, stretching from the Qattara Depression in the south to the small railway junction of El Alamein in the north.

It was in anticipation of the climactic battle of El Alamein that Glueck was assigned to survey the Sinai peninsula, the Negev, and Transjordan and to locate ancient roads and available supplies of fresh water, in case the British would lose the battle and be forced to retreat eastward. The troops would have had to escape through the Sinai and the Wadi el-Arish (the biblical Brook of Egypt) into Palestine, and perhaps further. He was to map every trail, every spring, every cistern, and every unusual formation that would be of help in such a retreat. Glueck certainly knew the topography of that part of the world, including where water for thirsty troops could be found. Since it is axiomatic among archaeologists that settlements could only be built where an adequate supply of water was available, either by continual flow, by digging wells, or by capturing rain water in cisterns, his knowledge of the Patriarchal, Roman, Nabataean, and Byzantine settlements in the area was crucial.

Beatrice Magnes recalled the anxiety of the residents of Palestine in the tense days before the battle:

When the German Army had reached El Alamein, there was a
general feeling that the Jews of Palestine would become refugees.
Meanwhile, the English officials and their families in Egypt were
fleeing to Palestine. Where were all of us to go? During the lull
in the troubles between Arabs and Jews, our destination — so we
said — would be Iraq. JLM [her husband, Judah Leon Magnes] and
I each packed our old rucksacks with what we thought we might
need for such a trek.[12]

The battle lasted for fourteen days, from October 24 through November
6, and ended with a decisive victory for the British troops. Rommel lost
half of his men and most of his tanks and heavy guns. He was forced
to retreat to Sollum on the border between Egypt and Libya. It was the
beginning of the end for the Axis powers in North Africa. Winston
Churchill was moved to say: "Before Alamein we never had a victory;
after Alamein, we never had a defeat."[13] Four decades later, Helen, reflecting on her husband's wartime activities, recalled: "He often told me how
grateful he was that his plans were never utilized."

*

From late summer, 1943 until early 1944, Glueck was back in the United
States, although he constantly urged his military superiors to send him
on a new assignment. He spent a good part of August in Colorado on
vacation with Helen and Charles, then visited briefly in Cincinnati.
Glueck's brother Nathan, editor of the family newsletter, reported:

Nelson came home August 10 [1943] after being on the job for
sixteen months — that's a long time! — flying the 12,000 miles in
four days by way of Egypt and Iceland. No beds on the trip — only
"catnaps." He is returning to Palestine in a few weeks to resume his
work as Director of the American School for Oriental Research at
Jerusalem.[14]

Throughout his years on assignment for the OSS, Glueck developed a
regular correspondence with his young son, letters that often featured
the adventures of Humpo the camel. One of Glueck's letters to his friend
Judah L. Magnes in the late fall of 1945 shows the father's pride in his
six-year-old child:

Dear Judah,

The enclosed clipping shows Charles Jonathan breaking into the news. He goes to art school at the [Cincinnati Art] Museum on Saturday mornings. He refuses to go to Sunday School any longer. He went four times this year, and then refused to go. I tell him a Bible story every night, and Mrs. Lotspeich, the perfectly remarkable head of the Lotspeich private school which he attends, tells the children one every morning.

When I tried to persuade C[harles] that he should go, he replied: "Mrs. Lotspeich tells us a Bible story every morning, and you tell me one every night, and that little Sunday School teacher, she can't compare to you or to Mrs. Lotspeich!" The argument was unanswerable, because he does get more in one week at home than he could get at Sunday school in 7 weeks. Every night after dinner he says to me: Please tell me another Bible story!

He is not a *wunderkind*, but is healthy, happy, sensitive, affectionate, obstreperous, companionable, not dumb, has a fine memory, and thinks for himself. This evening when I coerced him into putting something back in place, he called me a Haman and a Goliath! . . .

Nelson[15]

*

Back in Jerusalem, Glueck was able to spend some time with Aubrey (Abba) Eban,[16] a new acquaintance. A native of South Africa trained as a lawyer, Eban had joined the British Army in his native land and began serving in Palestine in 1941. He was soon working for both British Intelligence and the Jewish Agency.[17] Though each sensed the other's covert life, the matter was never discussed. The two men did discuss Middle Eastern history and oriental languages and chuckled over how foolishly mistaken Western perceptions sometimes were: an effort had been made to teach the Arabs about William Shakespeare, a topic as remote from their consciousness as flying to the moon. When they weren't engaged in close conversation, they could often be found on a nearby tennis court. Eban claimed that he was the only man in Palestine who played worse tennis than Glueck.[18]

Wartime restrictions prevented Glueck from doing any archaeological work, and his OSS assignments seemed not to fully occupy him. He mentioned in a letter to Helen that he had had five or six drinks with a friend the previous night, but "they didn't lift the gloom in which I find myself at present."

> I do not feel equal to going to the School right now, to be engulfed again by the loneliness for you that hits me particularly hard when I enter our house there, so full of memories of you. You playing with our dog, you digging in the flower beds, you with our boy, you in our bed, you with your voice which reaches my heart, and you with your starry gaze when you tell me with or without words that you love me.[19]

Despite this and many other expressions of affection for Helen, Glueck was not above teasing her about the many women available to those men who might be seeking such companionship: "This town is the maddest place I have ever seen, with thousands of men on the prowl for women. I sometimes think that when I am away from home, I too shall shoot quarry. But I never seem to get around to it." Then, perhaps realizing he had hurt her feelings, he continued, "Darling, your image is always in front of me"; then, quixotically, "Or maybe I'm too lazy."[20]

Shortly thereafter Glueck found himself in Cairo, still deeply missing his family and unable to concentrate on scholarly work. He went out to the cabaret one evening with other Americans, stayed until the wee hours of the morning, and remained aloof while "the fellows danced with the floozies standing about and bought drinks for them." He himself did not dance, but he did buy several highballs for himself.[21] Glueck remained in Cairo for several months, after which he was asked to travel to Aleppo in Syria and "such other places in the Levant states as may be necessary on temporary duty in connection with activities of the US Army Forces in the Middle East."[22] That assignment completed, he returned once again to Cairo. He arrived back in Washington in August, 1944, gave a full report to his superiors, and by November was restored once again to the Middle East theater of operations. He resigned from the OSS ten months later.

*

It is interesting to reconstruct the OSS perception and evaluation of Glueck both as a Jew and as a possible Zionist as they considered him for

wartime assignment. Dr. Walter Wright, Jr., who had received Glueck's
initial request to serve with the Office of Information, wrote to William
Langer on Dec. 12, 1941:

> Dr. Glueck is known to me personally. As a result of several years
> work as an archaeologist in Palestine and Transjordan, he is one of
> the best informed men in the world on this region. In particular, he
> has been engaged in the mapping of Transjordan. He is an Ameri-
> can Jew of non-Zionist background. I have just received a note from
> him offering his services unconditionally to the Government.[23]

Another memorandum sent from John A. Wilson[24] to Colonel Donovan
contrasts Glueck's credentials with those of another Jewish candidate
for OSS responsibilities:

> Mr. Baxter[25] tells me that you are considering the possibility of
> having a personal observer in Saudi Arabia. This memorandum
> brings together some sections based on three lines of thought.
>
> First, I assume you want a reliable man, and that you want a
> general observer and not a specialist of any kind. Second, time is
> limited. We should examine possible candidates who are already
> out and in the Near East. Third, any Westerner in Saudi Arabia is
> as conspicuous as the Negro in a New England village. Inevitably
> his every movement is watched, and he has not the possibility of
> blending with the landscape.
>
> Mr. Baxter tells me you are considering [name deleted by cen-
> sor]. The fact that he is obviously Jewish and is the son of a promi-
> nent Zionist rules him out immediately. This is not true of another
> Jew, Nelson Glueck, who is doing an archaeological survey of Trans-
> jordan. Glueck has spent several years doing archaeology among
> desert Arabs. His Jewishness is not a factor in any sense.
>
> In the first place, he has no visible characteristics, and it is prob-
> able that the Arabs have always thought of him simply as an Amer-
> ican. In the second place, he is one of the few thoroughly balanced
> Jews who have survived residence in Palestine through the trou-
> bled times (1936–1939). I have the highest admiration for the way
> in which he maintained his head and retained the respect of all

parties in Jerusalem at a time when Arab-Jewish violence was at
its height. Glueck could move easily into Saudi Arabia and do an
admirable job of observation.[26]

Glueck indeed blended in well. When he traveled with the Arabs he wore
a *keffiyeh* and rode camelback because that was how they dressed and
how they traversed the desert. He also enjoyed the romantic image he
thus conveyed as a Jewish "Lawrence of Arabia." His resemblance to the
World War I figure — who captured the attention of the world with his
capacity to recruit and lead Arab tribes in raiding Turkish facilities and
blowing up sections of the Hejaz railway — went further than his dress.
Helen recalled his telling her that he had made plans, should the Germans have broken into Palestine and Transjordan, to organize a guerrilla
band of picked Arabs whom he had known for many years, and together
with similar bands under the leadership of the British, to fight against
the Germans. They would have found sufficient Arabs, he believed, to
carry on such warfare for a very long time.

If not looking Jewish was one of Glueck's qualifications for serving
with the OSS, not being a Zionist was equally helpful. In August 1943
he wrote a twenty-page document clarifying Arab fears of massive
Jewish immigration:

> Palestine is not a vacuum — the Arabs are going to live there and
> they have every right to live there. No country in the world, cer-
> tainly not Great Britain or the United States, will take steps to evac-
> uate them and give their land to the Jews. There is, and Zionists
> ought to be the first to be aware of it, among the Arabs of Palestine,
> a lively fear of being flooded out by uncontrolled Jewish immigra-
> tion to Palestine. The Arabs should be assured that there will be
> positively no Jewish settlement whatever in Transjordan, Syria, and
> Lebanon, no matter what settlement may be permitted in Palestine.
>
> We have learned in this war that a sore spot anywhere in the
> world sooner or later affects us. The sore spot in Palestine is no ex-
> ception, and is of vital concern to the USA. The situation is loaded
> with dynamite. Both sides are armed to the gills.[27]

Later in the report, Glueck claims that if the United States and Great
Britain were to give the Zionists everything that they were asking for,

he could envisage the possibility that "the granting of these demands might so inflame the Arab world that riots would spread beyond the borders of Palestine."

Given Glueck's ongoing contact with the Arabs and his sympathy for the British — plus the basically anti-Zionist position that characterized a segment of the Reform Jewish movement in America even well beyond the establishment of the State of Israel — it is easy to understand these sentiments. Albright would observe years later that Glueck always cherished warm feelings toward the Arabs. Successive wars between Arabs and Jews hurt him deeply, but he remained essentially neutral.[28]

Almost alone within Palestinian Jewry, Glueck was in favor of the continuation of the Mandate. He made it quite clear that he appreciated the capability of the English to govern territories like Palestine and Transjordan:

> I consider Transjordan to be one of the best-governed English territories in the world. There, a few amazingly capable Englishmen run the government from behind the scenes, letting the Arabs occupy the large majority of the offices. There, too, for instance, the Arab Legion, at present under the command of Colonel Glubb,[29] is run along similar lines with Arabs holding offices as high as second in command.[30]

Glueck with Glubb Pasha and two Arab tribesmen during World War II. (*American Jewish Archives*)

*

At the same time, however, Glueck conceded that in Transjordan, even an enlightened mandatory policy did not create an environment friendly to the British: "Despite the exemplary manner in which the English have governed Transjordan in the period preceding the driving back of the Germans from El Alamein, I should say that seventy-five percent of the Arabs in Transjordan were more pro-Axis than pro-British."[31]

Thus Glueck penned a note to the American Jewish Committee in the summer of 1946 expressing his deep concern about a proposed British Federal Plan for Palestine, which he called "pernicious and malevolent, a sugar-coated petrifaction of the 1939 White Paper. It would preclude most of the Galilee, almost the entire Jordan Valley, and even the Dead Sea concession from the orbit of possible Jewish settlement."[32]

*

After three and a half years in the service of the OSS, Glueck resigned his commission on August 14, 1945, the very day that the Japanese accepted the terms the Allies had laid down at Potsdam. He filed his final report of field conditions in the Middle East at OSS headquarters in Washington a few days later. Though he felt he had made a significant contribution to the Allied cause, his name does not appear in the standard literature of the OSS, and he never described his experiences, even to Helen. She referred to his "protective amnesia." He told her that when he first returned home he could not even recall his simple code name (Bill), even though he had used it daily for communicating with confidential contacts. He simply blocked it out.[33]

His war service did not go unnoticed, however, and not everyone viewed it positively. Some professional archaeologists in particular were upset that he, in their opinion, had compromised their field by using archaeology as a cover for spying.[34] Writing many years later in his book *American Archaeology in the Middle East*, Philip J. King, director and then the historian of the American Schools of Oriental Research, criticized Glueck for working for the OSS. He argued that by compromising his political evenhandedness during World War II, Glueck lost the confidence of Arab friends. "It is an unwritten law in the Mideast," he wrote, "that archaeology and politics should never be mixed; when they are, it is always to the detriment of archaeology."[35]

King's comments certainly reflect a lack of understanding both of

Glueck's patriotism and what the consequences would have been had the British been defeated at El Alamein. Glueck's pioneering work in topographical archaeology had nothing at all to do with the politics of the Middle East. There is no hard evidence that the Arabs knew either that he was Jewish or that he was reporting to the OSS. After the war, when harder lines were being drawn with respect to attitudes toward a sovereign Jewish state, politics would indeed play a role, but not here.[36]

King's remarks also reflect a lack of awareness of how common it was for archaeologists to serve their countries as spies. H. V. F. Winstone's *Woolley of Ur* gives a full description of Sir Leonard Woolley's clandestine work on behalf of the British government during both World War I and World War II: "Woolley had joined with T. E. Lawrence in carrying out a military survey of Sinai and Transjordan in 1912, and traveled with a certain Captain Newcombe, whose instructions were to seek out disaffected tribesmen who would act as 'news agents' for Britain in the event of trouble with their Ottoman masters."[37]

Glueck's own feelings about his work for the OSS are reflected in a letter he wrote home exactly a month after he arrived in Cairo, on June 4, 1942, his forty-second birthday:

> Our interests in Oriental Research are naturally conditioned by our American tradition and our American outlook on life. The passionate sense of freedom and democracy that pervades our fair land of the United States of America is loosely akin to the essential religious teachings, which, anciently sprung from the soil of the Holy Land, remain as young and meaningful as ever. It is to preserve our American way of life that we must win this war. And what is more important, we must win the peace that shall follow it. No one can know better than an archaeologist what it means to look to the future with an eye to the past. No one can hope more ardently than the historian, that those who will run towards the horizons of tomorrow will yet find time to scan what may be read from the ruins of days gone by.[38]

Whatever virtues Glueck ascribed to archaeological neutrality in time of peace, they were obscured for him when the fates of nations and peoples were at stake.

Glueck believed that the Germans also were using archaeologists as undercover agents. He suspected that the Nazis sent archaeologists into Egypt before the battle of El Alamein to plant caches of gasoline and other supplies for the *Wehrmacht*. Fritz Frank, a German scholar who, like Glueck, specialized in topographical surveys, was, according to Glueck, also employed as a spy.

*

Meanwhile, the situation in Palestine grew increasingly unbearable for its inhabitants and for the British. Both Jews and Arabs were restive under the Mandatory authority, and the British faced significant international pressure to allow Holocaust survivors in European DP camps to enter the country. A seasoned observer noted that whatever chances the Mandatory authorities had to head off a Jewish revolt against their rule were lost when the British government wavered in regard to implementing three unanimous conclusions of the Anglo-American Commission in 1946: the immediate admission to Palestine of 100,000 Jews, a continuing large immigration, and the cancellation of the 1939 White Paper restricting Jewish purchases of land from Arabs. Elements of the Jewish underground blew up a wing of the King David Hotel on July 12, 1946, killing nearly a hundred civilians, including some of the most senior Jewish officers in the administration. The bombing shattered any illusions the British might still have held regarding their ability to maintain the security of officials of the Mandatory government.[39]

Along with English Socialist Harold Laski and Sir William Fitzgerald, Chief Justice of the Palestine administration, Glueck was a key player in the effort to maintain open lines of communication between the British, the Arabs, and the Jews. An unidentified source noted about Glueck: "He contrived to retain to the end friendly relations with Arab cultivators (*fellahin*) and nomads (*bedouin*) as well as with the *effendis* and the *sheikhs*. His school was an Inn of Friendship, like the Inn of the Good Samaritan, in the bleak landscape of divided Jerusalem."[40]

At ASOR, activities were minimal: it took some time for travel restrictions to be lifted so that new students and visiting professors could come to Jerusalem. As late as June 1946, getting to the American Schools was sometimes a scary experience. Marvin Pope, an American biblical scholar who studied at ASOR and later became its director, recalled his visit during that period:

The taxi-ride from Haifa had been hair-raising. The driver was scared out of his wits. There was a dusk to dawn curfew in Jerusalem and the driver was anxious to get there before sundown. . . . On Saladin Road we encountered a British tank with hatch open and machine gunner scanning the street, but they let us pass to the school.[41]

Pope was one of only three students at the school. Grateful for their presence in such tumultuous times, Glueck treated them well and took them on field trips all over the country. Primarily, the group traveled to the sites east of the Jordan River, where Glueck was reviewing and updating the information he had gleaned from his original surveys in the 1930s. Pope commented:

We revisited many sites and picked up thousands of potsherds and brought them to the *mudir* [Arabic for "director"] to see what he would call them. . . . Back at the school we had lectures and seminars on ceramics, and I began to think about the possibility of switching from Semitic philology to Palestinian pottery for a dissertation topic.[42]

In 1946, Glueck's second popular work, *The River Jordan: Being an Illustrated Account of Earth's Most Storied River,* appeared in print.[43] Millar Burrows, Professor of Biblical Theology at Yale Divinity School and President of ASOR, noted on the book's jacket:

Not many scholars who are acknowledged by specialists as international authorities are at the same time able to write books which can be enjoyed by the general reader. Nelson Glueck . . . has shown that he is one of the few. He has written of the Jordan with an almost unique combination of learning, personality, and spiritual feeling.

After completing his service with the OSS, Glueck stayed on as director of ASOR for another two years while maintaining his position as a member of the Hebrew Union College faculty. Soon yet another opportunity would appear in Cincinnati — one that would enable him to make a significant contribution to the religious life of American Reform Jewry.

7

A New Career Beckons

Hebrew Union College . . . is very precious to me.

Hebrew Union College marked its seventieth anniversary in the fall of 1945 with a national conference entitled "Judaism and American Democracy." Its president, Julian Morgenstern, however, had fallen ill with pneumonia and was unable to attend. His eventual recovery left him perceptibly weaker than before, and his personal physician, Hiram B. Weiss, urged him to consider retiring.[1] Morgenstern hesitated, knowing that a project he had been contemplating for some time — negotiating a merger with Stephen S. Wise's Jewish Institute of Religion in New York — was finally becoming a viable option.[2] He realized, however, that his own energy was limited, and that, after the war, HUC would be taking on new responsibility for rabbinical training and Jewish scholarship. It was too much for Morgenstern. He announced his retirement to the HUC Board of Governors in May of 1946, to take effect on June 30, 1947.

Two years earlier, Morgenstern had unofficially chosen Nelson Glueck as his heir-apparent. Glueck acknowledged the selection in a letter to Helen from Jerusalem dated June 6, 1944:

> I am coming home to Cincinnati and staying there, and perhaps in a while we will return here for a dig. I have ten years worth of publishing ahead of me with materials I now have in hand. Besides, it is becoming increasingly evident that I shall sooner or later have to take a hand in the Hebrew Union College, which in spite of all I say or have said, is very precious to me.
>
> In his last letter to me, Morgenstern again (!) says openly that he expects me to succeed him. Whether things will turn out that way or not I don't know, and don't particularly care. . . . I do know that I won't lift a finger to try to get the presidency of the college, but if it is offered to me, I shall take it and devote my energies to making as good an institution of it as is possible.
>
> I should be just as satisfied, or perhaps more satisfied, to remain a professor there and get occasional leaves of absence to come over here with you and the boy for a couple of months at a time.[3]

Morgenstern was persistent; Glueck responded (in a May 1946 letter) by listing his perceived inadequacies: he had never had to raise any money and did not think he would be successful doing so; he avoided committees whenever he could; he never attended rabbinical conventions, and did only what little administrative work he could not avoid. Only in August 1946, while Helen and Charles were visiting him in Palestine, did he communicate to Morgenstern that he had made up his mind to accept the offer. By then Morgenstern's retirement announcement was already public knowledge.[4] Helen later recalled Glueck's hesitancy:

> He always knew he wanted to stay in scholarship, and I think if destiny hadn't been what it was he would have stayed there.
>
> He took the presidency with a great deal of reluctance. He knew the school was bankrupt. He knew it would divert him from his first love, which was scholarship. I think if he had just done what he wanted to do — what was closest to his heart — he would have just been a great archaeologist.[5]

Nelson, Helen, and Charles Glueck at the director's house, ASOR, Jerusalem, 1946. (Courtesy of Barbara Glueck)

At any rate, in response to Morgenstern's announcement, a search committee headed by Lester Jaffe, who chaired the Board of Governors, was appointed. The committee included, among others, Dr. Maurice Eisendrath of the UAHC and Mrs. Arthur Hays (Iphigene) Sulzberger of the *New York Times* publishing dynasty. Mrs. Sulzberger's roots in the Reform movement were deep; her grandfather was Rabbi Isaac Mayer Wise.

Many names were suggested for the HUC presidency, among them Abba Hillel Silver,[6] Solomon Freehof,[7] and Joshua Loth Liebman[8]— men of renown, pulpit rabbis of unusual distinction, far more widely recognized among American Reform Jewry than Nelson Glueck. Rabbi Silver's magnificent oratory on behalf of the Jewish people before and during World War II had made him an unofficial spokesperson for all of American Jewry. These men were eminently capable of leading the College with distinction. And unlike Glueck, they were used to working with Boards of Trustees and speaking on behalf of Reform Judaism at regional and national meetings.

There were other candidates put forward as Glueck's hesitancy became widely known. Bernard Bamberger[9] became Morgenstern's choice after he began to believe that Glueck was only lukewarm about taking the job.[10] Even after Glueck had been offered the position, Jacob R. Marcus was asked to help persuade him to accept it, and if he failed to convince him, to consider the offer himself.

According to a letter from Herman Snyder, then Rabbinic Alumni Association president, Glueck's name was at the bottom of the list of candidates compiled by the alumni of the College.[11] But Mrs. Sulzberger wanted Glueck and only Glueck, and her will prevailed.[12] Nor was Glueck a unanimous choice among the students of the College. Irving Aaron Mandel remembered that there was a concern that Glueck's explosive temper might cause problems for him as president.[13]

What specific experiences, what unique aspects of his character, prepared Glueck for this honor and awesome responsibility? In a piece written for the special inaugural edition of *The American Israelite* in March 1948, Morgenstern described the process that had led to Glueck's appointment as a member of the HUC faculty in 1928, identifying his scholarship as "painstaking, thorough, and effective." Further, Glueck "quickly became known as a compelling teacher, one who drove his students urgently, but in a manner which was rewarding and which called

Glueck with Lester A. Jaffe, Iphigene Sulzberger, and Julian Morgenstern.
(*American Jewish Archives*)

for their appreciation, respect, and cooperation." Glueck was, according
to Morgenstern, "popular with both students and fellow-members of the
faculty, and revealed an unusual capacity for inspiring confidence and
good will and for winning and holding loyal friends."[14]

While there were other faculty members with equal claim to first-rate
scholarship and teaching skills, Glueck's pioneering work in the archaeological surveys of Edom, Moab, and Ammon, along with his discoveries at Meneiyyeh and Tell el-Kheleifeh had caught the imagination of
a much larger public. In addition, he had established himself as a good
communicator, at least in print, via articles in ASOR publications and
the newsletters that he himself published as director. The four volumes
of his *Explorations in Eastern Palestine* had been published, establishing his scientific credentials, and his first popular book, *The River Jordan*, conveyed in a fine writing style the results of his work. He had

also published several illustrated articles in *The National Geographic*, including "On the Trail of King Solomon's Mines" (February 1944), and "The Geography of the Jordan" (December 1944). Tens of thousands of readers of that magazine knew the name of Nelson Glueck.

To have found someone who had established an international reputation, who had a charismatic personality, and who could mesmerize people with his handsome appearance and emotion-filled speeches made the choice of Glueck easy to sell. Perhaps the more difficult part was convincing him to take the job. He was still ambivalent about leaving Palestine:

> Whether it be for a short or a long interval, it is always difficult for me to leave Palestine and to go away from our school here and the work which is bound up with it. I have made quite a few trips to and from America and Palestine during the last five years, and I never leave the Holy Land without sadness in my heart, and I never return to it without my heart breaking in gladness.
>
> I have spent most of the last twenty years here and in Transjordan, and have sunk deep spiritual roots in this part of the world. I am inclined to believe this is the center of the universe and that everything else is peripheral to it. However I shall *inshallah* [in Arabic, God willing] soon return.[15]

Ultimately, it was the influence of his cherished friend Judah Leon Magnes that swayed Glueck to accept the position. Magnes told Glueck that he simply had to respond to the call of the College to fulfill his destiny as a leader of American Reform Jewry. So, however reluctantly, and fully intending to continue his work as a biblical archaeologist in Palestine — either under the Mandate or in whatever kind of entity would emerge after its conclusion — Glueck became the fourth president of HUC.[16] His appointment was reported in the *New York Times* on May 9, 1947:

> Nelson Glueck, internationally renowned archaeologist, educator, and author, was elected president of the Hebrew Union College, America's oldest Jewish seminary, by the institution's Board of Governors here today, effective July 1 of this year. He succeeds Dr.

Julian Morgenstern, who requested several months ago that he be
granted retirement after having served as president since 1921. Dr.
Morgenstern will continue to serve the college as a member of the
Board of Governors and Professor of Bible and will devote much
of his time to writing and research.

The article also pointed out that Glueck's completion of the archaeological exploration of Transjordan marked the first time in which an entire
land had been archaeologically studied square mile by square mile, using
the modern technique of pottery identification.

The *Times* article was written by staff member Samuel Johnson Woolf.
In it, Woolf (who always sketched his interviewees) described how, while
waiting for Glueck to arrive, he thought of the bearded and patriarchal past HUC presidents Kaufmann Kohler and Julian Morgenstern:[17]
"When I opened the door for Dr. Glueck, I saw a young looking, smooth
shaven man, trim of figure, wearing a light colored overcoat, a gray suit,
and a flowered tie. A hearty, gracious smile spread over his face and his
dark, intense eyes, under heavy brows, beamed."

During their wide-ranging conversation, Glueck spoke with Woolf of
his approach to religion, Judaism, the Bible, and archaeology. The writer
noted that Glueck was very attuned to what was happening in the outside
world and believed that religion was an important part of humanity's
response to the world's problems. As Woolf wrote: "He sees in religion
the only salvation for the world in these confused days — not necessarily
in his religion but in any faith that upholds the moral and spiritual law."
Woolf asked Glueck about his hesitancy to take up the position as head of
America's outstanding institution for training liberal rabbis, and Glueck
responded by recalling an experience that helped him make up his mind
— one of his wartime journeys aboard a troop transport:

It was crowded with young men, all of them ready to make the
supreme sacrifice for their country. For weeks I lived with them and
shared their thoughts. I realized more than ever the need for religion. I thought of my own little boy and wondered if by the time he
was grown up war could not be regarded as an obsolete horror.

It was then that the cave men who lived near Haifa began
to lose their importance for me. The memory of those living,

hopeful boys on that boat loomed large in comparison with the prehistoric tools and weapons of primitive men. I decided that I could do more good teaching eternal laws, which, if understood and followed, would do away with future wars. And I knew of no better place to teach those laws than in an institution such as the Hebrew Union College.[18]

Glueck also felt a need to explain his decision to many of his friends. He told Eleanor Bisbee[19] that he felt accepting the presidency was a moral obligation and that, furthermore, it was time he stayed home for a while with his family.[20] To Lewis Leary, managing editor of *American Literature*, he wrote: "I took this job because I felt that I had to do everything I could towards the creation of a healthy society in these perilous times."[21] To Gershom Scholem, then teaching at the Hebrew University, he explained:

I have been delayed answering your note of congratulations not so much because there were so many similar letters to answer, as because it took months for me to overcome the pain of not being able to return immediately to Jerusalem and somehow or other writing to a person like you made that feeling stronger. I am writing now not because I am less attached to Jerusalem or less determined to maintain my connections with it, but because I have achieved an inner balance and a complete realization of the fact that I must meet, to the best of my abilities, this mature responsibility which has been entrusted to me.[22]

The opportunity came at a challenging moment in the history of the Hebrew Union College. As Board of Governors chairman Lester Jaffe put it:

The inauguration of the fourth president would be, at any time, a momentous event. But the utter extinction of the many great institutions of Jewish scholarship in Europe during the last decade, and the attendant challenge to American Jewry to fulfill a role as the new repository and creator of Jewish learning and culture for the years ahead, gives to the inauguration of a new president of the Hebrew Union College an enhanced significance.[23]

Two further challenges faced the new president: how to prepare the American Jewish community for its new leadership role in world Jewry and how to strengthen ties with the yet unborn and undefined Jewish state in Palestine. Al Segal, writing for the Indianapolis *Jewish Post and Opinion*, knew that Glueck's explorations required that he stay on friendly terms with Palestinian Arabs and that he never let himself be caught up in the political conversations about Palestine. Segal surmised that Glueck wanted to see in Palestine a state governed jointly by Jews and Arabs. Similarly, Morris Schulzinger, a family friend and fellow Cincinnatian, recalled his visit with Glueck in the fall of 1947:

> Like most teachers at HUC at that time, Glueck was lukewarm towards Zionism and was strongly opposed to the creation of a Jewish state. He was an active member of *Brith Shalom* [Covenant of Peace], an organization of intellectuals headed by Dr. Judah Magnes, which advocated the establishment of a bi-national Arab-Jewish state on the model of Austria-Hungary before World War I.[24]

Glueck's attitudes toward a Jewish state, of course, changed radically as events of 1947–1948 unfolded.

Unlike his brief stint with the UAHC five years previously, when Glueck seemed to lack a cohesive plan for the institution's future, at the College he knew exactly what he wanted to accomplish: HUC would prepare congregational rabbis for the burgeoning American Reform Jewish community and equip them with the tools of scholarship they would need in order to deepen their own Jewish knowledge and authenticity.

The fall of 1947 found Glueck busily engaged in establishing his imprint on the institution. First of all, he had to reckon with a new kind of student. Despite the largely Germanic beginnings of the College, during his undergraduate years, between 1915 and 1920, half the students, like himself, were the children of Russian or Polish parents, and more than half of the student body identified their parents as Orthodox. By 1930, over eighty percent of the HUC students were of Eastern European background.[25] A generation later, after World War II, the situation changed significantly yet again. Unlike previous generations — like Glueck's — the College no longer primarily served poor Jews as one of the few available ladders to social and financial success. Students now came mostly from middle-class families of sufficient status to assure their offspring an alternative career of equal prominence should they not be interested in the rabbinate. The number coming from Orthodox homes decreased steadily after the war. In addition, unlike their predecessors, these new students were motivated less by the desire for renown as great pulpit orators than by the wish to work with Jewish youth and to provide counseling for Jewish families. In the early 1950s, recently ordained Reform rabbis began recruiting rabbinical students to staff the regional summer camps that were being set up across the country. These camps in turn became recruiting grounds for the next generation of Reform rabbis, cantors, and educators.

During his first address to the College community as its president in October 1947, Glueck delivered a strong statement about the relationship between American Jewry and the long hoped for independent Jewish state that was about to emerge from Mandatory Palestine. He said, "The moral direction of the world can be determined in part by its relationship to Jews and Jerusalem, and there is an indissoluble connection between justice in Palestine and peace on earth."[26]

Recalling his own rabbinical education a quarter of a century earlier, he spoke of the requisite qualities of the American Reform rabbi:

> The modern rabbi requires not only the authority and inspiration of Jewish lore, with its indispensable discipline, but also the insights and techniques of the growing sciences of human relationships. He must know himself and be serene in his own soul, and be full of integrity and humility before he can guide others to clarity of mind, quietness of heart and the quickening of human sensibilities.[27]

With his new perspective as head of an American institution, Glueck was deeply concerned about the amount of American Jewish money that was being sent overseas to Europe and to Palestine. In a letter to Morris Lazaron, rabbi emeritus of Baltimore Hebrew Congregation and a long-time friend, Glueck wrote:

> I am increasingly alarmed by the fact that a very large proportion of the doing, thinking and giving of American Jewry is being centered upon charity abroad. Not that I would have one cent less sent

abroad for the helpless and homeless, but that I conceive it to be a great danger for American Jewry to have so many people feel, consciously or unconsciously, that they are fulfilling their duties as Jews by writing out each year an ever larger check for the welfare of our co-religionists abroad.

What will our future be if this school for serving God, which the HUC is and must increasingly be, is not strengthened and built up in every possible way? If we American Jews cannot be conscious of, live up to and spread the teachings of our religion, and have properly trained rabbis to teach and interpret it, then all of our charity will be of no avail. At present, we spend most of our efforts and practically all of our funds for anti-defamation purposes and for helping our people abroad. These are good purposes, but they cannot possibly take the place, as I need not tell you, of bringing the message of American Judaism to the homes and hearts of American Jews.[28]

Glueck, however, was unwilling to accept any government money for HUC, even when the GI Bill was making funds available to students at any accredited school.[29]

By early 1948 Glueck was ready to submit a blueprint for the Hebrew Union College of the future. It called for an eight million dollar fundraising campaign and projected not only an expansion of the rabbinical school of the College, but the introduction of a number of new programs: a department of human relations designed to bridge the gap between religion and the social sciences, a new School of Sacred Music in New York, a radio workshop, a summer institute for rabbis, and a program of training for laymen. It also included plans for the expansion of the dormitory and the physical plant of the College, new facilities for the training of religious school teachers throughout the country, a traveling museum, and the addition of new fellowships, both for young rabbis and for Christian ministers and theological students. His long-standing and productive relationships with many Protestant and Catholic scholars during twenty years of archaeological work in Palestine and Transjordan had convinced him that Christian scholars should also be part of the student body at HUC; their time at the College would make them not only more knowledgeable interpreters of Judaism but also more sympathetic to the contemporary Jewish agenda.[30] As a scholar, Glueck was eager to establish a new graduate program that would serve as the College's response to the need for training Jewish scholars in America.

Augmented income for the College allowed Glueck to increase the administrative machinery of the school. In Morgenstern's time the seminary was run by the college president, his assistant, and a secretary or two. Glueck had no intention of sitting behind a desk in his office and managing the institution. Instead, he engaged a cadre of young rabbis to assist him: Alvin Fine, recently ordained, was moved from director of field activities to the new post of assistant to the president, while Fine's job was taken over by Robert Katz, ordained in 1943. Abraham Klausner was made head of public relations and publicity and Bertram Korn handled arrangements for Glueck's inauguration ceremonies, scheduled for the weekend of March 12–14, 1948, eight months after Glueck assumed his new responsibilities.

Inaugural events were coordinated by a committee chaired by Benjamin Katz, prominent Cincinnatian and member of the Board of Governors. Glueck's mother, Anna Rubin Glueck, served as one of three honorary chairs of the Ladies Committee.[31] The services, symposium, discussions, and special events of the weekend functioned as a showcase for Reform leaders. The consecration service, created by David Polish of Chicago, took place Friday evening at the Rockdale Avenue Temple.[32] At that event, Rabbi Joshua Loth Liebman[33] spoke glowingly of his cherished colleague:

> And now I turn to you, my dear friend, Nelson Glueck, world famous scholar, who has opened up absolutely new pathways of understanding about Palestine . . . whose volumes on Biblical archaeology are acknowledged by experts throughout the world as master works. You have brought rare distinction to the name of the Hebrew Union College in the societies of the learned here and abroad, and now you bring to the high office of President a brilliant synthesis of love for the Jewish past, deep concern for the Jewish present, and passionate vision of the Jewish future.
>
> Reform Judaism will find in you the humble tentativeness of the scientist, the reverence for facts, the patient quest for truth, and at the same time the daring experimentalism of the American thinker and the prophetic statesmanship of the Jewish dreamer who in our

generation will make the *Mishkan* into a new *Mashkon* — the Temple of learning into the source of spiritual, moral and intellectual security for Judaism and Israel. May you and your gifted wife be blessed in this life of building.[34]

At the inaugural service, held at Isaac M. Wise Temple the following morning, Rabbi Stephen S. Wise was among the speakers. According to him, Nelson Glueck could

> resuscitate the very stones of Palestine, making them live and tell their thrilling story, and such a person could do even more to bring back to life and vitality some of the unvital tendencies of contemporary Judaism, Orthodox, Conservative, and Liberal alike. By reason of the compulsion of his catholic personality, he is likely more than ever to give leadership not to a sect or a party, but to the entire Jewish community. Many-sidedness must not lapse into fragmentation. Tolerant of every intellectual and doctrinal difference, Jewish indifference alone must evoke our intolerance.

Toward the conclusion of his address Wise alluded to Morgenstern's long-cherished dream — a merger between the Hebrew Union College and Wise's institution, the Jewish Institute of Religion in New York: "This day you are inaugurated as successor to President Julian Morgenstern. Someday, it may be, you will also be inaugurated as my successor, as President of the Jewish Institute of Religion."[35]

But it was the remarks of Julian Morgenstern himself that stood out among the weekend's many speeches. This was the man who had ordained Glueck a quarter of a century earlier; who had encouraged him to go abroad to study, just as he himself had done; who had found scholarship funds to enable him to obtain his Ph.D. in Germany; and who had long hoped that Glueck would follow in his footsteps as president of the College.

> It is a responsible mission upon which you are sent, a very high mission. Through the force of historical circumstance, our Hebrew Union College has suddenly been projected into the role of one of

the leading rabbinical seminaries in the entire world, the oldest
upon this continent, situated in the midst of the largest Jewish community in the world.

This is your charge. Into your hands this leadership role has fallen.
You will be the guide of the next generation. It will be your privilege
to teach and to inspire many disciples who will look up to you with
faith, with hope, and seek inspiration from you. It is a high charge.
In many ways, the destiny of Israel and the destiny of Judaism are
in your hands from this moment on.[36]

In his response, Glueck blended his passion for the ancient history of
his people with his concern for the future of American and world Jewry

With Stephen S. Wise at Glueck's inauguration, 1947. (*American Jewish Archives*)

in a time of crisis. He asked, "Who could have foretold not quite three-quarters of a century ago, that this first and still foremost college of its kind in America would be one of the few left in the world to continue, already largely through scholars it has trained, the teachings of the Torah, the Moral Law?"[37]

He referred to the small company of those who had received, voiced, and lived the fundamentals of Torah, from Moses to Rabbi Yohanan ben Zakkai, to the creators of the *Mishnah*, to the leading voices of the academies of Babylonia, to the Masoretes[38] in Tiberias, and to the luminaries of Toledo in Spain, of Alexandria in Egypt, and of Volozhin in Lithuania. Then he asked:

> Who has not marveled at the mystery of the revelations of God in the Holy Land? In the lush fields of Moab, in the sharp silence of the Southland [Negev], in the stark hills of Ephraim and Judah, in all the wondrous areas east as well as west of the Jordan, the presence of Divinity may yet be perceived. Jews and Christians and Moslems alike are drawn to it as a lodestar.[39]

Glueck praised the efforts of the United Nations to bring a peaceful solution to the current crisis in Palestine. Having shifted his view in favor now of an independent Jewish state, he addressed the partition plan, which had been approved by the General Assembly the previous November 29:

> The United Nations plan of partition to resolve the present perplexities of Palestine is literally under fire. To abandon it because it is being attacked is to give pretext to perfidy and lend license to terror. The nettle of enforcement of its decisions must be grasped by the United Nations, else it simply cannot survive. If its members accept of its edicts only what is convenient and comfortable, how can international amity be achieved and common catastrophe avoided?
>
> The spreading violence in Palestine must be stemmed forthwith, that the peaceful cultivation of its vineyards and fields and the building up of its commerce and industry may continue, not only for the benefit of all its inhabitants, but in the interests of mankind itself. The sacred soil of Palestine will not sustain nor will the stage of history support those who spill innocent blood. The consequences of violence there will be visited upon the entire world.[40]

In his address, Glueck found yet another way to blend the truths he had learned as an archaeologist with the work of the rabbis on whose shoulders he now was standing:

On the sides of mounds covering ancient settlements in the Jordan Valley, I have found fragments of pottery fashioned almost seven thousand years ago. Turned then on the potter's wheel and fired into enduring firmness, they remain mute witnesses to the lives of multitudes long since crumbled into dust. From the tarnished artifacts of thunderous hosts which once swept whole states and societies aside, I have learned much of the meaning of mortality.

But what the archaeologist and the historians gather through research, the teachers of the Torah, as indeed all men of real religion, know from perception of the order of God. "If ye have not faith, verily ye shall not endure"[Isaiah 7:9]. These words of Isaiah are as significant for our own day as they were in his. Israel had sought support from mighty Assyria, and the kingdom of Israel succumbed to the protection it invited. Somewhat later, the small kingdom of Judah, too, was fatally heedless of Isaiah's admonition to rely absolutely on God alone.[41]

He addressed the role of the Jewish community in America:

The genius of our American nation of nations and commonwealth of cultures is to emphasize the good of our differences and to encourage the enlargement of our common contributions. Ours is the opportunity and obligation to keep sharp and clean the values of our spiritual inheritance, all of which underscore the American promise. Through the invigorating understanding of our historic personality, we Jews shall be better prepared to participate in the building of the America of the future, and to cope with the problems that assail all souls. Here we take our stand with our fellow Americans to help preserve in this country and to restore elsewhere a spiritual climate in which freedom of expression, liberty of conscience, and equality of opportunity shall prevail.

Who can turn aside from such an assignment? I could not. You cannot. We dare not. And I know of no better way to meet it for myself and my son than after the fashion of my fathers to face up to the challenge of my faith. Let us labor, all of us, for the time in days to come, when according to the words of the Lord to the prophet:

> This will be the covenant which I shall make
> with the house of Israel:
>
> *I shall implant my law in their minds,*
>
> *And write it upon their hearts,*
>
> *And I shall be to them a God,*
> *and they will be to me a people.*
>
> *Then they will no longer need to teach*
> *one another*
>
> *With the words 'Know God!'*
>
> *For they will all know me,*
>
> *From the least of them unto the greatest of them,*
>
> Saith the Lord. Jeremiah 31:33–34[42]

On the evening of March 13 a great banquet was held at the Netherland Plaza Hotel in downtown Cincinnati. The keynote address was delivered by the eminent theologian and survivor of the Terezin concentration camp Rabbi Leo Baeck, who spoke about the shift in the centers of Jewish population that the Holocaust had created:

> If forty years ago a day like this had been celebrated, then it would have been an occurrence which only concerned American Jews. Now this day of consecration is an event which should stir the whole of the Jewish people. Centers have been shifted, the centers of the existence, life and hope of the Jewish people. Centers have shifted to America which is now to become a focus. Shaping the character and molding the futures of American rabbis has become a concern of all Jews all over the world. Two-thirds of all Jews are American Jews; two-thirds of all rabbis are American rabbis. As it were, the rabbinate is put into the hands of American teachers. This College is responsible to the world Jewish community. It will be called to account by the entire Jewish people.[43]

Those who attended the inauguration weekend were treated to a panoply of speakers and a vision of the future of American Reform Judaism. However, the inauguration weekend, splendid as it was, could not long occupy the attention of the Jewish community of Cincinnati. During the spring of 1948 events in Palestine were on everyone's mind. With the ending of the Mandate on May 15, 1948, the independent Jewish state of Israel was born, only to be immediately engulfed in war with its Arab neighbors. Nonetheless, Glueck was ecstatic and with tears in his eyes told the senior students in his Bible class: "Boys, you are the first rabbis in two thousand years to be ordained while an independent Jewish state exists!" He added: "Some day, I want to build a school there!"[44]

8

Academic Growth and Institutional Challenges 1947–1952

*My friends, the Hebrew Union College is not going to
move from Cincinnati. Over my dead body!*

Once inaugurated, Glueck turned attention to his first major challenge as
HUC president: successfully negotiating the proposed merger between
the College and Stephen Wise's Jewish Institute of Religion. Whether the
merger would have taken place if someone other than Nelson Glueck
had been chosen president of HUC in 1947 is a matter for speculation.
What is not at all in doubt is that the timing of Glueck's accession to
his new post was crucial: Wise was nearing his seventy-third birthday
and had found no one to continue the work he had begun a quarter of
a century earlier.[1]

With a long history of negativity to be overcome, however, concluding
the merger was less than a foregone conclusion when Glueck entered
upon the scene. Even though Wise had almost matriculated at HUC for
his own rabbinical training, for most of his adult life he had held HUC in
disdain — and there were members of the HUC faculty and Board with
similar feelings towards JIR. Just prior to JIR's first year of operation in
1922, the president of HUC's Board of Governors had wagered his "hat"
that JIR would never open its doors. After it did open, HUC maintained
a cool reception to JIR initiatives. When Lee K. Frankel, chairman of the
JIR Board, proposed to Dr. Morgenstern an exchange of professors, students, and credits, HUC's president turned him down, arguing that no
parity existed between the two institutions.[2]

In the late thirties, conversations were again initiated to discuss various
kinds of cooperation and coordination between HUC and JIR. These discussions were encouraged by Rabbi James G. Heller of the Isaac Mayer
Wise Temple in Cincinnati. Heller's position as an active member of the
Central Conference of American Rabbis, an alumnus of HUC, and a

confirmed Zionist made him an appropriate intermediary. It was all to
no avail. The unwillingness of some of the HUC Board of Governors and
faculty to accept religious liberalism in place of classical Reform — plus
their utter rejection of Zionism — still stood in the way.[3]

Morgenstern ultimately resolved the impasse when, at the CCAR convention held in Chicago in 1946, he renounced anti-Zionism as a part of
the program of the College. With Glueck's accession to the presidency
of HUC — an American-born rabbi with a great love for Zion, though
not formally a Zionist — the final obstacle to the merger had crumbled.
In addition, Maurice Eisendrath argued that it would be more than
appropriate to have a branch of the College in New York. He pointed out
that Isaac Mayer Wise had insisted that the college he founded would
have to serve all of American Jewry and not just the southern and western congregations that had founded the UAHC in 1873.

Glueck was clearly excited at the prospect of a combined HUC-JIR.
In May 1947, less than two weeks after accepting the presidency of HUC,
he wrote to Stephen Wise:

> I look forward with eagerness to seeing you. . . . You say that as the
> oldest of the seminary presidents, you offer me your hand and heart
> in welcome to the most youthful of the presidents. I thank you for
> that offer and extend my hand and heart to meet yours. A great task
> has been entrusted to me. I count on your help. I hope that our two
> institutions can unite to labor mightily for our single task.[4]

When the JIR's ordination exercises were held in June 1947, both Glueck
and Morgenstern received honorary degrees in New York. Within the
year, this symbolic act of connection between the two institutions was
followed by serious, detailed negotiations. A joint statement was eventually issued:

> The Hebrew Union College and the Jewish Institute of Religion
> resolve to unite for the strengthening and advancement of Judaism
> in America and throughout the world. The right to serve the Jew-
> ish people in its entirety [*klal yisra'el*], with freedom for faculty and
> students alike, is axiomatic.
>
> This united institution shall continue to maintain schools in

Cincinnati and New York, with Nelson Glueck as president, and Stephen S. Wise and Julian Morgenstern as presidents emeriti. Upon this union we invoke the blessing of God.[5]

When Glueck was inaugurated as president of HUC in March 1948, Wise was there with words of encouragement and support. The last few steps needed to complete the merger were soon taken. In June the JIR board accepted Wise's resignation, elected him president emeritus of the Jewish Institute of Religion, and made Nelson Glueck its president in his stead. The final official step took place in October, when Wise installed Glueck as president of the JIR. Unfortunately, Wise died on April 19, 1949 and did not live to see the merger completed. His legacy was to be that he bowed to necessity with grace and candor.[6]

*

In accordance with the dictum that "all beginnings are difficult," various problems surfaced for the newly expanded institution. The most controversial issues were geographical. From the beginning, Glueck insisted that Cincinnati would be the primary campus and New York would be its subsidiary. Knowing that Reform's roots were deeply set in the Queen City, and believing that New York's frenetic pace of life and many distractions would make it difficult for students to concentrate on their studies, he drafted his plans accordingly, and the board approved them. Notices were sent to second-year students at the New York branch (JIR) late in the spring of 1951 that they would be required to spend the next three years in Cincinnati and be ordained at the Cincinnati campus.

It was an ill-advised directive, and the JIR students were furious — their Institute was essentially being reduced to a two-year preparatory institution instead of a five-year seminary where candidates for the rabbinate could be ordained. Jacob R. Marcus, who served as unofficial "chief of staff" in Glueck's presidency, never wavered in his opposition to Glueck's plan to downgrade the New York school. He argued, "If we do not establish a five-year complete school in New York, a rival school will arise, receive support from the Union [the UAHC], and cause an infinity of headaches."[7] The battle over where the students would study and in which city they would be required to reside during their rabbinical training was fought out over the next four years, until the issue was finally resolved: students could spend the entire five years of their rabbinical studies in New York and be ordained there. It was a stinging rebuke to Glueck — the most significant defeat he had to endure during his tenure as president of HUC-JIR.

A second major challenge to Glueck's vision of Cincinnati as the center of Reform Judaism had arisen soon after the war. The organization that Glueck had once briefly and unsuccessfully headed, the Union of American Hebrew Congregations, was now firmly in the charge of Rabbi Maurice Eisendrath. Like Rabbi Edward Israel earlier, Eisendrath proposed a plan to move the executive offices of the UAHC to a city with a much greater concentration of Jews and organizations connected with Jewish life. Israel's choice had been Washington, DC; Eisendrath wanted the UAHC moved to New York.[8]

A "Committee for the Removal of Headquarters of the Union" was established in 1946, and on April 26, 1947 its chair presented the committee's recommendation to the executive board, which at the time was comprised of fourteen members from Cincinnati and twenty-five non-Cincinnatians.[9] Serious reservations were expressed about the move, and the board voted to bring the matter to the next Union Biennial, to be held in Boston the following year. Its recommendation, however, was that the executive headquarters be moved to New York.

The proposal became a declaration of war; emotions ran high on both sides of the issue, and the next twenty-two months were filled with argument, accusation, and political maneuvering. The basic question was whether Reform Judaism was prepared to place its headquarters in the heart of the mainstream of American Jewish life — in the metropolis of New York — or whether it wished to remain in a city perceived to be more and more peripheral to what was happening in the Jewish world in order to preserve its proximity to HUC and its classic German roots.

As Michael Meyer described it, "Cincinnati, the center of the American Reform movement for seventy five years, had come to represent what the movement stood for in its classic phase: integration into an optimistic, forward-looking America, untroubled by ethnic strife and industrial conflict."[10] Those who felt strongly that the UAHC should remain in Ohio wanted to preserve that tradition. The UAHC must have an "American outlook," rather than a "New York outlook," argued Iphigene Ochs Sulzberger. Sylvan Lang of San Antonio, another congregational delegate, stated; "We regard Reform Judaism primarily as a religion. Move the headquarters to New York and whether it be the State of Israel or the Taft-Hartley Act, our Union will inevitably become embroiled in politics."[11] Those against the move also feared that "pure Reform" would be overwhelmed in New York, and thereby lose its focus as well as its adherents. It would become contaminated by a radicalized Jewish constituency, or be taken over by more traditional congregations who would seek to enter the Union.[12] Either way, they said, New York would spell disaster for the movement.

In contrast, Eisendrath and his supporters saw New York as providing exciting challenges to the Union. Social justice could become a central feature of its work. He spoke of New York as the "heart" of American Jewry, while Cincinnati was the "shrine" of Reform. If you wanted to visit Reform's American origins, then go to Cincinnati. If you wanted to work for Reform's future, come to the "House of Living Judaism" to be built in New York:

> New York is the organizational center of American and world Jewry; many Christian denominations have their headquarters in New York City; New York is the home of the largest Jewish community both in America and the world, and New York is the supreme focal point of contact with the constituent members of the Union.[13]

The deciding vote was taken at the UAHC Biennial Convention in Boston on November 16, 1948, where a substantial majority favored the move.[14] Glueck was not among them, the roots of his disdain for New York's Jewry having been laid bare. He felt that as long as Union headquarters were in Cincinnati, he could maintain a strict watchfulness on its activities. No doubt he had little regard for the New York Jewish community, as evidenced by his effort to diminish the role of the JIR in the combined seminary. In short, he preferred Cincinnati to New York for some of the same reasons he preferred to excavate at Tell el-Kheleifeh and the even more remote Khirbet et-Tannur with a small crew of professionals and a few local workers.

Once the UAHC had actually moved, rumors cascaded from all directions suggesting that the College too would soon move to New York. Glueck was even more adamant in his opposition to this suggestion than he was to the Union's move. In the earthy way he often talked, he said: "My friends, the Hebrew Union College is not going to move from Cincinnati. Over my dead body!"[15] His vision for the institution had begun to take on a very different geographical aspect. While the Union might prefer to operate out of New York, Glueck dreamed of establishing a College-sponsored Reform institution in the newly restored homeland of the Jewish people. His explorations in Palestine and Transjordan had given him access to many of Israel's leading public figures,[16] and he had discussed with the Israeli authorities the possibility of acquiring land in Jerusalem and establishing a Hebrew Union College "House" there. The building would contain a library, a chapel, a small lecture hall, an office, a workroom, and about ten dormitory rooms, and would serve as a hostel and headquarters for students, faculty, and graduates.[17] But it would also serve as a base for the projected activities of a department of biblical archaeology. Because it was easier to raise funds for archaeological endeavors than for rabbinical studies abroad, and because the American Schools for Oriental Research in the Arab portion of Jerusalem was no longer accessible to Jews, the first building would become known as the Hebrew Union College-Biblical Archaeological School.

The merger with JIR and the move of the UAHC to New York were not the only major challenges Glueck faced during his initial years as president; they were simply the most controversial. Serious budgetary concerns had to be addressed in the spring of 1950, and while the merger with JIR provided many tangible and intangible assets, cash on hand was not one of them. As a first step toward economizing, he proposed that support for the New York School of Religious Education, a project begun with high hopes two year earlier, be withdrawn — but that support would continue for New York's School of Sacred Music, the only school of its kind in the country. The motion was passed, then rescinded. Both schools remained open. In his message to the board, Glueck acknowledged that the institution faced grave financial problems but cited the successes of the College-Institute's new department of human relations and its museum, which was then on tour throughout the country.

*

When the Korean War broke out in June 1950 and American troops began fighting and dying there, Glueck saw the conflict as a prelude to the apocalypse. He had been thoroughly frightened by President Truman's authorization of the development of the hydrogen bomb, and wrote to the alumni of the College:

> During the approaching High Holyday season, all of us will be offering up our prayers to *ribono shel olam* [Master of the Universe], that the threatened holocaust which now imperils humanity may be averted.
>
> We shall need to utilize every spiritual and intellectual resource at our command to strengthen our people for whatever is to come. If God sees fit to answer our prayers, and the world-wide conflict is avoided — there will still be drastic readjustments for all of us to make. Already the young men of our congregations are being called to active military service. Our ministry to them and to their families will create a heavy drain upon our emotional and spiritual energy. Again we are being called upon to advise young couples caught up in the frenzy of war-time hysteria. Some of our colleagues may soon be called or recalled to active duty in the chaplaincy. All of us, and all human beings will be affected by vast social and economic changes whose outcome no one can predict.[18]

Glueck's overreaction to the 1950 threat perhaps reflected his tendency to misread the significance of current events, just as he had done in Berlin twenty-five years before.

*

Throughout his twenty-four years as president of HUC-JIR, Glueck was able to enrich the rabbinical students' experiences by calling upon the many Jewish scholars in Germany and in Israel whose acquaintance he had made during his years of travel. While Glueck was a student in Germany in the 1920s he had attended a number of Sunday afternoon gatherings where he listened to the words of Rabbi Leo Baeck, the heroic leader of German Jewry during the Holocaust. The author of *The Essence of Judaism*,[19] Baeck had declined offers of refuge in America, choosing instead to buoy up Jewish spirits in Nazi Germany and later in the Theresienstat concentration camp. As noted above, Baeck spoke at Glueck's inaugural banquet in March, 1948. There, he defined what he thought a rabbi should be:

The rabbi must be a man of the Jewish way of life, and perhaps the Jewish way of life means also a bit of Puritanism, a bit of asceticism. The new rabbi does not mean the fashionable rabbi. His sermons must be a part of his own life. The rabbi must live the Jewish life, and then he will give not only sermons and speeches, but he will give himself.[20]

During his presidency Glueck brought Baeck and other outstanding scholars to the Cincinnati campus for a semester or more of teaching and research. Several came from the Hebrew University in Jerusalem: Gershom Scholem (eminent scholar of Jewish mysticism), Isaiah Tishby (Kabbalah and Hasidism), Gershon Shaked (modern Hebrew literature), and Uriel Tal (modern Jewish history).[21]

While attending to his administrative duties, Glueck did not neglect his own scholarly efforts. In the spring of 1951 he gave a lecture at the Library of Congress on the occasion of the publication of a major scholarly work to which he had committed himself fifteen years earlier: *Explorations in Eastern Palestine*, Volume IV, published by the American Schools of Oriental Research in New Haven. Glueck had spent most of the previous summer working on the volume.[22] He would henceforth focus more on his popular archaeological books, which would eventually include *The River Jordan* (1946), *Rivers in the Desert* (1959), and *Deities and Dolphins* (1965), along with a revised edition of *The Other Side of the Jordan* (1970), originally published in 1940.

In his first years as president of HUC-JIR, Glueck could claim a number of significant accomplishments. He had completed the long-delayed merger of HUC and JIR, giving the College a strong presence in New York City. He had enlarged the faculty, expanded the administrative arm of the College, and instituted significant new programming and curricular emphases. In addition, he had provided ample role models for the scholarly endeavors of both students and faculty. Scholarship, as he frequently argued, was of utmost importance both for the Reform rabbinate and for the Jewish community it would serve.

9

Glueck and Eisendrath:
Enmity in Velvet Gloves

Since when must the child be utterly subservient to the parent?

With the increasing visibility and influence of the UAHC in its New York headquarters, the stage was set for a decades-long struggle for supremacy between the Union and the College, the two main institutions of American Reform Judaism. The rivalry was personalized by the differences between the leaders of those institutions — Nelson Glueck and Maurice Eisendrath, both of whom could claim rabbinical authority and the right to speak for the movement nationally.

That there should be such a struggle for pre-eminence within one of the three major branches of Judaism in America is an anomaly. In the Orthodox world, the rabbis who head the most renowned *yeshivot* gain the most widespread influence. There is no lay organization powerful enough to challenge that authority. In the Conservative branch, the head of the Jewish Theological Seminary in New York has always been the spokesperson for the movement, while the lay organization, the United Synagogue, comprised of representatives from the constituent congregations, has had relatively little influence.

When in 1942 it became clear that Glueck's commitment to the OSS precluded his meeting his responsibilities at the UAHC, Maurice Eisendrath had already stepped forward as interim director. By the end of 1942, Eisendrath was officially appointed to the position vacated by Glueck and would direct the UAHC for more than thirty years. Ordained in 1926 at the College, Eisendrath had served a congregation in Charleston, West Virginia for a few years and then moved on to Toronto, where he became the spiritual leader of Canada's leading Reform congregation, Holy Blossom Temple.

From the summer of 1929 through the fall of 1942, Eisendrath established himself as the voice of Reform Judaism in Canada through his regular broadcasts on a national radio program called "Forum of the Air," which he used to promote his social action agenda.[1] Holy Blossom had undertaken to build a new synagogue during his tenure, and Eisendrath had good reason to stay in Toronto. He evidently believed, however, that it was his responsibility to Reform Judaism to respond to the Union's call.[2]

Glueck had publicly endorsed Eisendrath's nomination as the full-time head of the UAHC. It would be reasonable to suggest, however, that the seeds of their lengthy and often bitter rivalry had already been firmly planted. Glueck wrote to his close friend Judah Magnes indicating his displeasure with the appointment: "The UAHC is on its way to being captured more or less by the Zionist Organization. The Zionist crowd was pushing [for Eisendrath] strongly."[3] As for Eisendrath, it is anybody's guess as to whether he was miffed to be only the second choice, or whether he and Glueck would, in any event, have squabbled over whether to move the headquarters of the UAHC to New York, over the extent of the control that the UAHC would have over HUC, and over how to allocate the moneys collected for the Reform movement in an equitable fashion.

It is interesting to note that before Glueck and Eisendrath entered into the institutional settings from which they publicly sparred with one another, they had enjoyed a collegial friendship that developed while both were students at HUC in the 1920s. Indeed, in August 1929, en route to Charlottesville, Virginia to deliver a set of lectures at the University of Virginia, Glueck spent a few days in Charleston with Eisendrath and his wife Rosa. He wrote them a gracious thank-you note: "I thoroughly enjoyed my visit with you and am glad that I didn't know I was supposed to be here [in Charlottesville] instead. Charleston was delightful and it was exceedingly pleasant to talk to you a bit."[4]

During the Toronto years, Glueck and Eisendrath presumably had little contact. Since Glueck rarely attended CCAR conventions, that venue would not have provided opportunities for them to meet. During the late 1940s and early 1950s, setting aside for the moment the disagreement about moving the Union to New York, the relationship between the two was cordial. Exchanged pleasantries are recorded in the proceedings of the UAHC biennials. In the Annual Report of the UAHC for 1951, Glueck is described as an "eminent scholar and teacher in whose capacities for great accomplishments we have firm and enduring faith and to whom we pledge our loyalty and co-operation."[5]

Eisendrath himself offered an important public affirmation of Glueck's role, along with an assessment of the importance of cooperation between the Union and the College-Institute when he addressed the UAHC Board in the spring of 1952:

> I was overjoyed to hear at the recent meeting of the Board of Governors, in the course of a comprehensive report of remarkable progress during the five-year incumbency of the honored post of President by Dr. Glueck, his own vigorously voiced insistence that "the cause of the College and the Union is one and indivisible," and that "neither can conceivably advance without the other."
>
> I do sincerely reciprocate this sentiment, not alone because of my growing esteem and affection for my colleague and co-worker, Dr. Glueck, but because of the historic heritage, the present necessity, and the future indispensability of such complete co-operation between Union and College-Institute.
>
> I know that the Board joins with me in my heartfelt felicitations to Dr. Glueck upon the completion of five years of Herculean effort and rich attainment at the helm of our cherished Alma Mater, and that we pray that he and we will be blessed with unnumbered years of future labor and ever more abundant accomplishments together.[6]

In the fall of 1956, Eisendrath acknowledged with pleasure receiving a number of Glueck's letters posted in Israel, and his reply indicated that he was looking forward to a "long conversation about so many matters." By the end of the decade, however, their rivalry heated up. Both had been serving as institutional leaders for more than a decade, and profound differences between them had emerged. Eisendrath's biographer, Avi Schulman, suggests that part of Eisendrath's problem was his ego. Glueck stood in the way of Eisendrath being perceived as the pre-eminent spokesperson for both American and Canadian Reform Jewry.[7]

The other divisive issue was the relationship of the College-Institute to the UAHC. Glueck's intention was to maintain the College as the primary source, not just of rabbis, but of authority in the movement. Michael Meyer suggests that "unlike his predecessors, Glueck did not conceive the College to be a ward of the Union." On his part, Eisendrath "did not see the principal role of the Union to be the support of the College. Each believed his own institution should possess primary influence."[8] Eisendrath felt that the Union, through its biennial assemblies, reflected the collective will of Reform Jewry and should therefore direct and control all national activities, including the training of rabbis. Glueck, regarding the College-Institute as an autonomous institution, hoped to move beyond the current system of collecting dues from each congregation and splitting the proceeds evenly.[9]

In the foreword to *Like A Raging Fire*, Albert Vorspan[10] referred to Eisendrath as a "stormy petrel," eager for controversy. But "he truly believed that liberal Judaism had both the mandate and the power to transform the world,"[11] and that he would be the one to lead the transformation. Glueck saw things differently and did not hesitate to say so. Speaking at an HUC Board of Governors' meeting in January 1958, he responded to the statement that the proper relationship of the College to the Union was that of a child to a parent: "Since when must the child be utterly subservient to the parent, and what kind of parent attempts to exact that kind of obedience in this day and age, or ever could in any age? And besides, how long does it take for a child to grow up? This child is only three years younger than its parent and is now 83 years old. Some child!"[12]

The two men clashed over funding, over control of the California College of Jewish Studies, and even over ownership of the main HUC campus in Cincinnati. After strenuous effort had failed to dislodge the title for the property from the UAHC, Glueck retaliated by ending a longstanding custom of having Union leadership sign HUC ordination certificates. Eisendrath responded by giving less exposure to the College-Institute at the Union biennials and in the pages of its publication, *American Judaism*,[13] thus making it more difficult for Glueck to increase his base of individual supporters.

Cognizant of and alarmed by the growing public awareness of this deep division in the Reform movement, Rabbi Jacob Rudin, then president of the Central Conference of American Rabbis, declared in his 1958 presidential message to the hundreds of rabbis in attendance: "Reform Judaism cannot afford the instability of uncertain peace, nor the luxury of unamiable controversy. This is not a contained, limited struggle. Reform Judaism in America is the casualty. Everybody gets hurt. Every national interest [of the Reform movement] is endangered."[14]

Despite Rudin's call for peace, matters went from bad to worse. One flashpoint was the combined campaign for Reform Judaism and the

Endowment Fund: both parties felt that they were due more than fifty percent of the proceeds. Another was disagreement about the number of seats on the HUC Board to be allocated to the Union. In December 1962, Sidney Meyers, who chaired the Board of Governors of HUC-JIR, addressed the Union's executive board on the matter: "This is the most important talk I have ever made. We are at a dangerous crossroad, and I sincerely hope I can properly express all the cogent facts and thoughts."[15] Meyers went on to describe his frustration in trying to get Judge Emil Barr, head of the Union board, to call a meeting of the joint liaison committee (established specifically to deal with this matter) during the summer of 1962, while Eisendrath was vacationing on his private island, Tamagami, and "out of touch." In January 1964 Irvin Fane, who served on both the College Board of Governors and on the UAHC board, also weighed in on this issue:

> I wish to add only this one personal commentary. In my remarks on the occasion of my installation as Chairman of the Board [of the UAHC] I said that I wanted to devote generously of my energies in the next two years toward the achievement of peace within our Reform movement. I further stated that for far too many years the leaders of our movement have been agonized by conflicts, and I asked the rhetorical question whether our movement would not have been further advanced if our leadership had been permitted to use its energies for programs as against destructive battling for position over rights, or with respect to other disagreements.
>
> These were not idle words. I meant them in great depth when I first spoke them, and feel them even more strongly now. We cannot afford the luxury, or the indecency of a civil war in Reform Judaism, for there will be no winner and no loser; a civil war is always brother against brother.[16]

No matter what the level of public animosity between the two institutions, however, Glueck continued to show friendly personal feelings toward the Eisendraths in his correspondence with them. During the latter 1950s most of their interchanges concerned Rosa Eisendrath's health. A telegram that Glueck sent from Bombay in April 1958 conveyed his concern: "I pray for Rosa's speedy recovery. I meet you with full heart for our single cause. God bless you both." A letter sent from Cincinnati in May began: "Dear Maurice: I hope strongly that Rosa has greatly recovered, or, even better, is completely well again, and that you too have been getting some rest."[17]

The sudden death of Rabbi Barnett Brickner, a prominent Reform colleague, in an automobile accident, deepened Glueck's awareness of the fragility of human life and impelled him to make a concerted effort to remove the roadblocks in the relationship between himself and Eisendrath:[18]

> Let us count our blessings while we may, my friend. How can we be so foolish as to be angry at one another. I clasp your hands and vow to do everything possible — as inwardly I believe I always have — to work with you for our single cause. There are times when we will not see eye to eye, but let it be regarded as honest differences of judgment and let no one whisper in our ears that it is animosity. Life is difficult and short. The work is great and the cause is enduring and the workers are all too few. And however much we succeed in advancing the work of God entrusted to us, it must inevitably fall short of what remains to be done. And so I salute you and Rosa with all my heart and pray for your health and well-being and for the blessing of everything we hold dear. Your success is my gain, and your happiness my enduring hope.[19]

Early in September 1958 Glueck wrote to Eisendrath from Israel:

> I have been wondering about you and Rosa, and my strong hopes that both of you have had a wonderful and restful summer. I pray that all vestiges of Rosa's indisposition have disappeared, and that you are restored to your usual, extraordinary state of creative vigor. I have been thinking about the progress of the UAHC under your leadership, and it has been quite remarkable. I take delight and pride in what you have been able to do thus far for Reform Judaism and thus for all of us. I pray that you and Rosa may be spared for long years to come to accomplish still more for the sacred cause to which we are devoted.[20]

In a letter three years later Glueck referred to a "heartwarming meeting" they had had, and wished they would meet more regularly, because "if we continue these meetings and this kind of spirit prevails, much of the misunderstanding and anguish that sometimes occur could be removed. You repeated one remark, which I have made at various times, to the effect that when we stand together, nothing can stop us."[21]

Glueck invited Eisendrath to give the sermon at ordination for the graduating class of 1962, and later wrote telling him that he had given a "most excellent message."[22] But a letter from Eisendrath dated the following day presumably crossed Glueck's in the mail and provided new fuel for their ongoing disagreements. Eisendrath began:

> When you spoke to me after the ordination and suggested that we get together before we both leave the country for the summer, you will recall that I said that I was contemplating writing you a letter which, hopefully, might lead to the same goal. However, I was postponing the writing of it until there would be some attenuation in the very strong feelings which some of your comments during the last week or so evoked in me. Only the lateness of the hour at our own Board of Trustees meeting prevented my dealing with several facets of your comments there which [I found] most misleading.

He continued by referring to Glueck's mentioning —"and not for the first time"— his concern about the Union's interference in the academic freedom of the College:

> You know full well, Nelson, that regardless of what at times might have been my own feelings, neither I nor any member of our leadership have made any suggestions regarding anything that had to do with the faculty, the student body, the curriculum, with anything that is in any way identified with academic freedom. Neither I nor any of our leaders have at any time communicated with any member of the Board of Governors [of the College], directly or indirectly, on matters bearing on this subject.

Eisendrath labeled Glueck's charge unfounded and unfair, and continued:

If we are to meet, we will certainly have to discuss such fundamental matters as this rather than merely the details of either of our funding campaigns. If you are prepared to strive, once again, to reach some kind of profounder understanding between us in the hope that we may seek to establish that sense of concord which is so imperative if our movement is to go forward — then I would welcome such a conference with you. But I think we should definitely allow sufficient time to cover the entire ground.[23]

After years of illness Rosa Eisendrath died on July 2, 1963, and Nelson and Helen each sent hand-written condolence notes. Eisendrath's replies were posted to Nelson on July 10 and to Helen on July 24, both from European cities whence Eisendrath had gone to assuage his sorrow; in them he expressed his gratitude at their kind expressions of sympathy, and the profound sense of loss he felt as he faced life without the presence of his beloved Rosa, to whom he had been married for thirty-six years. To Nelson he wrote:

Close as I was to my dear one, I now realize how many days, hours, moments, I squandered on that which was useless, insignificant, sinful. Much of the waste of precious, never-to-be-recaptured instants of joy had to do with you and me. Too swiftly the "repent one day before your death, for every day, any day, might be so fated"— that admonition was lost amid the corrosion of the commonplace. Only now do I comprehend that wise rabbinic utterance when it is too late for what mattered most.[24]

That year the Union biennial was scheduled for Chicago; Eisendrath wanted a special HUC Convocation — and the granting of honorary degrees — to be part of the 90th anniversary of the Union's founding, but he was advised that "provisions of the Hebrew Union College charter seemingly make it impossible for you to grant degrees in any state in which we have no schools."[25] Eisendrath expressed his regret about not being able to create such a "most impressive event."

The Chicago biennial provided a platform for yet another controversy, this one reflecting the different worlds in which the two men moved. Eisendrath had established a tradition that at each biennial he would deliver a presidential message, which he called "The State of Our Union." The message usually lasted over an hour and gave the delegates a comprehensive exposition of his current thinking. In his "State of Our Union" message to the delegates assembled in Chicago, Eisendrath responded to the news that the Catholic Church might revise its official doctrine regarding Jewish culpability in the crucifixion of Jesus.[26] He called upon his fellow Jews to reappraise the "often jaundiced" view of Jesus that appeared in statements and publications of the Reform movement. He characterized the Christian Savior as "a Jew who offered a lofty yet simply stated message that was thoroughly grounded in prophetic and rabbinic thought." "How long would it be," he queried, "until Jews would reclaim Jesus as one of their own and admit that [his] influence was beneficial, not only to pagans, but to the Jews of his time as well, and that only those who later took his name in vain profaned his teaching?"[27]

Glueck was livid. His attitude was that "the only possible way in which Jews could make any rapprochement with Christianity or a reappraisal of their attitude towards Jesus would be tantamount to accepting some of their doctrines with respect to Jesus' divinity." In his view "there was nothing of Christianity and its theological definitions that we could accept." What annoyed Glueck most of all was the statement "Let us render unto Jesus that which belongs to Jesus." Glueck recognized the reference to the text in Matthew: "Let us render unto Caesar that which is Caesar's" and fulminated that there was no way that Judaism could agree with such a statement. Meanwhile, his differences with Eisendrath received international attention.

Glueck's concern also stemmed from the hard-fought battles in which he had engaged with the Orthodox establishment in Israel as he tried to obtain land upon which to build a Reform institution in Jerusalem. Orthodox Jews feared a "Reform incursion," and the last thing Glueck needed was an American Reform Jewish leader talking about a rapprochement with Christianity. "Statements such as Dr. Eisendrath had made, even if he didn't mean them in the way they seemed to be understood by others, would set back the progress of Liberal Judaism in Israel for forty or fifty years." He explained:

The Orthodox rabbinate in Israel had been saying with regard to me in particular, that I was the envoy of assimilation and that Reform

With Maurice Eisendrath, 1968. (*American Jewish Archives*)

Judaism meant an intermediate step on the road toward assimilation to Christianity. . . . It is fortunate that the international press carried my very strong objection to Dr. Eisendrath's statements and that my strong objection was featured in the newspapers in Israel.[28]

TIME magazine, which would soon feature Glueck on its cover, quoted him as saying that "Eisendrath's statement made it seem as if American Reform Judaism was prepared to put Jesus in a central role as a great rabbinical leader."[29]

It has been suggested that Glueck created difficulties for himself by trying to be all things to all people. Yet when he felt that the image of Reform Judaism was in danger of being tarnished, he spoke out clearly and forcefully in defending his point of view. He was similarly forthright when it came to protecting the academic freedom of HUC faculty as well as the rights of students to participate in protest marches and invite controversial speakers to campus.

The Six-Day War in 1967 between Israel and her Arab neighbors provided Glueck with an opportunity to speak to American Jewry with perhaps his most eloquent voice. His *Dateline Jerusalem: a Diary*[30] was a moving testimony about his love for Zion, his long-time relationship with the Jewish state and its past and present leadership, and the enduring bridge Glueck had built through the Hebrew Union College-Biblical Archaeological School.

Eisendrath, on the other hand, had exercised his prophetic impulses by speaking out for the civil rights movement in America and against the war in Vietnam. Each man had followed his passions, the one for Israel, the other for social justice. American Reform Jewry was the richer for their diverse interests, even if it had to endure their quarrels.

Less than four years later Glueck was gone from the scene and Eisendrath himself had only a short time to live. In an interview held a year after Glueck's death and a year before Eisendrath's demise, the UAHC president seemed to have put his differences with Glueck into perspective. He suggested that "it would have been a miracle if two such ambitious men, heading their own respective institutions, had not disagreed." He stated that their disputes were largely over money and harmoniously resolved: "I don't think we were enemies. We each respected the other. There were times when I felt that deep inside I was very fond of Nelson Glueck."[31] "There were times"—"deep inside"— qualifiers both; the public controversy is what most of their contemporaries most vividly recall.[32]

10

Surveying the Negev

Hunger and thirst are its patrimony.

Just prior to the establishment of the State of Israel in 1948, a new and exciting era in biblical archaeology began. In the winter of 1947, a young-ster from the Taamireh Bedouin tribe happened upon ancient manu-scripts secreted in jars in a cave at Qumran, near the Dead Sea. A Qumran expedition was subsequently carried out by G. Lankester Harding of the Palestinian Department of Antiquities and Fr. Roland de Vaux of the École Biblique. William L. Reed, director of the Jerusalem branch of ASOR from 1951 to 1952, also participated in the examination of thirty-nine caves and crevices containing artifacts. The most sensational find of this campaign was the copper scroll that contained a list of Temple treasures with their location. All of these ancient manuscripts would come to be known as the Dead Sea Scrolls.

In other archaeological settings during this period, James Kelso in 1950 excavated Khirbet en-Nitleh, possibly the biblical Gilgal. Joseph Free of Wheaton College conducted excavations at Tell Dothan, thirteen miles north of Nablus, from 1953 to 1964. In 1959, 3,200 ceramic and metal vessels from a rich tomb dating from circa 1400–1100 B.C.E. were uncov-ered there. Gradually more and more sites with biblical strata became the loci for active archaeological work within the borders of the new State of Israel. New political realities, however, limited the scope of archaeo-logical discovery after 1948. With the former Mandatory Palestine now divided into Israel and Jordan, Nelson Glueck, as a Jew, could no longer visit his former office or the library of ASOR. Nor could he examine the exhibits in the Rockefeller Museum, also now in Jordanian hands. More-over, he could not gain access to any of the sites in the Hashemite king-dom east of the Jordan where he had wandered virtually unhindered for the first twenty years of his archaeological career. No longer could he traverse the highlands of Moab and Edom seeking to discover their occupational history and suitability for potential Jewish settlement in the twentieth century[1] or meander through the Arabah in search of pot-tery sherds and copper mines. For the next twenty years these political realities would deny Jewish archaeologists the opportunity to visit Tell el-Kheleifeh and Khirbet et-Tannur.[2] The deep frustration resulting from this situation weighed heavily on Glueck's mind. Moreover, given his new responsibilities as president of the Hebrew Union College, he understood that he would have to curtail his field work in the Middle East. Instead, for five years he consolidated his role as president of HUC and implemented some of the major elements of his vision for the College, later the College-Institute.

Nevertheless, he could not stay away for long from the excavations he loved. By 1952 he had made up his mind to explore the Negev, Israel's southern desert, in the same comprehensive manner as he had proceeded to survey Transjordan decades earlier, locating ancient settlements, dating them, and carefully recording water resources. In other words, he could continue his unique contribution to Near Eastern archaeology — identifying sites of historical importance — often with the Bible as his handbook.

There were many questions to answer: Was the Negev truly a desert or only seemingly so? Was it actually as barren and inhospitable to sedentary occupation as had been assumed for so many centuries? Where were the camps, fortresses, guard posts, and sources of water that must have existed there in the past? Which were the tracks that Abraham and his retinue had followed on their journey from Canaan to Egypt and back again? Was it possible to figure out from the topography of the country, together with biblical descriptions, the lines of march that the Israelites of the Exodus had wearily pursued through the Negev en route from Sinai to the Promised Land?

There were other reasons to explore the Negev, with much more at stake than confirming the historical record. Glueck could increase his knowledge of the culture and civilization of the Nabataeans, whose temple at Khirbet et-Tannur he had excavated in 1937; and he could obtain more detailed information about ways to conserve the sparse rainwater that fell in the desert. If he could discern, using aerial topography and information on the ground, how the Nabataeans had sustained their large communities there, then the lessons could be applied by Israeli agronomists and irrigation experts, and the Negev could sustain tens of thousands of immigrants to the Jewish state who might be sent to settle there.

Glueck approached his self-appointed task within the framework of his poetic vision of Israel's southern desert:

Bare landscapes, bold colors and fiercely bright light stand out in the picture of the Negev. The picture is one of strength and simplicity. Hunger and thirst are its patrimony, but there are great treasures of ore and oil concealed in its most desolate wastes. Its hills are gaunt and there are lunar-like craters and massive depressions imprisoned below almost sheer cliffs. It has some fertile plains and innumerable patches of good soil in carefully terraced creek beds.

Wide stretches of *hamada* desert are covered with flint and slate and sandstone pebbles as if the earth in abject mourning had strewn itself with sackcloth and ashes. A few springs and infrequent wells accentuate the general poverty. It is a land ravaged by drought, but where on rare occasion freshets tear through normally dry stream beds.[3]

In order to answer the questions he had posed, Glueck was prepared to examine every square mile of the desert from Sde Boker[4] to Eilat[5] and to carefully consider the topography, the pottery, and the habitations of the Negev. He would spend his summers traversing the area in Land Rovers and command cars to accomplish his objectives. Camels would no longer suffice. But he would still use time-tested Bedouin techniques to find water that was readily accessible. In numerous instances, Glueck and his entourage found *thamileh* (holes sunk to a shallow depth until a moderate amount of water was obtained).[6]

Whereas Yigael Yadin, his Israeli colleague, would hire workers from the development towns near his sites, Glueck preferred to gather volunteers from nearby kibbutzim. Using different approaches, both men were participating in the process of helping the native Israelis (*sabras*) — as well as recent arrivals from Europe and the Middle East (*olim*) — to identify with Israel's past. Glueck preferred the *kibbutznikim*; he wanted people who could be presumed to know something about the history of the places they were excavating.

Only when the project was already underway did he realize its enormity. To complete it he would also need to engage amateur archaeologists, including Israeli soldiers, and to make of them professional observers of a

desert ecosystem.[7] He also needed help at the highest political level of the
new Jewish state. One person who shared Glueck's vision and whose support was critical to the success of the initiative was David Ben-Gurion,
the Polish immigrant who had made *aliyah* to Palestine in the early
twentieth century as David Green and had become, in time, the ac-
know-ledged leader of the *yishuv* and then the first prime minister of
Israel. Glueck and Ben-Gurion were kindred spirits, linked by their political *savoir faire*, their love for the land and the Bible, and their vision
of the Negev's future.

There had been personal contact between Glueck and Ben-Gurion
prior to the establishment of the state, but it was during the early 1950s
that their relationship truly flourished. On one occasion when Glueck
– known to all Israelis as "Ha-Professor" (the professor) – was a dinner
guest at Paula and David Ben-Gurion's home, he turned to his host and
said, "I have a gift for you." He presented Ben-Gurion with something
black and mysterious, a piece of asphalt that he had found floating on the
surface of the Dead Sea, somewhere between Ein Gedi and Sodom. Ben-
Gurion was delighted with Glueck's find. It meant there might be recov-
erable oil in the area, a major requirement of a modern nation-state.[8]

In a letter to Glueck early in 1954, Ben-Gurion indicated his pleasure
at having heard from him regarding his most recent discoveries in the
Negev:

> I await your return with great anticipation, though I am more inter-
> ested in the eschatology of the Negev than I am in its archaeology.
> But I am sure that the ancient artifacts of the Negev are close to your
> heart and from the early history of the Negev we can learn much
> about its future, in a manner indicating that all of our interests
> are shared.[9]

What Ben-Gurion was really interested in was the number of people that
could be settled in the Negev and sustained by available water resources.
He knew that only about eight inches of rain fell in an average year in
the Beersheba area, and less than an inch in Eilat on the shore of the
Red Sea. How could agricultural or irrigation techniques make the Negev bloom with such paltry rainfall, most of which, coming in torren-
tial storms, disappeared into the sand without irrigating anything?

Ben-Gurion was convinced that the Negev, virtually uninhabited in modern times except for its complement of Bedouin tribes, could be restored to significant levels of human habitation. He knew that during earlier historical epochs the Negev was populated and productive. Glueck knew this as well. There was yet another consideration, vital to a Jewish entity that was, from the moment of its inception, an island in a sea of enemies. As it was, the Negev provided easy access for infiltrators, and Israel was vulnerable to terrorist attacks on the isolated Jewish settlements in the area. If it could be settled and developed, then Israel's borders with Jordan and Egypt would be more secure and defensible.

Ben-Gurion considered the "taming of the Negev" the primary challenge to Israel in his time. In his introduction to Yaakov Morris' *Masters of the Desert: 6,000 Years in The Negev*,[10] he wrote: "The supreme test of Israel in our generation lies not in its struggle with hostile forces without, but in its success in gaining domination, through science and pioneering, over the wastelands of its country in the expanses of the South and the Negev."[11] Cyrus Gordon, the Semitics scholar who had met Glueck at ASOR in the 1930s, reviewed the Morris volume in the *Saturday Review of Literature*, making references to Glueck's discoveries and summariz-

With Yigael Yadin, 1956. (*American Jewish Archives*)

With David Ben-Gurion, 1960. (*American Jewish Archives*)

ing the book's wildly optimistic hypothesis: that Israel could support a population of some eight million through known techniques of producing food. "Since the Negev constitutes the larger part of Israel's area, the development of the nation resolves itself in large measure on transforming the Negev from wasteland to habitation."[12]

Some fifteen years earlier, in 1938, Walter Clay Lowdermilk, then the assistant chief of the United States' Soil Conservation Service, had studied the area with great care. His conclusions appeared at a critical point in the process of molding opinion about the Negev and provided Nelson Glueck with ample scientific evidence about its possibilities.[13]

The casual observer may well conclude that its general appearance does not fortify hopes of much restoration. Experts, however, are more hopeful. Sir John Simpson, who was sent by the British government in 1930 to make a survey of agricultural possibilities of Palestine reported: "Given the possibility of irrigation, there is practically an inexhaustible supply of cultivable land in the Beer-Sheba area. Up to the present time there has been no organized attempt to ascertain whether there is or is not an artesian supply of water."[14]

He also mentioned that T. E. Lawrence and Sir Leonard Woolley expressed their opinion in a report entitled *The Wilderness of Zin*[15] that, with ordinary methods of farming, the Negev could be as fertile as it ever was. Moreover, decades earlier, Sir Flinders Petrie had done a small experiment on a hill south of Gaza and found that productivity could be markedly improved.[16]

The Negev also offered a gateway to the Red Sea. With its sea lanes under their control, a Jewish state could reach out to Africa and Asia, just as the Bible described Solomon doing in the tenth century B.C.E. The establishment of Eilat as a major port on the eastern branch of the Gulf of Suez, with its potential for opening Oriental markets to Israeli commercial ventures, was an urgent requirement of the growing Israeli economy.

As with everything else he did in his archaeological endeavors, Glueck framed his view of Eilat as part of Israel's millennial history. Attending the annual meeting of the Israel Exploration Society[17] there in 1962 on the shores of the Red Sea with Tell el-Kheleifeh visible on the horizon, he said: "The significance of our gathering in Eilat cannot be described by any other word than 'miraculous.' The historical sequence of events which enabled us to gather at this modern Israeli seaport cannot be explained completely in terms of scientifically rational factors. Well over thirty centuries ago, many of the Children of Israel stood on these very shores after having spent a long generation of sojourn in Sinai." Glueck continued:

The principle of keeping the way open to the Red Sea became and always has remained one of the cardinal and undeviating fundamentals of all Israelite and Judean foreign policy, and it is and can be no different today. There is no question in my mind but that it was basically over this issue, aside from the mineral riches of the Aravah, that fierce war was waged at frequent intervals with Edom over a period lasting for several hundred years. Israel and later Judah had no choice in this connection, any more than modern Israel has any choice today, if it is to survive and grow into the greatness of its historical mission.

Paraphrasing I Kings 4, he concluded: "How wonderful it would be, if future records of our own time were to read, 'and Ben-Gurion presided over the State of Israel, whose southwestern boundary extended to the Brook of Egypt and he had peace on all sides around about him.'"[18]

Glueck was given the title of "honorary citizen" of Eilat during this conference. One cannot overemphasize the importance of these annual meetings of the Israel Exploration Society in propagating the idea of the Land of Israel as the age-old home of the Jewish people and helping to form an Israeli identity during the early years of the Jewish state. During the 1950s and 1960s, its meetings drew audiences of several thousand to hear academic lectures on the archaeology, geology, and history of Israel. Presidents, prime ministers, and army generals were often in attendance, and not just as honored guests; most were very active participants. The IES deliberately chose to hold its meetings in out-of-the-way places, corresponding to, say, Cheyenne, Wyoming or Las Cruces, New Mexico, in the United States. The academic settings were conceived as capable of supplying tangible proof to the claims of the Zionist narrative, and to support an integrative national culture for a society of immigrants.

It has even been argued that IES meetings shared characteristics with other Zionist rituals established in Israel within a few years of its creation — specifically *yom ha-zikaron* (Day of Remembrance), when all of the soldiers who fell in Israel's battles were memorialized, and y*om ha-atzma'ut*, the anniversary of Israel's independence (May 14, 1948 — the 5th of Iyyar, 5748). The IES events were an annual occurrence; they involved significant numbers of political leaders; and they centered on cherished national values, especially the sacred bonds between the present and the past and between the people and the land.[19]

*

Ben-Gurion, like many of Israel's founders, was a completely secular Jew.[20] Typically he would say: "I am not religious, nor were the majority of the early builders of modern Israel believers. Yet their passion for this land stemmed from the Book of Books. That is why the single most important book in my life is the Bible."[21] He viewed the Third Jewish Commonwealth (the modern Jewish state) as an opportunity for unparalleled creativity:

> And I am sure now that we are home again, we shall once more be creative as a people. We have already begun to be so. Today, we are in the process of writing a new Torah, not only with scribes, but with pioneers and farmers, artists and scientists, teachers, engineers, legislators, collectivists, citizens, in every walk of life. All speak the language of Moses, and even the freethinkers among them study deeply in the Book, the source of inspiration, provider of a past and a vision for the future. Our new Torah is still being written now, but its best chapters are yet to come. It is my conviction that they will tell the story of the taming of the desert.[22]

Like Ben-Gurion, Glueck had profound respect for the biblical text. Glueck was known to carry a Bible with him on his explorations and to read aloud to his guides, staff, and volunteers about the areas they were exploring and the sites they had found. In a piece he wrote for *Horizon Magazine* in November 1959, he discussed at some length the role of the Hebrew Scriptures. Referring to the discovery of the Hebrew inscription in Hezekiah's tunnel in Jerusalem, he noted:

> The Biblical statement [in II Kings and II Chronicles] and this rock-hewn tablet [which Glueck had seen in Istanbul] form a classic example of how historical memories and records in scriptural accounts are confirmed or supplemented or clarified by archaeological finds. The archaeologist's efforts are not directed at proving the correctness of the Bible, which is neither necessary nor possible, any more than belief in God can be scientifically demonstrated. It is quite the other way around.
>
> The historical clues in the Bible can lead the archaeologist to a knowledge of the civilization of the ancient world in which the Bible developed and with whose religious practices and concepts the Bible so radically differs. It can be regarded in effect as an almost

infallible divining rod, revealing to the expert the whereabouts and characteristics of lost cities and civilizations.

The biblical account was most important for Glueck, and, under the influence of Albright, his thinking about the historicity of the Bible assumed proportions often associated with those who asserted that every word of the Bible was Truth. Although in matters of theology Glueck was no fundamentalist, he did possess a sense of mystique about the land he traversed; it was part of his faith. The dark star-filled nights in the Negev aroused a deep religious fervor. It was the response of a man who felt a profound connection with the parched soil he was surveying. He mentioned this feeling a number of times to his photographer, Beno Rothenberg,[23] when the two of them were alone in the evening.

It was clear to Glueck that wherever there was or is water in the Negev, it is possible to find the remains of ancient settlements. Many of those settlements antedated by millennia the beginnings of historical time.[24] The well of Bir Hafir provided one such water supply. Glueck approached the well and exchanged greetings with the Bedouin. They gave him a cool drink and gently poured water over his head to wash away the dust and sweat of the Negev. On another trip, he arrived at the pool of Ain Yerka, hidden in a muddy hollow at the base of sheer walls that slanted upward and inward to a small skylight opening at the top. Glueck studied soil and natural resources in order to understand how they were used in the past. His thorough knowledge of pottery identification enabled him to further the scientific effort of his Negev explorations. This knowledge had set him apart from the archaeologists of the preceding generation, who were unable to use this valuable tool to establish the historical sequence of a site.

Another advance in archaeology — the use of carbon 14, which became available after World War II — provided much greater accuracy when dating the strata of a site. Archaeologists were now in a position to determine the age of any artifact that, being composed of organic material, had contained that element. When a living organism dies, it stops taking in radiocarbon. The radiocarbon then decays at a constant rate, allowing the archaeologist to measure the age of the material. This new technique allowed Glueck to accomplish much more in the Negev than he had in Transjordan.

Using air surveillance as a tool, Glueck was able to identify more than five hundred ancient sites between Beersheba and Eilat. As the pilot flew east of Beersheba through several significant *wadis* (normally dry stream beds, capable of quickly filling and flooding), Glueck noted the natural boundaries and the major highway that paralleled their entire length. One of the *wadis* led to the foothills of the mountains of Hebron. Especially important was what he found at Tell Arad. The scraps of pottery found at the surface of that tell established its identity as a massive and strategically located ancient site. He concluded that the multi-tiered ruins of successive biblical and pre-biblical cities buried within Tell Arad reached back well over five thousand years to the Chalcolithic period.

In the border area of the high uplands facing the approaches to Kadesh-Barnea — usually identified as the oasis where the former Hebrew slaves spent most of their forty years after leaving Egypt — Glueck discovered a large number of ancient sites. Among them, the one he numbered site 345, not far from Bir Birein, was about a third of a mile long and over two hundred yards wide. It was in Glueck's mind a sort of county seat from the Middle Bronze I period (Abrahamitic). With the exception of a small number of sherds from the Roman and Byzantine eras, the pottery was solely Middle Bronze I. The break in habitation concerned Glueck greatly: he asked himself why there had never been a continuous chain of settlement in the Negev.

Eventually he concluded that long temporal stretches of emptiness alternated with the periods of habitation, which he was able to trace through the pottery. Using material that he garnered from Egyptian literary sources,[25] Glueck proposed a theory: Was it possible that the destruction and annihilation wrought by Chedorlaomer and his allies from Syria to Sinai through Transjordan and the Negev during the patriarchal period might have been distant forerunners of the eruption of violent forces that resulted in the invasion and conquest of Egypt by the Semitic Hyksos?[26] For three hundred years — from the beginning of the twenty-first century through the eighteenth century B.C.E. — tranquility prevailed in Transjordan, the Negev, and Sinai. The town dwellers of this period may have purchased the peace they required through tribute to the Bedouins. "Twelve years they served Chedorlaomer and in the thirteenth year they rebelled" (Genesis 14:4).

Glueck followed his teacher W. F. Albright in declaring the Middle

Bronze Age I as Abrahamitic. The memory of Abraham's physical and spiritual adventures in the Negev lingered on in Glueck's consciousness. He supposed that the abundant artifacts and sherds that he found from the Middle Bronze were from the time of Abraham. The "Pax Abraham-itica" that Glueck proposed stood in sharp contrast to the more turbulent period of sedentary occupation marked by stone buildings and pottery and cisterns. The strong fortification walls with regularly spaced guard towers and high embattlements indicated enemies at the door. These were the stoutly built fortresses from the time of Solomon, where every town of importance needed to be guarded — Hazor, Shechem, Lachish, Tell Beit Mirsim, and Tell el-Ajjul, among others.

Glueck continued to explore the Negev season after season during the 1950s. Fascinated with the work, he was determined to complete his top-ographic survey of Western Palestine. He spoke of a fifth volume in the series he had begun, *Explorations in Western Palestine*. Taking the pro-posed title from the great survey done by the British in the 1880s called *The Survey of Western Palestine*,[27] he thought of his work as companion volumes. Indeed, he viewed himself as part of the tradition of the great British topographers of the nineteenth century. After Glueck's death in 1971, the noted archaeologist Yigael Yadin eulogized his colleague affec-tionately: "If Glueck had been born of British lineage, rather than Amer-ican, he would have been referred to as 'Lord Glueck of the Negev.'"[28]

*

As in the 1930s, archaeological surveys in the 1950s had their share of amusing moments. During one of his 1958 forays into the Negev, Glueck was accompanied by three Hebrew Union College students. Based in Beersheba, the group spent several hours a day over several days driv-ing through *wadis* looking for signs of ancient settlement. One day the group went much further south and west than before, arriving close to if not beyond the border with Egypt. Around midday they arrived at an ancient well and, nearby, found a large hollowed out rock into which, presumably, shepherds would pour the water they drew from the well for the flocks. Exulting in the discovery, Glueck asked two of the students to haul the rock up the hill and load it into the command car. He exclaimed: "This will be worth thousands of dollars to me at home!"[29] Oblivious to the oppressive heat, Glueck watched as two of the students struggled up the hill with the stone. They were almost at the top when a Bedouin child appeared out of nowhere. The youngster jabbered at Glueck in Arabic; Glueck jabbered back. After a few moments, Glueck yelled to the students: "Bring it back! They're still using it!"[30]

*

The publication in 1959 of *Rivers in the Desert: A History of the Negev* marked the conclusion of Glueck's Negev topographic explorations. Just like in his first book, *The Other Side of the Jordan*, describing his work in the 1930s, Glueck published his new survey in a non-scholarly form so that the general public would have ready access to the information without being bogged down with graphs and statistics. His work was comprehensive, reaching back to prehistoric times when Palestine Man first walked on the earth, and continuing through the Chalcolithic period near the end of the fourth millennium B.C.E., when the inhabitants lived in mud-brick villages. The book then discussed the Early Bronze I period, which lasted through the third millennium. For that period Glueck took note of the settlements in the Northern Negev and the Central Negev. The conquests and settlements of the Judean kingdom were noted in all parts of the Negev during the Iron Age II period between the ninth and sixth centuries B.C.E. Finally, the most intensive period of Negev settlement was Glueck's favorite: the Nabataean-Byzantine era, extending from the second century B.C.E. to the seventh century C.E. This eight-hundred-year stretch of time was the longest continuous period of civilization in the Negev's storied past. Commerce thrived and the population grew as never before.

In publishing *Rivers in the Desert,* Glueck traced the long and fascinating history of the rise and fall of civilizations in the Negev better and more thoroughly than any of his predecessors had done. He argued that gaps in the story of its settlements could be ascribed to wars and economic blights rather than changes in weather. With this publication, Glueck filled in the Negev's empty spaces on the map, just as two decades earlier his explorations had located boundaries and settlement sites in the ancient lands of Edom, Moab, and Ammon.

During this period of his work, Glueck came into frequent contact with the emerging cadre of younger native-born or Israeli-trained archaeologists. Among them were Ruth Amiran and Trude Dothan, both of whom were impressed with Glueck's romantic flair. According to Dothan:

> He was quite a figure, covering his head with an Arab *keffiyeh*, wearing rolled up sleeves. Glueck in the fifties was the old man of the archaeologists. He was always accompanied by soldiers on his expeditions, traveling by jeep wherever he went. He cut a dashing figure. He was tall and thin, usually wearing sunglasses. He talked well and was comfortable with everyone. Everyone knew him. We were surprised to learn that he was also a Reform rabbi.[31]

Glueck also made a profound impression on a young American Reform rabbinical student, Seymour Gitin.[32] In 1959 Gitin asked Glueck if he could accompany him on his next expedition into the Negev.[33] Glueck agreed, and Gitin found that he could scarcely keep up with the nearly sixty-year old man, who was in top physical condition, "deeply dedicated and physically hard working." Eventually Gitin would be called on to serve the American Schools of Oriental Research in the same capacity as his archaeological mentor. But not all the reactions to Glueck and his work were positive. He had to deal with criticism directed at him by some of the same Israeli archaeologists who praised his energy and flair. He was accused of attempting to "prove" the correctness of the Bible, when in fact he was simply utilizing it as an important tool for his research, just as one might use geological information, Arabic place names, or *ostraca* (pottery with inscriptions) to help forge conclusions about a site. Archaeological study of the Negev served to determine whether biblical descriptions were accurate. Glueck noted that scores of archaeological findings confirmed in clear outline or in exact detail historical statements in the Bible.

Despite his spirited defense, the criticism was never completely refuted. A serious re-evaluation of his work at Tell el-Kheleifeh was about to be published, a volume that would cast a shadow on the accuracy of Glueck's interpretation of the archaeological evidence he had uncovered at that site, regarding both its dating and its purpose.

11

Tell el-Kheleifeh Refined

'I still believe it to be King Solomon's.

By the early 1950s, Glueck had accomplished much. He had expanded Albright's method of the scientific study of sherds into a systematic discipline that would be of enormous help to all future archaeologists. He had surveyed Transjordan and drawn a complete archaeological picture of the localities and sites in the area, thus providing a firm basis for its further exploration. His excavations at Khirbet et-Tannur illuminated a fascinating civilization, heretofore little known, and yielded not only historical treasures, but insights for modern agronomy. And his excavations at Tell el-Kheleifeh had convinced him that he had discovered King Solomon's seaport, Etzion-geber. This last archaeological announcement — building upon his earlier work sketching for the Jewish people the landscape of the Patriarchs — had especially thrilled the *yishuv*, and "Ha-Professor" became a household name among Palestinian / Israeli Jews.[1]

Against the backdrop of Glueck's enormous achievements and larger-than-life reputation, a hitherto unknown young man began to raise questions and eventually to challenge Glueck's identification of Tell el-Kheleifeh as Solomon's seaport and its purported smelter as evidence of an Israelite copper industry during Solomon's reign. It all began in 1952, when Beno Rothenberg, a photographer with a passion for exploring the desert, attended the annual conference sponsored by the Israel Exploration Society in Tiberias. As noted above, these conferences were generally held in areas populated by new immigrants, the intention being to engage the newcomers in the historical experience of the people whose future they would be sharing as they became citizens of Israel.

Eager for an opportunity to explore the Negev with the famous archaeologist, Rothenberg volunteered to join Glueck as his photographer. Moreover, he was willing to let Glueck make use of his newly acquired Land Rover to facilitate his explorations. Glueck was "taken" with Rothenberg, and soon included him in all his journeys into the Negev.

Somewhere along the way, Rothenberg became skeptical of Glueck's ability to assay the value of copper ore, i.e., to determine if it would be suitable for smelting and thus of commercial value. After some time, he concluded that Glueck did not know enough about metallurgy as practiced in the ancient Near East to justify his conclusions. Glueck, of course, never claimed to be a metallurgist, and consistently relied on experts in England and America before reaching and publishing his conclusions, which were perfectly reasonable, given the state of archaeology at the time of his discoveries. However, Rothenberg was determined to become more knowledgeable about metallurgy: he attended courses in London from 1959 to 1962, claiming afterwards that he had obtained a Ph.D. in the subject from a German university.[2] His next step was to undertake his own surveys of the western Arabah, where Glueck believed that King Solomon's mines had been. Gathering his own staff, Rothenberg set about searching systematically for ancient habitations, roads, and activities, with special attention given to evidence about a mining industry.

During their initial season in 1959, the members of Rothenberg's western Arabah expedition were willing to accept Glueck's Solomonic dating for the Timnah mines, but then their skepticism grew. Since Glueck's theories were never tested *in situ*, his conclusions could not hold their own against increasingly contrary evidence on the ground. The same held true for what Glueck had insistently called the "smelter" at Tell el-Kheleifeh; Rothenberg's team suggested that the large structure that Glueck had described in such detail and published about in so many places was really a granary, used for the storage of food; an alternative theory posited that the building was a fortress, and yet a third supposition was that it was a combination granary/fortress.[3]

Rothenberg worked in the Arabah through four seasons during the years that he also studied in London, concentrating most of his efforts in the Timnah valley and including in his purview Be'er Ora, Nahal Amram, and Nahal Jehoshaphat west of Elath. Whereas no such evidence was found at Tell el-Kheleifeh, in the Timnah area Rothenberg found well-preserved workshops and habitations as well as significant signs of copper smelting in the form of slag heaps and furnace fragments on hilltops and slopes.

Glueck had theorized as early as 1935[4] that the Solomonic copper industry of the Arabah was connected to the slag found at Timnah, but Rothenberg determined that what Glueck had found was not the by-product of any roasting process. The "true" copper ore of that region did not require roasting prior to its reduction to copper in a one-step smelting process. If the process could be done in a more cost-effective manner on site at Timnah, there was no need for a furnace/smelter at Tell el-Kheleifeh.

Rothenberg asserted that some of what Glueck had understood to be high grade copper ore, based on the expert opinion of metallurgists in England and America, was in fact only tinted sandstone or stones with very low grade ore of no possible commercial use.[5] On the other hand, together with geologist Yigael Bartura, Rothenberg had found truly high-grade green copper ore at the top of a cliff. This ore, identified as chalcocite, constituted clear evidence of material suitable for mining and smelting at Timnah. The problem was that there was no evidence that the mining was "Solomonic." Rothenberg's discovery led to the identification of three distinct periods of mining at Timnah: Chalcolithic, Iron Age, and Roman-Byzantine. But unless there was proof that what Glueck found at Tell el-Kheleifeh was indeed a refinery and that King Solomon was responsible for building it, there was no evidence for an Israelite mining industry during the period of the Israelite kings.

*

Given Glueck's reputation and the enthusiasm with which the yishuv had greeted his discoveries in the Moab highlands regarding the patriarchal period and the Exodus, as well as his identification of Timnah and Tell el-Kheleifeh with King Solomon, it is not surprising that Rothenberg's efforts to argue for and to publish his conclusions met with a stone wall of resistance and denial from Israel's archaeological establishment.

Rothenberg wrote to Glueck challenging his dating of the site in the tenth century B.C.E. and identification of Tell el-Kheleifeh as a smelter. At the time, Rothenberg had come to no independent conclusion about the actual dating of the Iron Age remains or which nation was involved with the industry. (The remains were eventually determined to be Late Kingdom Egyptian — end of the fourteenth century to the middle of the twelfth century B.C.E — because of the discovery at Timnah of a Temple dedicated to the Egyptian goddess Hathor.)[6] In Glueck's initial response to Rothenberg, he expressed certainty that if the building he had excavated on the northwest corner of Tell el-Kheleifeh was not a copper smelting furnace, then such a furnace could be found on the eastern side of the tell; further, Glueck insisted: "I still believe it to be King Solomon's." Faced with Glueck's perseverance, Rothenberg wrote to Glueck's mentor, Albright, and asked him what to do. Albright's response was: "You must publish."[7]

Rothenberg followed Albright's advice, and his article appeared in *The Palestine Exploration Quarterly* in 1962. Scarcely anyone who read that report took it seriously. Glueck's suppositions about the site and his published evidence, along with his reputation as an established authority in Negev pottery dating and exploration, were too powerful to challenge. One of Glueck's long-time friends, French archaeologist Jean Perrot, told Rothenberg, "It's difficult to face you, because what you say simply cannot be true. The whole archaeological world has taken up Glueck's theory, and what you say is utter nonsense."[8]

Albright published a response to Rothenberg's article in *Bibliotheca Orientalis* (1964, p. 67) in which he refers to Rothenberg's piece as "a useful monograph on the ancient copper industries in the western Arabah," but says that Rothenberg's conclusions would have to be weighed carefully, since he did not participate in any of the original excavations at Tell el-Kheleifeh in the 1930s.

In 1962, as noted above, the annual meeting of the Israel Exploration Society was held in Eilat, the Israeli town that straddles the shore of the Red Sea just a few kilometers west of Tell el-Kheleifeh. There Rothenberg sought an opportunity to present his findings to the assembled archaeologists and interested laity. Having been told that he applied too late and that there was no room for another speaker, he was not offered a place on the program. As a result, he was furious, but it is unlikely that there were a dozen people in the room who would have supported his views or even wanted to hear from him.

The opening presentation was given, as was the custom, by the Conference chair, Yigael Yadin, who then introduced Glueck. Glueck presented his conclusions about the Solomonic dating of Etzion-geber (Tell el-Kheleifeh) and his evidence for the use of the site as a smelter for copper for commercial use. Yosef Aviram, later to become the head of the IES, and Zalman Vinograd, an amateur archaeologist, were impressed with Glueck's "objectivity and Zionist fervor."[9] Not surprisingly, Beno

Rothenberg derided the presentation as a public relations effort, an appeal to the pride and passion of the citizens of a new nation eager to recover their biblical roots.

As word of Rothenberg's challenge to Glueck's hypotheses gained somewhat wider currency, more and more people, including graduate students like David Gerrish at Cambridge, weighed in — on Glueck's side. Gerrish sought Glueck's response to Rothenberg's challenge in a letter he wrote to him at the end of October 1962:

> Perhaps I am too conservative, but I regard some of Rothenberg's statements as sweeping and dangerous, and [I] can't really believe that you could be as mistaken as he points out. I find it difficult to believe that the great work you did at Tell el-Kheleifeh could be so widely acclaimed by so many and yet seriously questioned without a visit to the site. It would therefore be most kind of you if you could say if there are any points wherein Rothenberg has misunderstood or if it be too much for a busy man, whether (and where and when) a defense of your original hypothesis will be published.[10]

Glueck responded to Gerrish by asserting that Rothenberg was irresponsible and his claims made no sense: "For him to say that the flues were not flues is ridiculous. After the excavation of the refinery was completed and the debris removed, by placing our hands against the flues we could feel the drafts of air entering the building."[11] Glueck also challenged Rothenberg's interpretation of the meteorological phenomenon; Glueck was referring to the effect of the frequent sandstorms that made the archaeological work and its interpretation so difficult at a site like Tell el-Kheleifeh.

Nevertheless, Rothenberg did not give up. He continued to prepare his fundamental reappraisal of Glueck's work at Tell el-Kheleifeh and his interpretation of what was found at Timnah. Meanwhile, Glueck continued to defend the Solomonic dating (tenth century B.C.E.) even though the Bible was totally silent on an Israelite mining industry in the area. The most relevant biblical text, found in I Chronicles 18:8, records that David, as King of Judah, took a vast amount of copper from Tibbath and Cun, cities of Hadadezer, a king allied with the Arameans. Those cities were located northeast of the Dead Sea, and not in the Arabah.

By 1965 Glueck was finally persuaded to step back from his insistence on a large-scale metallurgical operation at Tell el-Kheleifeh. In its place, he posited that a small measure of metallurgical activity had taken place there at various times. He also conceded, "It had been our thought, which we now abandon, that the apertures [in the building he excavated at Tell el-Kheleifeh] served as the flue-holes [for the smelter] during period I of the building."[12] Glueck now accepted the use of wooden beams laid laterally and vertically for strengthening purposes as a widely used building technique, in no way an exclusive feature of smelters. In fact he carefully documented parallels to this construction technique throughout the ancient Near East.

Glueck rejected his earlier theory about the smelter and accepted the suggestion of Rothenberg and others that the structure was a granary or storehouse. Many of Glueck's archaeological colleagues, including Yadin and Aviram, were impressed by his capacity to change a cherished conviction when a more likely option was presented to him. His graceful acceptance of the situation enabled the archaeological community to affirm its commitment to scholarly truth, and Nelson Glueck's reputation was further enhanced.[13]

Neither Rothenberg's challenge nor Glueck's response had much of an impact on an Israeli public that had "grown up with" Glueck's understanding of a Solomonic smelter at Tell el-Kheleifeh. In a popular history, *My People: The Story of the Jews*, published in 1968, Abba Eban, Glueck's friend from pre-war days, still accepted without question the identification of Tell el-Kheleifeh with Etzion-geber:

> Solomon was a determined builder. He fortified towns of strategic and economic interest. . . . Though Israel was mainly an agricultural people, little prone to commerce on a larger scale, Solomon saw great possibilities in the development of trade. He built a magnificent fleet and established Etzion Geber on the Gulf of Aqaba as the home port. From there his ships undertook mysterious voyages to the land of Ophir, bringing "gold and ivory, sandalwood and precious stones, apes and peacocks." (I Kings 10:22).

Nor was there a scintilla of doubt in Eban's mind about the extent of copper being traded during Solomon's reign: "One of Solomon's outstanding economic enterprises was the building of copper mines and refineries for the smelting of metals near Timnah in the Negev."[14]

＊

It was abundantly clear that Glueck's discoveries had fired the imagination of an entire people. Nearly thirty years had passed since the original
excavations at Tell el-Kheleifeh, and Israel of 1965 was a very different
place from British Mandate Palestine of the 1930s. The 600,000 Jews
who lived in Palestine in 1948 when Israel became an independent state
had burgeoned into a well-established community of more than three
million Jews, with more arriving on a daily basis. Villages had become
towns, towns had become cities, and Israel was well on its way to being
a regional power economically and militarily. Archaeology had become,
in some respects, less a national obsession than a popular hobby. Israel's
economic progress and first-world status could now provide the sense
of positive identity that archaeology had provided in the past; Glueck's
"new conception" would not faze them, and served instead to strengthen
the public's perception of his character.

Furthermore, with Tell el-Kheleifeh's identification with Solomon's
empire rejected and the copper mining industry of the Western Negev
no longer attributable to any Israelite monarch, it was Glueck's Middle
Bronze I survey of the Negev, his work with and interpretation of the
Nabataean civilization, and his four-volume publication of his *Explorations in Eastern Palestine* that would maintain his place of honor among
those contributing to Israel's knowledge about past events and present
opportunities. His younger contemporary G. Ernest Wright argued that
the *Explorations in Eastern Palestine* would be rated as "one of the two
most important individual contributions to the field of Palestinian archaeology in our generation."[15] Moreover, as discussed above, Glueck's
discoveries about the water-collecting and irrigation systems of the
Nabataeans had great practical value for modern Israel, which contin-
ues to find increasingly effective ways to irrigate arid areas both at home
and in third world countries. Glueck's 1930s vision of settling thousands
of Jews in the Moab highlands never came to fruition. But Ben-Gurion's
dream of settling thousands of Jews in the Negev certainly came true.
And even though Solomon has been removed from any connection with
the Negebite copper industry, the aura of his name and powerful feelings aroused by its supposed connection with that region far outlasted
the controversy between Glueck and Rothenberg.[16]

12
At the Helm
1952–1963

[Glueck's] vision and energy have opened new horizons

— Abba Eban

With the initial challenges of the merger with the JIR and the College's relationship with the UAHC seemingly met, Glueck decided that he could turn his attention to influencing the prayer life of the College-Institute. He began his sixth year as president by emphasizing the importance of daily and Sabbath chapel services in both Cincinnati and New York. Every faculty member and student at the College during the years of Glueck's tenure knew that the president would be attending the daily service in one of the two places, and that they were expected to attend as well.[1]

Glueck also took steps to ensure the smooth administration of the expanding College-Institute by appointing Jacob R. Marcus to be in charge while Glueck was in Israel pursuing his archaeological interests. A memo to Marcus in May 1954 informed him, "During my absence from the country, the Board has appointed you as Acting President." Glueck hastened to add, "Now that I have caught you in this situation, I am thinking of staying away for a very long period indeed."[2]

Unfortunately for Glueck, the newly stitched relationship between the College and the Institute began to unravel. Despite the appointment of Paul Steinberg, the director of the School of Sacred Music in New York, as Dean of JIR and Ezra Spicehandler, a popular lecturer on Hebrew literature and a veteran of Israel's War of Independence, as a full-time faculty member, the New York staff and full-time faculty remained inadequate for a complete program leading to ordination. When students and faculty realized that Glueck's intention was to make the JIR a two-year "feeder program" to HUC — instead of the fully vested ordaining institution it had been under Stephen S. Wise — a full-scale rebellion erupted in New York.[3]

Rabbi Louis I. Newman, once an assistant to Stephen S. Wise at the Free Synagogue and then the rabbi of the prestigious Rodeph Shalom congregation on Manhattan's Upper West Side, gathered together a group of colleagues who believed that a full five-year Reform rabbinical school should exist in New York. Through their efforts, the Academy for Jewish Higher Learning was established at Rodeph Shalom. A faculty consisting of Newman, Edward Klein, Cyrus Gordon, and Moses Hadas attracted a total of thirty pupils. Their determined stance and the relative success of the academy eventually forced Glueck to bow to the inevitable. In June of 1956 it was agreed that the New York school would be a full five-year institution, with the authority to ordain its graduates.[4] That settled, New York and Cincinnati graduates could meet as colleagues as well as HUC-JIR alumni.

But the battle wasn't over. Efforts initiated by Glueck to change the name of the combined institution[5] aroused the wrath of Justine Wise Polier, Stephen S. Wise's daughter and a judge on the bench of the Domestic Relations Court of the City of New York. She wrote to Glueck in February 1957:

> I find it hard to understand how you can, in good conscience, recommend what amounts to the obliteration of the Jewish Institute of Religion under the guise of changing a "long and difficult name." Without talking about the legal aspects of this matter, you know, as I know, that there was a clear agreement when the merger took place, that both institutions would be continued as two co-equal institutions in the future, and that the suggestion of the retention of the "Hebrew Union College" and the elimination of the "Jewish Institute of Religion" under the guise of a change of name is a violation of the spirit if not the letter of that agreement.[6]

The name was not changed. It had taken Glueck ten years to work through the issues relating to the merger. Resolving them confirmed Glueck's ability to serve effectively as president of the combined schools.

*

Providing opportunities for his faculty and other leading academicians to publish their work was another priority for Glueck during the 1950s. HUC-JIR continued its publication of the *Hebrew Union College Annual*, which had begun in 1924 and now included a larger proportion of articles dealing with the modern period. Although rabbinical students and pulpit rabbis rarely contributed to this scholarly journal, its publication reflected Glueck's vision of the Hebrew Union College as more than just a professional school.

Indeed, like any academic institution, HUC-JIR sought far and wide for scholars, literary figures, humanitarians, philanthropists, and political figures to grace their commencement exercises and other public ceremonies, granting each an appropriate honorary degree. In addition, ordinees of the College-Institute could obtain the honorary degree of Doctor of Hebrew Letters upon completion of twenty-five years of service. On one such occasion Glueck decided to award honorary degrees to Rabbis Morris Lazaron of Baltimore and William Fineshriber of Philadelphia. Both were national leaders of the anti-Zionist American Council for Judaism. Over the strong protests of Rabbi Roland Gittelsohn, who argued that "when so much effort is being expended to help the development of a non-Orthodox type of Judaism in Israel, I feel that these honorary degrees will set the cause of Reform Judaism back by perhaps as much as half a century."[7] Glueck, however, never wavered, explaining that the degrees were given not for their views on Zionism but rather for their service to their congregations.

At the beginning of 1954 Glueck took two additional steps to enhance the program of the College-Institute. He hired the College's first Christian faculty member, Lowell McCoy, who, as Professor of Speech, was charged with responsibility for helping students deliver their sermons effectively. And he proposed the establishment of a summer camp of six to eight weeks duration for incoming rabbinical students, to be held at Towanda, Pennsylvania and staffed by members of the faculty. In principle, its purpose was to provide an introduction to the history and philosophy of Reform Judaism and to enable students to attain a basic competence in reading Hebrew texts.

At about the same time, Glueck initiated important changes at the administrative level in Cincinnati. Sheldon Blank, professor of Bible, had served as chair of the faculty for many years before deciding to step down in 1955.[8] Shortly thereafter, Glueck came to the conclusion that the academic as well as the general administration should be handled by a single individual with the title of provost, who, in addition to directing the Cincinnati School, would also coordinate the activities of both campuses. Samuel Sandmel, an eminent scholar of Hebrew Bible, New Testament, and Hellenistic Literature, came from Vanderbilt University to fill the post.[9]

*

In October 1957, Glueck marked the tenth anniversary of his accession to the presidency and was feted with a testimonial dinner at which his archaeological mentor was the featured guest. On that occasion, Albright noted that Glueck had "created a revolution in the methods of surface exploration in his archaeological survey of Transjordan and then the Negev." Israel's ambassador to Washington, Abba Eban — Glueck's old friend from their war-time years in Jerusalem — noted that Glueck's vision and energy "opened new horizons for theological, literary, and historical scholarship both at the College in Cincinnati and the Institute in New York." Frank L. Weil, Board Chairman, suggested that in the ten years of his leadership, Glueck "added to the distinction given the College by his great predecessors, and added a special luster of his own."[10]

Those attending viewed a new Israeli government documentary film depicting Glueck's archaeological explorations of the Negev and their significance for the development of that portion of modern Israel. A lovely and dignified portrait of Glueck by artist Joseph Margulies was unveiled, a gift of the leaders of the Combined Campaign for Reform Judaism, whose annual fund-raising effort was initiated that evening. The portrait is displayed, along with those of the previous HUC presidents, in the foyer of the Administration Building in Cincinnati.

Secure in his position and sure of his vision, Glueck lost no time in challenging the Board to look boldly into the future:

> We are at one of those junctures in the history of our college where we can proceed in any one of several directions. We can act with confidence and a certain calculated boldness and risk and meet thus the compelling needs of the present and the obvious challenge of the future, or we can sit tight and inevitably go backwards. It is utterly impossible to stand still.[11]

*

Two extraordinary women who worked for the College-Institute during the 1950s and 1960s were of tremendous help to Glueck in attaining his goals. Rissa Alex came to work at HUC in 1962 and soon became a very important supporting player. In the words of Kenneth Roseman, who served as Dean of Students during a portion of her tenure: "As Executive Secretary, she held 'the keys to the kingdom,' allowing only those people to see Dr. Glueck whom she felt were important enough to be seen." In so doing she enabled Glueck to focus on his most important tasks — developing a vision for the College-Institute and communicating that vision to his faculty and the Board of Governors. Alex screened all of Glueck's calls, handled his correspondence, made his travel arrangements, set up appointments with people in distant cities, and took care of a myriad of other details, large and small. When Glueck was away from the office, as he frequently was, Alex was the "go-to" person with questions about what was happening at the school.

Eleanor Vogel, on the other hand, had nothing to do with the administration of the College, but everything to do with keeping Glueck's archaeological notes and publications in order. She was initially hired as the Efroymson Fellow in Archaeology and then appointed Archaeological Assistant. Working at the College from 1961 to 1979, she was single-handedly responsible for the various editions of Glueck's extensive bibliography and likely had a major role in the preparation of Glueck's last archaeological volume, *Deities and Dolphins*.

The concluding years of the decade of the fifties were marred by renewed tension between the College and the Union of American Hebrew Congregations. In 1958 Glueck spoke to the Board of Governors about "the completely undesirable and wholly unnecessary stress in the relationship of the HUC-JIR and its patron organization, the Union of American Hebrew Congregations, which has again come to the fore."[12] The comment was provoked by the decision of the Union's Executive Board to separate the Los Angeles College of Jewish Studies from the California School of HUC-JIR. The Union's educational program in Los Angeles had preceded the College's investment in a rabbinical seminary there, and now that the seminary's branch was a reality, the Union feared its involvement would be overshadowed. However, this effort to create two wholly separate institutions did not come about.

*

By June 1958, Glueck's son Charles had completed his sophomore year at Harvard and had established a significant relationship with a young woman from Chicago, Barbara Weinberger, a student at Radcliffe. In

spite of his many absences from the family, Glueck tried in his own way
to keep in touch with his only child and to give him fatherly advice:

Dearest Charles,

Riding along this afternoon in my command car, I was thinking
of you. Thinking of you with those deep and tugging feelings of
love that every father must entertain for his son or children.
I was wondering how you were getting along and whether or not
your thoughts were crystallizing about your future studies. I was
thinking that I wish I had urged you to study in Chicago this
summer. . . . It surely would have been a more successful and
pleasant summer for you than this constant commuting to
Chicago [to see Barbara]. However, who knows? Perhaps the very
effort of your peripatetic demonstrations of your devotion may
be influencing your lady love.

The nicest time of the day in the Negev is from about four
o'clock on. As we were gliding along, in the soft and gently
colored and perceptibly changing afternoon light, with curves
and panoramas taking the place of harsh lines and blinding
white views, we were engulfed with a sense of peace. I remember
your once telling me of a similar feeling overcoming you when
you have been sailing on Lake Charlevoix. The world seems
simple and sane and serene, not raucous not competitive, not
consuming. This feeling is accentuated by the fact that all day you
have been delving into the so-called distant past, whose destruc-
tive antics have been smoothed over in the perspective of great
distance in time. . . .

Be that as it may, this is simply to let you know that I have been
thinking of you and wishing that you were traveling with me,
and that Mother and Barbara were here too, because at this stage
of the game, I can't see you going off alone a long distance away
from Barbara. I am sure that when you are married, you won't be
following my bad example of leaving your wife and love for long
periods of time. That is one of the advantages of getting married
when you are young. I was 31 before I got married, and was a
hardened donkey by then, who has never learned to change his

habits. Not that I didn't warn your Mother about me. For my sins I repeat what Heine once said: "le bon Dieu me pardonnera, c'est son métier." To you and Mother and Nannie [Helen's mother] I send all my love.

        — From your devoted [signed] *Father.*[13]

*

Fifteen years after he had resigned his position with the Office of Strategic Services, Nelson Glueck was invited to represent a significant portion of American Jewry at an important moment of American national life. The nation's first Catholic president, John F. Kennedy, arranged for Glueck to offer the benediction at his inauguration on January 20, 1961. On a Sunday morning in November, at a relatively early hour, the Gluecks received a phone call. The conversation, which Helen later recalled, went like this:

> *Glueck:* "Hello."
>
> *Caller:* "Is this Dr. Nelson Glueck?"
>
> *Glueck:* "Yes."
>
> *Caller:* "We need to know, Dr. Glueck, if you are a Democrat."
>
> *Glueck:* "Who's calling?"
>
> *Caller:* "Senator John Sparkman, Chairman of the Joint Congressional Committee on the Inauguration of John F. Kennedy. The president-elect would like you to offer the benediction on that occasion."
>
> *Glueck:* "In that case, Senator Sparkman, I'm a Democrat."[14]

January 20, 1961 was a snowy and blustery day. Special heaters were installed on the inaugural platform to keep the guests from getting frostbite. Those who attended or watched the proceedings on TV remember people huddling inside their overcoats trying to keep warm, and poet Robert Frost's papers blowing every which way along with his shock of white hair. When Glueck rose to speak, he intoned the prayer he had prepared, concluding with the *birkat kohanim*, the priestly blessing from Numbers 6: 24–26:

May the Lord bless thee and keep thee.

*May the Lord cause His countenance to shine upon thee
and be gracious unto thee,*

*May the Lord lift up His countenance unto thee
and give thee peace.*

Perhaps from nervousness, Glueck stumbled over the text, diminishing
the pride his friends and associates had felt at his receipt of the high honor.

*

On the Cincinnati campus, a new student literary effort, replacing the
defunct *HUC Monthly,* appeared for the first time in the 1960s. It was
entitled *variant*, with a lower-cased "v." By way of introduction, Richard
N. Levy, eventually to become a president of the CCAR, wrote a thoughtful editorial challenging the faculty to provide a more creative and indi-
vidually oriented curriculum for those preparing for the rabbinate:

Things aren't quite the same these days in the once architecturally
dormant seminary on the hill. In their new offices on the top of the

gleaming new library, administrators of the College-Institute look with pride at the shiny new buildings they have built, and work on plans to finance and fill them.[15] But four floors below, in the classrooms and corridors, students look with somewhat less pride at the sameness they perceive in their curriculum.

For there are those whose interests are in an active, practical rabbinate, keyed to service to congregants and community, to meaningful worship and stirring sermons, who feel that there is something wrong with their text courses and not enough materials to guide them in the non-academic paths of their calling. There are also those who would live a scholarly rabbinate, even those who wish to become scholars first and rabbis second, and who are dissatisfied with the preparation they are receiving for a career in Jewish scholarship.[16]

Efforts to redress the grievances expressed in Levy's editorial would continue for more than a decade. The tension between Glueck's perception of the College-Institute — as a place to train students in scholarly methodology and textual analysis — and the students' avowed needs in preparing for the practical rabbinate was palpable in the 1960s and continued on into the 1970s. A series of committees, some comprised of faculty only, and others involving students, would study the issues and make their recommendations. Eventually, an acceptable compromise was reached. Certain scholarly standards would be maintained, but more attention would be given to practical matters and to the development of opportunities for internships and other connections with rabbis in the field.

Much of Glueck's time and energy in the late 1950s was taken up by the need to enlarge the Cincinnati campus. Given the increasing size of the entering classes of rabbinical students, Glueck also raised funds for a new dormitory to supplement the limited space provided by the Sisterhood Dormitory, built in the 1920s. The new dorm was constructed. However, many more students were now married, and the costly new structure, with its single rooms, was never fully utilized.

Despite this serious miscalculation, Glueck continued to be highly regarded. His presence was sought on many boards and commissions, and he was given significant recognition by the State of Israel. In March 1962 he received an invitation from Mayor Sam Yorty of Los Angeles to attend a State of Israel Commendation Dinner in November, where Harry S.

Truman would present Medallions of Honor to him and to nine other outstanding supporters of Israel who were not themselves citizens of the state. Glueck was nominated in recognition of his conspicuous contribution to the cause of human progress "in the broadest sense," and in particular for his personal role in strengthening the relationship between the United States and Israel.[17]

By then Glueck was a familiar figure in the Los Angeles area, and the Los Angeles program of HUC-JIR had come a long way from its modest beginnings. The years since World War II had seen a significant population shift, both general and Jewish, from the east to the west coast. In Los Angeles, for example, Jews settled in such numbers that its Jewish community was soon the second largest in the country. In view of this new reality, it was not surprising that voices had been raised since the early 1950s calling for the establishment of an official branch of the Hebrew Union College in Los Angeles.

One of the most influential of those voices was that of Jack Skirball, a 1921 ordinee of the Hebrew Union College. Skirball had made his way to California and had become a highly successful businessman with strong connections to the film industry. He was appointed to the Board of Governors in 1950. The following year he called for HUC-JIR to initiate the creation of a rabbinical campus in California, noting that there was already competition from the Jewish Theological Seminary, which had opened a branch on the West Coast.[18]

At a meeting of the Board of Governors in 1953, Glueck expressed the hope that a campus would soon be established in Los Angeles that would provide the first two years of rabbinical training and offer the Bachelor of Hebrew Letters degree. In Glueck's vision, the new branch would serve exactly the same role on the West Coast as the Jewish Institute of Religion would serve on the opposite end of the country: with relatively small faculties, both would channel all their students to Cincinnati for the final three years of rabbinical training and ordination. The failure of Glueck's proposed down-sizing of the JIR in New York left HUC-Los Angeles as the only "feeder" school. Ordination would not be granted there for another half century.[19]

By the fall of 1956 preparations were well under way for the acquisition of an abandoned home for asthmatic Jewish girls on Appian Way in the Hollywood Hills to serve as the home of the Los Angeles School, heretofore housed at the Wilshire Boulevard Temple. Glueck reported to the Board of Governors that the school already had three strong programs: the rabbinical school, leading to the BHL and DHL degrees; the School of Sacred Music; and the Education department, which granted a Master's Degree in Jewish Religious Education. In January 1957, the Appian Way property was acquired.

Two months later Glueck appointed Alfred Gottschalk, a 1957 ordinee who would later become his successor, as dean of the newest campus. Gottschalk described how he learned about the opportunity:

> On a rather cold and blustery Cincinnati day early in the month of March, a distracted senior was on his way to class. An unmistakable voice suddenly jarred him out of a reverie.
>
> Dr. Nelson Glueck had summoned me to his office. In his inimitable persuasive style, he painted a picture of California: its promise, a chance to make history, carry the spirit of HUC-JIR west, the future of Jerusalem and Los Angeles, and so on. I came home and told my wife of the fabulous offer and Glueck's bold dream. The possibility of failure, the experimental nature of the project, the likelihood of an aborted beginning, were all words which he used with me. I chose not to hear them, or at least, not to share them with my wife. I accepted the offer, and sight unseen, we went West.[20]

On September 8 the founders of the California School gathered for dedication ceremonies in the Hollywood Hills. One speaker after another rhapsodized about the growth of the school, the zeal and commitments of its founders, and the hopes for its future.[21] In the next few years, the California branch of HUC would become an increasingly vital part of Jewish life in Southern California and take its place along with the Cincinnati and New York campuses as a significant setting for the training of rabbis and other Jewish professionals.

*

Like many of the years of Glueck's presidency, 1963 was replete with accomplishments as well as moments of sorrow.[22] The national tragedy of Kennedy's assassination on Friday, November 22 obviously affected Glueck deeply. He delivered a powerful eulogy in the HUC chapel that evening,[23] and a month later he began weeping while speaking of the president on a local television program.[24]

Just three weeks later, on December 13, Glueck's portrait appeared on the cover of TIME Magazine, calling attention to its lead article, "The Search for Man's Past." It was not the first time Glueck had appeared in the magazine; an article in the Science section of the July 27, 1959 issue described Glueck's intention to "uncover traces of people who inhabited the Negev back to Moses' time and before it, and through them study ways of colonizing that sun-eaten land." Glueck himself was described as "lean and as leathery as Joshua."

It is unlikely that his administrative responsibilities at HUC-JIR would have gotten Glueck onto the cover of TIME,[25] but the fame he achieved thereby certainly increased his ability to raise public awareness of the College's existence and to enhance his fund-raising efforts on behalf of both the California School and a future HUC-JIR presence in Jerusalem.

13

Establishing a Foothold in Jerusalem

Today the Jerusalem landscape is enriched — "the stone which the builders rejected has become the chief cornerstone."[1]

Shortly after Israel's successful struggle for independence, Nelson Glueck made a fateful decision: he would provide the new Jewish state with an institution comparable to the American Schools of Oriental Research in East Jerusalem, no longer accessible to him or to any other Jewish archaeologist. That way he could guarantee the continued involvement of Israeli archaeologists in the efforts of their non-Jewish colleagues in the Middle East. Glueck's bold, even visionary idea paved the way for ever-increasing participation of the Israeli public in archaeological discoveries.

Glueck recognized that the nascent State of Israel, facing enormous challenges, would have few financial resources available for archaeological exploration. From a nation surrounded by implacable enemies, recovering from a war that had cost the lives of six thousand men and women, and soon to accept and resettle refugees from the four corners of the earth, it was too much to expect government money for archaeological research. ASOR had been an invaluable funding resource, and without its assistance, very little could be accomplished. The staffing and supplying of one significant excavation could cost tens of thousands of dollars each season, even with the help of scores of volunteers.

Funds would have to come from sources such as those Glueck had already cultivated in America: the Cincinnati Art Museum and universities with established programs for archaeological study — most notably Pennsylvania, Chicago, and Harvard. Later, Glueck himself, with the help of Dean Paul Steinberg of the New York school, would obtain significant funds from the Smithsonian Institution. These sources of support would eventually be augmented with resources from the various theological seminaries that traditionally had supplied funds to ASOR. Over time, Glueck's vision and diligent efforts would create a consortium of universities and seminaries to support projects in Israel through operating funds, trained archaeologists, and organizational expertise.[2]

Glueck rightly feared that failure to act expeditiously could result not only in losing the funding necessary for archaeological endeavors, but also the people needed to carry out the work. There were only a handful of Palestinian Jewish archaeologists in 1948 — most prominently Eliezer Sukenik, his son Yigael Yadin, Avraham Biran, Moshe and Trude Dothan, and Binyamin Mazar — and no funding available from university sources in Israel. Given the many important sites located in other parts of the Middle East, Glueck understood that Protestant and Catholic archaeologists likely preferred to work where there was political stability, no restrictions on access, and adequate funding.

Language was also an issue. When the government of Israel established a Department of Antiquities in 1949, the language to be used in its communications was Hebrew. Glueck believed that a parallel English language program had to be maintained — one that would enable non-Hebrew speakers to be fully involved in the government-sponsored program and give them full access to archaeological sites, funding, and library resources.

All of these considerations led to the construction of the Hebrew Union College Biblical Archaeology School (HUC-BAS) in Jerusalem. The School was destined to play a major role in the proliferation of archaeological excavations all over modern Israel through the remainder of the twentieth century and beyond.[3]

Glueck was uniquely suited for the task of founding such an institution: his rabbinical training and significant experience made him an appropriate, indeed a cherished colleague for the graduates of the Protestant and Catholic seminaries with whom he often worked, while his non-halakhic approach to Judaism resonated well with the secular Israeli Jews whom he usually met in the field of archaeology.[4] The contacts he had established over his three terms as head of ASOR (1932–1934, 1936–1940, and 1942–1947) gave him ready access to the people and connections he would need.

Glueck also understood that he would have to use his prestige and influence as a leader of American Reform Judaism if he were to succeed in this project. The problem was that only a handful of American Reform Jews cared about archaeology or saw it as more than a pastime. In developing his proposal to create an ASOR equivalent in West Jerusalem, Glueck "fired up" his American constituency with the idea that if the Hebrew Union College could build a branch in Jerusalem, then liberal Judaism could gain a foothold there: rabbis and rabbinical students, and eventually educators, cantors, and communal service students could come and acquaint themselves with the reality of modern Israel. It was the combination of these two visions, the new ASOR and the new center for Reform Judaism, that would guarantee the success of his program.

Glueck's warm personal relationships with people like David Ben-Gurion, Israel's first prime minister, Moshe Sharett, its second elected leader,[5] and Yitzhak Ben-Zvi, its second president,[6] helped remove many bureaucratic obstacles. Ben-Zvi, for example, exemplified the unusually strong relationship between high public office and scholarship in the Jewish state. Asked by Glueck, who was then working on *Deities and Dolphins*, whether there were any Hebrew sources on the concept *dolphinim*, Ben-Zvi found one in the Talmud:"Dolphins procreate like human beings. What are dolphins? Rav Yehuda replied: creatures of the sea."[7]

Initially, however, Glueck's most important contact was with Avraham Biran, one of the archaeologists who had worked with him at Etzion-geber. Shortly after the War of Independence, Biran was appointed Jerusalem's District Governor and was in a position to give Glueck considerable support. Biran took responsibility for negotiating the arrangements with the Israeli Government after it had agreed in principle to make land available to the Hebrew Union College.

With two objectives, then — the creation of a school for biblical archaeological research and a Jerusalem address for Reform rabbis and rabbinical students — Glueck set out to remove the obstacles that stood in his way. It took ten years for the shaping and refining of his vision (1948–1958) and then five more years to overcome all the difficulties that plagued the building's construction.

First he had to convince the HUC-JIR Board of Governors that the Jerusalem project was both necessary for the growth of the movement and feasible in terms of cost. The Board first learned of Glueck's plans for Jerusalem in November 1952 — long before HUC's troubled relationship with the students and alumni of the Jewish Institute of Religion was smoothed over, and a few years before the school in Los Angeles became a major part of the system. Returning from his summer explorations in the Negev that year, Glueck told the Board of his suggestion to the Israeli government that the College-Institute was prepared to erect a building in Jerusalem that would contain a library, a chapel, and a small lecture hall, plus a number of other components. It would serve both as a headquarters for students and faculty while studying in Jerusalem and a base for the operations of the proposed department of archaeology.

He added, "We have a firm and repeated verbal commitment on the part of the [Israeli] Government that it will give us a choice site free of charge in Jerusalem, if we go ahead with the scheme."[8] There was, as yet, no discussion of a budget for creating a presence in West Jerusalem. But in the summer of 1953 the Board was called into special session when Glueck was offered a piece of land adjacent to the King David Hotel and overlooking the tank traps and barbed wire separating the two Jerusalems. The Board authorized him to accept it on behalf of the College. A great divide had been crossed.

Glueck referred to the Jerusalem project again in speaking to the Board in October 1953, reiterating the need for a chapel in the proposed plan. This small detail would loom large as the plan moved from dream toward reality.[9] Because the Israeli Orthodox establishment would oppose such a chapel, that part of the proposal was not mentioned in releases to the Israeli press.

By the summer of 1954 things began to move more quickly. Biran had notified Glueck on May 16 of the precise dimensions of the plot that the Jerusalem municipality was prepared to offer the College. He referred to the project as "The Hebrew Union School of Oriental Studies," reflecting the only aspect of the project that Glueck wished to promote in Israel; he added in his memo that the area in question would be leased to the College for a period of forty-nine years.[10]

In August 1954 the *Cincinnati Enquirer* published an article about the project. Its readers, however, could scarcely conclude from its account, any more than one could from Biran's report, that HUC-Jerusalem had anything to do with the training of rabbis:

> The school would train a score of scholars each year. They will study archaeology, history, geography and languages of the Holy Land. There will be both Jewish and Christian religious students, as in the case of the parent institution in Cincinnati. The school will have its own chapel, which presumably will reflect the reformed [sic] Judaism of the American college.[11]

The first major step had been taken, but Glueck still had much work to do before the new school could become a reality. First, he had to find an architect. Seeking advice from his Israeli friends and noting certain buildings whose style of architecture caught his eye, he eventually chose Heinz Rau, a German-born Israeli. Glueck later described Rau as a man with the reputation of being "the most difficult, the most cantankerous, the most bad-tempered, the most stubborn, and the most honest man in Israel, and he was all of these."[12] Rau's saving grace was his ability to actualize on drafting paper Glueck's description of the school he wanted.[13]

In the fall of 1954 Glueck was able to estimate construction costs at approximately $500,000. The new campus would serve as a graduate department of HUC-JIR and be intended primarily for its own students, alumni, faculty, Board members, and friends.[14] At this point Glueck was building an institution for his American constituency. His supporters in the U.S. were not terribly interested in the second part of the project — the institute for archaeological research. In May 1955 he wrote an article for the annual publication of the World Union for Progressive Judaism describing in some detail the features of the property for which he had successfully negotiated.[15] He referred to it as "the very choicest piece of ground" in Jerusalem: "This eight dunam [two-acre] plot of ground, which is very near the property of the King David Hotel, and which commands a wonderful view over the Valley of Hinnom to the walls of the Old City,[16] has been leased to us for the symbolic rental of one Israeli pound a year. Five years rental was paid in advance!" He continued:

> The plans are to provide for a chapel or temple to seat between 350–400 people, a library large enough to hold about 50,000 volumes, five classrooms, a workroom, a photographic laboratory, a small number of dormitory rooms, a suite for an annual professor and a suite for a resident director. This is to be the Jerusalem school of the HUC-JIR.[17]

With the WUPJ readership in mind, Glueck spoke about having an impact on Israel's perception of liberal Judaism: "We expect to provide," he wrote, "our own type of liberal services in our own synagogue, and all those who care to attend or to join as members will be welcome." He considered the project capable of serving the "real hunger of most of the people of Israel for an attractive form of Judaism, separated from State authority."[18]

In laying out his expectations, Glueck recognized that he was building a bridge between American Reform Judaism and the Jewish state, a bridge set on solid foundations but one that would also face enormous challenges as the Orthodox establishment began to treat liberal Judaism as a cancer on Israel's "body religious," to be excised at all costs.

Rumblings about Glueck's project surfaced in March 1955. A member of Israel's parliament, Eliahu Genichovski, representing the Orthodox Agudat Yisrael faction, asked about "the erection of a Reform synagogue . . . which has symbolized over the last century and a half alienation and betrayal of Jewish values. I indignantly ask: Is it possible that the government of Israel is ready to betray Jewish history?"[19]

Glueck also received a letter that month from Rabbi I. L. HaCohen Maimon, a leader of Mizrachi, the less fervid, more pro-Zionist Orthodox faction. Maimon had been named to Israel's first cabinet as Minister of Religious Affairs. He knew of Glueck's archaeological work, though they had not met:

> I am a traditional Jew, I oppose Reform Judaism, and yet I have many friends who are Reform Jews, among them Dr. Stephen S. Wise — who presented me with an honorary doctorate — and Dr. Abba Hillel Silver. . . . I have heard that the honorable Professor Glueck is considering establishing a Reform Temple in Israel. . . . I turn to you in my request made in the name of the Land of Israel and its unity, and in the name of all those who seek the brotherhood of unity in our land and our state, not to take this step. . . . "Do not touch my anointed"— let the Land of Israel remain in its perfect holiness and purity.[20]

More evidence of just how strongly the Orthodox felt about Glueck's project surfaced during the summer of 1956. Glueck needed a permit from the local authorities to build his school. The Jerusalem Municipal Council was responsible for that decision, and Glueck's name attached to the permit raised a red flag with its Orthodox members. Various objections and delaying tactics meant that four months and twelve meetings of the council would pass before a majority of the eighteen-member group was prepared to approve the permit. In the process, the coalition — which included the Orthodox members and had enabled the mayor of Jerusalem, Gershon Agron, to exercise some authority — broke apart and a new coalition had to be formed.

In October 1956 Glueck answered the Orthodox in Israel, who were maintaining that "the Reform movement must not be allowed to take root in the country through the opening of synagogues."[21] Glueck's response was characteristically forceful: "It is not our desire to act as missionaries in Israel, but it is our determination to realize for ourselves the right which is guaranteed for all people in Israel to preach and practice and pray to the God of our fathers in accordance with our own understanding."[22]

The fight went on in the press, at countless meetings, and occasionally in the streets. It was an early exchange of fire in the continuing *kulturkampf* between the liberal branches of Judaism, allied with secular Israelis, and the Orthodox.

*

In May, 1957, Glueck was able to inform the Board of Governors that the Israeli government had given him 25,000 Israeli pounds (then worth about $12,000) towards the cost of the College branch in Jerusalem. A year passed. Contracts for the building of the Jerusalem campus of HUC-JIR were signed. When Glueck referred to the project at the October 1957 meeting of the Board, he presented the perspective that he usually reserved for an Israeli audience, saying: "We are building a Jerusalem School as a post-graduate research school devoted to Biblical and archaeological and related research." Evidently he felt confident that Board support of the project would not be withdrawn when its archaeological component emerged. He also announced at that time that the school would bear the name "The Jerusalem School of Archaeology of the Hebrew Union College." That name was eventually discarded in favor of "Hebrew Union College-Biblical Archaeological School (HUC-BAS)" and finally to "The Nelson Glueck School of Biblical Archaeology."

But all did not go smoothly. The following spring a dispute caused a significant delay when the Israeli contractor actually fenced off the site and permitted no access to it.[23] Rather than bring the matter into the courtroom, Glueck paid him off, and by October of that year (1958) a new contractor, Hillel Fefferman, was selected. This took some doing on Glueck's part,[24] and in order to prevent any similar problems in the future, he succeeded in obtaining a commitment to greater on-site supervision from several HUC-JIR Board members. But other problems — from squatters on the property who refused to move to an unending stream of objections by Orthodox opponents — delayed the building's dedication. Initially planned for spring 1961, it had to be postponed until July 1963.

The extended time frame necessitated a new architect to complete the project. Heinz Rau divorced his wife and moved to Switzerland. Ruth Melamede, an associate in Rau's office, quickly familiarized herself with Rau's plans and set about completing the task.[25] Working together on the construction and design of HUC-BAS, Glueck and Melamede, who shared a deep emotional attachment to the land, became intimate life-long friends.

With American Students studying in Israel in 1961. Rear: Stanley Garfein, Carl Seltzer, Jack Spiro, Tamar Kalom, Ronald Kalom, Bill Cutter. Front: Glueck, Ted Parris, Sy Gitin. (*American Jewish Archives*)

With Abba Eban, looking
over plans for HUC-BAS, 1958.
(*American Jewish Archives*)

With Jacob Rader Marcus and Associate Supreme Court Justice Arthur L. Goldberg, 1961.
(*American Jewish Archives*)

With renewed confidence that the project was indeed near completion, Glueck recommended that the Board of Governors should hold its February 1963 meeting in Jerusalem. That meeting did take place in Israel at the end of March, at which time Glueck proudly announced that the American Government had authorized a grant of more than $70,000 for the new school! Walworth Barbour, the American Ambassador to Israel, had provided the information to Nelson Glueck a few days earlier. Glueck referred to Barbour's generosity in a statement that he made at the Board meeting and released to the Hebrew press on March 27:

> We, the faculty and the Board of Governors of the Hebrew Union College-Jewish Institute of Religion, and honored guests, enter into this first academic convocation of a new American institution dedicated to higher learning in the Holy Land. The name of the institution reveals its purpose: The Hebrew Union College School for Biblical Archaeology in Jerusalem, Israel. The generous support of the Government of Israel and the deep interest and support of my own country, America, sustained the erection of this institution.
>
> . . . It is also quite significant that the Honored Ambassador from America, His excellency Walworth Barbour, brings the influence and participation of the United States at this historical gathering, partly by means of his high office, and partly for deeply personal reasons.[26]

In an impressive ceremony the HUC-BAS was dedicated on July 7, 1963. Glueck referred to his original dream of creating the equivalent of the American School of Oriental Research on the Israeli side of Jerusalem, "but with additional aspects and activities, and for all kinds of reasons preferably under the auspices of the HUC-JIR." He continued:

> It is to be an advanced American research center serving American and other universities, seminaries and museums as a base for Biblical and related studies and archaeological investigation in Israel. It will provide resources of scholarly exchange and communication in the fields of Bible, Biblical and post-Biblical archaeology and cognate fields.[27]
>
> A second function of the school is to serve as the headquarters for professors of the HUC-JIR coming to Israel from one of our Col-

lege campuses in Cincinnati, New York, or Los Angeles — at least one each year, to hold seminars in their specialized fields of study, and to co-ordinate the work of those of our own HUC-JIR students who spend a year of study in Israel.[28]

Thirdly, as we have already pointed out, an ever-increasing number of American institutions of higher learning active in Israel are concerned with academic teaching and research programs related to the Near East. It is envisaged that our School will serve as a coordinating agency for them.[29]

Having set forth his immediate objectives, Glueck turned to the matter of the chapel for the new building, designated the William Murstein Chapel in response to a generous donation from the Murstein family:

It would have been unnatural and out of character for the Jerusalem School to have been built without a synagogue. Our synagogue will seek no organized membership, have no dues paying congregation. But it is prepared to serve American and Israeli visitors who feel attracted to it, and who may undertake to create forms of worship growing out of the modernity of present day Israel, but rooted in the fundamental principles of our religious past.

He continued:

We have no desire, nor do we intend, to "missionize," but in all candor, we do believe that authoritarian concepts and controls of any kind, and especially in the area of full religious expression, are foreign to everything that Jewry and Judaism and Israel stand for. There are many facets to religious truth and many ways to express it — and, with the deepest respect for all other forms of Jewish religious orientation and devotion, we shall hold our own kind of religious services, and strive to achieve untrammeled freedom to practice Judaism in every aspect of our lives.[30]

"Untrammeled freedom" was not to be achieved for a very long time.

In November 1963, the new school produced a newsletter, which contained a report from Glueck reflecting his euphoria over the response to the first High Holy Day services held at the Murstein Chapel: "We made no public announcements whatever, but for several weeks so many Israelis wrote, phoned, or came in person with requests for seats, that the Chapel was packed shortly after we opened the doors on the eve of Rosh Hashanah." He continued:

> I must confess that it was an occasion charged with considerable emotion for me when I ascended the pulpit to preach in Hebrew on Rosh Hashanah eve. To realize that our Hebrew Union College Biblical and Archaeological School had finally been built and was functioning in the various ways that had been planned made me feel deeply that I had been greatly blessed. It is not often that one can dream a dream of this kind and witness its physical fulfillment and the beginning of the translation of its promise and potentialities into reality. How grateful I felt to all those who had assisted with time and labor and heart and funds in bringing all this to pass.[31]

Those services were held entirely in Hebrew, despite the fact that some among those attending, particularly the American tourists and HUC students, did not have enough command of the language to follow the service or understand the sermon. HUC was an American institution planted on Israeli soil, but it also reflected one of the key concepts of Reform Judaism, which was to offer prayers and sermons in the vernacular, the language the local population would understand.

Glueck announced that regular Saturday morning services had been instituted and would be enhanced by lectures given an hour before by Dr. Jakob Petuchowski, Professor of Rabbinics at the Cincinnati School and Director of Jewish Studies in Jerusalem. The first lecture series — with admission by card only — was called "Spiritual Resources for Twentieth Century Jews." Friday evening services were also being considered.

The Orthodox establishment clearly viewed these announcements as provocative. On September 18, 1963, the *Jerusalem Post* published an interview with Zerach Warhaftig, Israel's Minister for Religious Affairs. The minister was asked, "Do you believe that the Hebrew Union College Archaeological Institute and its Reform synagogue in Jerusalem constitute the threat which religious circles had anticipated?" Warhaftig replied, "Only a minute number of worshippers participate in the services of the Reform synagogue. However, this movement constitutes primarily a threat to Jewish unity because of its intention to undermine Halakhic control of marriage and divorce."[32]

Orthodox opposition notwithstanding, Glueck was confident that the "religious activities" of the Jerusalem school would exercise an ever-increasing force for good in Israel. Sooner or later, he reasoned, Reform rabbis and others would be authorized by law to perform all religious functions and ceremonies, and then absolute authority over marriage and divorce would be removed from the sole jurisdiction of the Orthodox. That has not yet happened.

But in many other respects, the creation of a branch of HUC-JIR in Jerusalem was a signal triumph for liberal Judaism, for biblical archaeology, and above all, for Nelson Glueck. The campus expanded in the following decades, adding an amphitheater, a library, a museum, a youth hostel, and administrative offices. It came to serve not only the Hebrew Union College, but the Reform movement in Israel and the World Union for Progressive Judaism as well. Its beautiful buildings became a major cultural center for the city of Jerusalem. Speaking at the dedication ceremonies, Abba Eban, then Israel's Minister of Education, summed it up nicely: "Today the Jerusalem landscape is enriched — 'the stone which the builders rejected has become the chief cornerstone.'"[33]

*

In accord with Glueck's intention for HUC-BAS to serve as the organizational heart of the Israeli archaeological community, he asked Paul Steinberg to organize the school's first summer Institute on Near Eastern Civilizations, to be held in July and August of 1963. It was a highly successful event. Some twenty American university professors participated in the lectures, field trips and the excavation at Ashdod,[34] as did several ASOR people who came over from Jordan. Glueck wrote with great enthusiasm to his friends and supporters about this initiative:

> I know of no program in America dealing with the relationship between Jews and Christians which is superior to the work that we are doing here. We are not trying to "missionize" the professors, but I am very sure that most of them will leave here with a better understanding of American Jews and of the significance of modern Israel.[35]

In the meantime, Glueck had invited the eminent Harvard professor Frank Moore Cross[36] to serve as the first annual director of HUC-BAS, a position precisely parallel to Glueck's own appointments at ASOR in the 1930s and 1940s.[37] Whereas Glueck was a surface archaeologist, Cross's specialty was textual analysis: he had achieved renown from his work interpreting the Dead Sea Scrolls. Arriving in Jerusalem in August 1963, shortly after the dedication ceremony, Cross chose to enter Israel from Jordan through the Mandelbaum Gate, the only legal entry point between Jordan and Israel from 1948 to 1967.[38]

By offering the first annual directorships to two important Albright disciples — to Cross and then to G. Ernest Wright in 1964 — Glueck was able to solidify an academic relationship with Harvard University. Glueck had approached the Harvard Semitic Museum (Wright was then its director) with a proposal that they share responsibility for a major excavation at Gezer, halfway between Jerusalem and Tel Aviv. The Hebrew Union College would provide financial backing and the administrative faculty, while Wright would bring students from Harvard as volunteers. In subsequent seasons a mixture of HUC and Harvard volunteers worked on the dig. It was certainly a coup to be allowed to excavate such a significant site as Gezer, with confirmed dating to the Iron Age II period. Glueck was no doubt enthused about Gezer because of his prior work at Tell el-Kheleifeh. The site was mentioned in the Bible as one of King Solomon's three fortress cities, along with Megiddo in the Jezre'el Valley and Hazor in the Galilee. Wright, for his part, had been interested in the area since 1937, when Albright suggested it to him as a dissertation topic.

*

During the first two decades of Glueck's tenure as president of HUC-JIR, Albright and his students Frank Moore Cross, G. Ernest Wright, John Bright, David Noel Freedman, and George E. Mendenhall exerted enormous influence on the substance and direction of mid-twentieth-century biblical and archaeological studies. Known as the "Baltimore School" because of Albright's long tenure at Johns Hopkins University in that city, these scholars were able to impose political and ideological hegemony in the field, and their dominance generated complex questions about the relationship of archaeology to religion.

Glueck could not help but notice with increasing discomfort the direction that the Baltimore School was taking. G. Ernest Wright was in the process of planning, and later would guide, a group known as the Biblical Colloquium. Composed of disciples of Albright who were eager to share their teacher's scholarship with the world, the group undertook, beginning in 1949, the task of reprinting Albright's books.[39] In 1956 John Bright brought out his *Early Israel in Recent History Writing*,[40] which helped join historical archaeological reconstructions with Protestant theology.[41]

With his long personal relationship with Albright, their shared scholarly interests and solid reputations, their commitment to scientific principles, and their similar approaches to biblical archaeology, Glueck was disturbed by the colloquium's "members only" approach. Why did it profess a commitment to a closed group of scholars who would "objectively" speak for Albright's approach? Why was it necessary to promote sectarianism in American biblical scholarship? Tensions quickly arose between Protestant and non-Protestant scholars, and Glueck represented the Jews who had been excluded.

Albright and David Noel Freedman were appointed editors of the *Anchor Bible* project, whose intent was to provide annotated translations of the biblical books, based on Albrightian principles.[42] The latent conflicts that were likely to erupt from such a project and the need to cater to theological sensitivities were huge issues for the editors — and no less so for Glueck, who was left on the sidelines. The editors, it seems, were not looking for archaeologists but rather for scholars who were preeminent as translators of biblical texts.[43] Among other concerns about the project, Glueck worried that the Anchor Bible would minimize the interfaith character of the series.

In time several major books were assigned to Jewish writers: Glueck's colleagues Avigdor Ephraim Speiser for *Genesis* and H. L. Ginsberg for *Isaiah*. Evidently Albright, though expressing some reservations, thought that Speiser and Ginsberg could be counted on to express conservative attitudes toward the text. At this point, Glueck's concerns about the nature of the assignments to Jewish scholars became more personal. Why was he not given one?

Freedman had written to Frank Moore Cross about Speiser:

After the old man [Albright] and Mendy [Mendenhall], Speiser would be the best choice, and the exigencies of the situation dictate that we must have at least one prominent Jewish scholar. Of them all, Speiser is the only one we could contemplate working with, and he has requested *Genesis,* for which you will admit he is admirably trained in all the necessary historical, archaeological, and linguistic disciplines, second perhaps only to Albright himself.[44]

There is more than a hint here of tokenism: it is indeed surprising that Glueck's name hadn't even been mentioned — especially considering the quality of his scholarly work *Ḥesed in the Bible*. Perhaps Freedman viewed Glueck primarily as a popularizer. Nevertheless, had Glueck been asked, it is hard to imagine that he could not have produced a credible translation with textual notes for the scholar and the untrained reader alike — just the intent of the series. Moreover, he would have been in a unique position to provide the Deuteronomic works (the "D" source in the Wellhausian system) with maps illustrating either the pre-monarchic or the monarchic periods.

Throughout the fifties the gap between the Baltimore school and Jewish biblical scholarship grew until it became a chasm. Despite his personal disappointment, however, Glueck worked to overcome these tensions and tried to think of a way to cooperate with a project of such importance. He wanted to build a bridge between Albrightian scholarship and the Jewish archaeological community, just as he had successfully brought together many disparate interests in creating the Jerusalem school.

*

Meanwhile, the dig at Gezer was launched. Ernest Wright proposed a small sounding there, and Glueck agreed. The results were encouraging. The next season Glueck hired William Dever as director and Darrell Lance as associate director,[45] with Wright and Glueck maintaining oversight as the advisory committee. Thirty post-doctoral students attended the 1964 Summer Institute and participated in the first season.

Initial excavations at Gezer had been conducted at the beginning of the twentieth century by R.A.S. Macalister, working on behalf of the Palestine Exploration Fund (PEF), which was established in London in the previous century. Setting up his expedition camp on the mound of Abu Shusheh, on the newly constructed railway line to Jerusalem, Macalister began his work on June 14, 1902. After erecting temporary buildings to house his staff and protect his equipment from the elements, he soon identified successive occupations at the site, including ancient burial caves, a Canaanite temple and high place, and the perimeter of the ancient fortifications. Limitations on the funding and increasingly chaotic conditions in the Ottoman empire before and during World War I precluded any further excavations. The HUC-BAS excavations were the next major effort to extricate the story of Gezer.

The 1964 excavations soon revealed the stone foundation for one of two enormous mud-brick towers flanking the southwest gate, the largest stone-based structure ever found in Palestine — fifty-one feet wide and fourteen feet high. Some of the larger stones were nearly five feet across.[46] The 1966 excavation uncovered a *glacis*, or plastered slope, built against the outer face of a wall. Yigael Yadin interpreted the glacis and wall as a defense against the battering ram introduced in that part of the world in the Middle Bronze Age II (seventeenth century B.C.E.). With this in mind, archaeologists were able to conclude that Gezer was among the most fortified sites in Canaan during that century.

Uncovering the layers of the site yielded much important information. Debris found in stratum seven indicated massive destruction in the fifteenth century B.C.E., perhaps to be attributed either to Thutmosis III in 1468 B.C.E. or to Thutmosis IV at the end of that century. An Astarte terra cotta plaque showing Egyptian influence was found and dated to the fourteenth century B.C.E. Philistine pottery found at Gezer indicated indisputably that this was the period when the Philistines, one of the five tribes of the so-called "Sea Peoples," had settled in the coastal plain immediately to the west of Gezer during the twelfth century B.C.E. Of special interest to Jewish archaeologists and scholars was the excavation of a Solomonic-era (tenth century B.C.E.) gate similar to the one that Yigael Yadin had found at Hazor and again at Megiddo. And some Hellenistic pottery was found in stratum two dating to the second century B.C.E. After that the site appears to have been uninhabited for several centuries.[47]

The ambiance that Glueck and Wright created at Gezer — a sense of intimacy with the land and of a connection between tradition and scholarship — forged a link between the students and the teachers. Glueck frequently lectured to the group about both archaeology and Reform Judaism. He also initiated seminars for which he brought in guest speakers — faculty from the Hebrew University as well as leading political figures such as his friend David Ben-Gurion. The Gezer project became the watershed experience for American archaeologists after World War II — in methodology and approach as well as in the student volunteer system that it developed and that became the model for future projects throughout the Eastern Mediterranean Basin. Gezer trained the next generation of American archaeologists, who went on to direct their own excavations in Israel, Jordan, Cyprus, Egypt, and Tunisia. The students who trained there, whether Jewish or Protestant, gained a respect for one another that helped dispel partisan theologies in America. This was Glueck's and Wright's legacy, their new "American School." The two men had successfully bridged at least the archaeological component of the religious gap in American biblical scholarship.

14

Issues and Events

1964–1970

*There is intellectual and spiritual freedom
at the Hebrew Union College.*

The assassination of a sitting American president in November 1963
initiated a period of almost unprecedented violence in America. Confron-
tations between blacks and whites, between blacks and the police, and
between demonstrators and counter-demonstrators became commonplace, especially in 1968, when Martin Luther King Jr. was assassinated on
April 4 and Robert Kennedy on June 5. Devastating riots occurred in Los
Angeles, Detroit, Newark, and elsewhere during the long hot summer
that followed. The ensuing fires leveled huge areas of those cities, while
anti-war demonstrators at the Democratic Convention in Chicago were
brutally beaten by police.

A generation of young people growing up in the 1960s learned to question any and all authority, whether that of their parents, their teachers
and school administrators, the police, or their government. Traditional
patterns of respect in the family, in religion, and in government were
dissolving; the pace of change had quickened so rapidly that many in positions of power were unable to find firm ground upon which to stand.

The Hebrew Union College, too, was buffeted by the winds of change
as long-standing attitudes were examined, debated, and adjusted to meet
contemporary challenges. One such issue focused on the chaplaincy and
military service in Vietnam. During World War II, HUC had provided
more chaplains to the Armed Forces of the United States, in proportion
to its enrollment, than any other theological seminary in America, Jewish
or Christian. In recognition of HUC's contribution, a Liberty ship, the
Isaac Mayer Wise, had been launched on December 21, 1944, at Jackson-
ville, Florida.[1] Rabbis had served with the military forces of the United
States since 1862, the year that Congress revised the requirement that
"chaplains be clergymen of some Christian denomination" to mean that
"no person shall be appointed a chaplain in the United States Army who is

not a regularly ordained minister of *some* religious denomination." Under this interpretation, rabbis were deemed eligible to serve as chaplains.[2]

Glueck fully intended that those under his charge as rabbinical students would "do their duty." In his tenure as president, from the Korean War until well into the sixties, each HUC student was considered to have the moral obligation to serve as a chaplain for two years following ordination. Not all were called to serve, but all who were called had to be willing to go if they could pass the physical examination that the Armed Services required.

As the Vietnam War heated up and more and more Americans were sent to Southeast Asia, students were increasingly reluctant to become chaplains. A chaplaincy procurement program had been jointly established by HUC and the CCAR and had for some time provided a system of selection based on categories of marital status. But the categories themselves exacerbated tensions among the graduating seniors. An article in the student quarterly *variant* in 1964 reviewed the concerns, anxieties, and miscommunications generated by the current system. It concluded:

> Most fervently we recommend to seniors who follow us an attitude: "I may not want to go into the chaplaincy, but neither do my classmates. In all honesty, any man who is physically able to undertake the civilian rabbinate is capable of serving as a chaplain. I will do my best to get into the chaplaincy, and I expect my classmates to do the same." Ultimately we choose the option of leaving it to chance [by way of a lottery] as to who must serve [rather than categories based on marital status]. . . . In this way, maximum fairness and minimum pain would be engaged in the process.[3]

Since there was already in place at each of the three branches of the College-Institute a kind of lottery system that helped determine who would serve at the most desirable bi-weekly and monthly student pulpits, the idea of a lottery for the chaplaincy also seemed fair. For his part, Glueck tried to sweeten the package by introducing a seminarian reserve program for the students. HUC-JIR men, obligated to serve in the military chaplaincy after ordination if called, would receive credit for the time they had spent as rabbinical students and have no military responsibilities until they actually graduated. They would enter the chaplaincy with a higher rank and higher pay.[4] Despite these efforts, however, a lottery for chaplaincy positions was never implemented, and the issue remained unresolved and increasingly contentious during the Vietnam War.

Early in 1966 Glueck explained his position to his Cincinnati staff. Students were to be told in writing of their moral obligation to enter the chaplaincy upon graduation; conscientious objection would not disqualify a student from being ordained, but he had to establish that status with his local draft board before applying to the Hebrew Union College. "I can assure you," he had said earlier to the Board of Governors, "that I shall ordain every student who enters the Hebrew Union College who passes all the moral and academic requirements that are imposed upon him by us, regardless of the chaplaincy."[5]

The moral dilemma of conflicting imperatives was passionately debated in the halls of the College-Institute. Glueck was aware that some graduate and professional schools, including his own campuses, offered a haven for those who wished to avoid the draft. His position was that a theological seminary should not provide any kind of advantage in this matter over other graduate programs. But by the mid-1960s some students who might have been willing to serve in the chaplaincy under other circumstances absolutely refused to be drafted into it for a war they did not believe to be justified. They were not swayed by the argument that Jewish soldiers, sailors, marines, and airmen would be serving in the war, fighting and dying in the conflict, and in need of spiritual counsel and communal prayer. Their consciences would not allow them to lend any support to their government's "wrongheaded" policy.

The issue was eventually settled in 1968 when the Central Conference of American Rabbis accepted selective conscientious objection as grounds for refusal to serve, and the following year made the chaplaincy itself totally voluntary.[6] But the Vietnam War became the catalyst for ever more dramatic expressions of its condemnation by students and by some faculty members, notably Sheldon Blank, a politically liberal professor of Bible. In the spring of 1968 students on the various campuses participated in the Mobilization to End the War in Vietnam. A climactic moment came in December when a student at the Cincinnati school stood up in chapel and proclaimed that he was sending his selective service card back to his local draft board and would face the consequences. Glueck felt impelled to respond immediately. He arose and said:

It isn't necessary for me to agree with everything you say, but it is necessary for me as president of the Hebrew Union College to practice what we preach here: that there is intellectual and spiritual freedom at the Hebrew Union College and that we in general and I in particular will do everything in our power to nurture and strengthen, and if necessary, to defend it.[7]

Glueck added that he didn't think the student's action would be effective, but it would not have any bearing on a decision as to whether or not he should be ordained.

The protests were not limited to statements in the chapel. One Cincinnati student scheduled an anti-war event to be held at the College but to which the general public would be invited. Glueck summoned the student to his office and told him he would have to cancel the event. The student refused, whereupon Glueck threatened to expel him. The student body convened, and emerged with a plan for a one-day boycott of classes, to be called a "Day of Deliberation," during which numerous resolutions were passed affirming the students' rights. Reporting to the Board on this incident, Glueck clarified the distinction he made between supporting the individual student's right to engage in political and social activities of his choice, and students not having the right to commit the entire College to their point of view without the College's consent.[8] After due deliberation, it was determined not to expel the offending student.

During the same period Glueck found himself under increasing pressure from both students and alumni of the College-Institute to make the curriculum more relevant for its rabbis-in-training. More relevant meant two new emphases: one on what would help the congregational rabbi do a better job in the pulpit; the other was on the role that social action initiatives could play in the life of a rabbi and his congregation. America's changing demography and most notably the struggle for equality and civil rights were having an impact on the preparation of rabbis for the Reform Jewish community.

The first issue was addressed by inviting successful congregational rabbis to visit an HUC campus for several days, sometimes for a week at a time, to meet with students in formal and informal sessions and to share with them the techniques they had learned after many years in the pulpit.

The second issue received attention when Glueck related to the Board of Governors in 1967 that the "translation of our religious idealism into the realms of living social justice was admirably met in both Isaac M. Wise and Stephen S. Wise and their associates." He went on to emphasize the importance in the rabbinical curriculum of religious leadership in programs of social justice and creative communal endeavor: "To be asked, as we sometimes are, whether or not we are living in an ivory tower of academia, remote from the world of reality, is to reveal a lack of knowledge of our curriculum past and present." Glueck then mentioned some well-known advocates of social reform, all contemporary Reform rabbis. "How could a school such as ours ever be accused of failing its students in this general regard?" He concluded:

> No student can be graduated from our School in any of the three American centers without first becoming well acquainted with both the powerful tradition of Jewish religious idealism as it affects the brotherhood of man, and without being well informed and considerably experienced in the tasks and techniques of translating the societal ideals of our religious faith into tangible acts and achievements and driving goals for food and fairness and freedom of opportunity for all human beings.[9]

Pressure for curricular change came, as well, from another source — alumni of the College-Institute who were part of the Central Conference of American Rabbis. At first only a few members of the CCAR criticized the training they had received. Then in 1967 the incoming president of the conference proposed a study of rabbinical education to determine whether the curriculum adequately prepared students for the challenges contemporary congregational life would present. A year later, when the conference passed a resolution suggesting that the College defer its capital funds campaign until meaningful curricular discussions between the Board of Governors and the CCAR were held, Glueck put his foot down. He believed the CCAR had no business interfering in the curriculum of his school, and he was prepared to deny CCAR members appointments to the HUC Board if they did interfere.[10]

The College had other matters on its agenda. Glueck announced at a

June 1966 Board of Governors meeting that many students were going to Israel to pursue their rabbinic studies, and that "financial aid for this purpose had been made available from the president's discretionary fund as a one-time commitment." It was Glueck's hope that grants-in-aid from other sources would be supplied for such study in the future. As it worked out, funding for the required first year, which began in 1970, would come from the Reform rabbinate, with most of its costs sustained by fundraising efforts among HUC-JIR alumni.

*

Barbara Glueck, wife of Glueck's son Charles, recalls that at summer's end, Nelson Glueck often took an arduous plane trip from Palestine to Pellston, a small airport north of the family's summer cottage in the resort town of Charlevoix, Michigan. After traveling for as much as thirty hours, he was completely exhausted and looking forward mostly to sleeping. On the other hand, Helen, his son Charles, and his sister-in-law Josephine and her family were ready for round-the-clock sports and entertainment. Even after Glueck had caught up on his sleep, he was utterly unmoved by activities such as golf and swimming, canoeing and sailing, fishing and flower-arranging; his favorite Charlevoix pastime was sitting quietly in the sun. When he went sailing, he carefully shifted from one side of the boat to the other, not because the boat needed steering — he just wanted to escape the shade of the sail.

According to Barbara Glueck, during the high holidays Glueck dreaded making the politically charged decision about which Cincinnati congregation to attend. Rather than choose one temple over another, he realized that escaping to Charlevoix would protect him from disappointing any rabbis or worshippers. Traveling with Helen, her sister and brother-in-law the Josephs, Bill and Jean Wolf from Hamilton, Ohio, and maybe Herb Bloch, Jr., he would hold short holy day services on the porch overlooking Lake Charlevoix, after the others had finished a golf game. The combination of sports and minimal religion suited the group just fine. Herb used to call Glueck "the Pope."

The Charlevoix house sat on about four acres on a bluff overlooking Lake Charlevoix on land purchased from the railroad in 1947 by Helen and her sister Jo. The tracks ran through the property, separating the beach from the upland portion. During Glueck's days there, the train still ran once or twice a day, and the youngsters would wave at the engineer when it passed. For a few years the wooded driveway contained a stick carved with the letters "HUC."

There were two structures on the property: an old farm house on concrete blocks that contained six bedrooms and a few baths, and a new one-story combination living room, dining room, kitchen, with the porch overlooking the lake. Nelson Glueck and Helen used the first floor bedroom, which was once the kitchen of the farmhouse, with the original kitchen cupboards still attached to the walls. Barbara Glueck recalls that at Helen's dinner parties, Glueck would make small talk with vacationers from Chicago or Detroit, but he was never caught up in the trivialities of the resort crowd. He would stay in Charlevoix up to a week to please his wife and son, who loved the place, but rarely longer.

Charlevoix had picturesque beaches and a harbor full of boats. Glueck would take obligatory walks to see the tourist spots, but it was easy to see that his mind was elsewhere. Travel in Europe ranked much higher in his priorities, and returning to work in Cincinnati or Jerusalem was highest of all.[11]

Toward the end of the summer of 1964, after the usual family vacation at Charlevoix, Glueck entered a new and immensely satisfying phase of his life: he became a grandfather. On August 31, 1964, David Samuel Glueck, the first of Glueck's four grandchildren, was born. David's middle name was given in memory of Helen's father. In due course, three other

With grandson Daniel Glueck, age two, February, 1968. (Courtesy of Barbara Glueck)

grandchildren arrived to augment his joy: Daniel, Deborah, and Susan. All would attend Walnut Hills High School, as did their grandmother and father, and all would graduate from Harvard with honors, as did their father.

During the last years of Glueck's tenure, the size, background, and character of the rabbinical student body underwent even more changes.[12] Enrollment increased at a steady pace, fueled by the expansion of the Reform movement; more and more candidates were needed to fill newly established pulpits and to provide assistants for senior colleagues whose congregations had grown. Nearly all the students were now American born, and many had a desire to work with Jewish youth and to help Reform Jews through counseling efforts. By 1968 about eighty percent of entering students came from Reform backgrounds, and most had been active in the National Federation of Temple Youth. Only the New York school still enrolled a significant number of students from traditional backgrounds.[13] The members of the largest entering class in the history of the school up to that time — fifty-six men — began their studies at HUC-JIR in the fall of 1966. The number alarmed some of the men in the field, who were afraid that despite the growth of the movement, a surplus of rabbis might make obtaining a "better" congregation difficult. Glueck assured them that his vision for the employment of graduates of the College-Institute extended well beyond the pulpit. As he told the Board, "increasingly some of our graduates are demonstrating their desire to become Jewish academicians."[14]

*

Another major change at HUC came about in 1964, when the opening of the fall semester in 1964 brought a young woman named Sally Priesand into the undergraduate program of the College. In the course of her eight years as an undergraduate at the University of Cincinnati and at HUC and then as a rabbinical student, Priesand would finally break the barrier to the ordination of women in the United States.[15] She represented the fulfillment of Glueck's long-cherished dream of guiding a woman to that hitherto unattainable goal.[16]

Priesand wrote to the College in the spring of 1963 as she completed her junior year of high school. Joseph Karasick, assistant to the provost, welcomed her interest in attending HUC but cautioned: "We would have to inform you candidly that we do not know what opportunities are available for women in the active rabbinate, since we have, as yet, not ordained any women. Most women prefer to enter the field of Jewish religious education."[17]

The year she entered the undergraduate program Glueck had told his Board of Governors that "the Hebrew Union College-Jewish Institute of Religion has always been prepared to accept properly qualified Jews, male or female, to study for the rabbinate. If a female student should complete the entire course, I, as the representative of the College-Institute would not hesitate to ordain her as a rabbi or as a rebbitzen in Israel."[18] Glueck evidently thought that the term "rebbitzen" would become the female equivalent of "rabbi."

Priesand later recalled first impressions of Nelson Glueck, his "handsome youthfulness, his regal bearing, and especially his eyes, which left nothing unsaid. Somehow they always reflected his approval." She added, "The knowledge that he would be the one to ordain me made the difficult times so much easier."[19]

Priesand entered the Cincinnati rabbinical program in 1968. Involved in student government, she met with Glueck on many occasions. As she began her fourth year in rabbinical school Glueck's serious illness was diagnosed, and she dedicated her rabbinical thesis to him. Glueck told Helen that there were three things he hoped yet to be able to do: attend his grandson David's Bar Mitzvah, live in their apartment in Jerusalem, and ordain Sally Priesand.[20] Sadly, none of these wishes were fulfilled. It fell to Helen to share with the young woman how deeply Glueck felt about the significance of her ordination.[21]

If ordaining a female rabbi was one of Glueck's greatest hopes, ordaining a student whose wife wasn't Jewish by birth or by conversion was out of the question for him. Equally abhorrent to him was the hiring of a faculty member, no matter how impressive his scholarly attainments, if he was similarly "encumbered" with a non-Jewish wife. Glueck's attitude toward mixed marriage also posed obstacles to couples planning a wedding in the HUC Chapel. In one instance he acquiesced in the case of the son of a faculty member — provided that only a rabbi would officiate at the ceremony and that the couple would promise to raise their children as Jews.[22]

*

Glueck entered his eighteenth year as HUC-JIR president in 1964. With HUC-BAS firmly established and its archaeological program in full swing, he could turn his attention to developments at the Los Angeles school, which was currently housed in a small and somewhat inaccessible building on Appian Way in the Hollywood Hills. In January 1964, he informed the board that half of the necessary property for a new facility for the school had been purchased near the campus of the University of Southern California, on Hoover Avenue, between 32nd and 33rd Streets.[23]

An intriguing set of coincidences had led HUC to consider this area, designated for urban renewal. Various other properties had been considered: one in Beverly Hills, another in West Los Angeles, and a third on Mulholland Drive, a site eventually purchased for the Conservative movement's University of Judaism. The Hoover Avenue property became an option when the University of Southern California closed its School of Religion and much of that school's faculty joined the Claremont School of Theology. Geddes MacGregor, an Episcopal priest and dean of USC's School of Religion,[24] along with Lesley Robb and some other faculty members decided to remain where they were. They were seeking to retain a viable program in their field at USC, and they recognized a timely opportunity in HUC's quest for a new site for its California School.

When Dean Alfred Gottschalk spoke with Norman Topping, USC's president, they readily agreed about the mutual advantages of locating HUC's new facility near the University of Southern California campus. Familiar with Glueck's archaeological work, Topping was strongly interested in relocating the HUC Museum of Judaica and Archaeology to a site nearby. When Glueck agreed to this condition, the Hoover Avenue location for the California branch of Hebrew Union College was assured.[25]

Topping invited Glueck to give the Baccalaureate address at USC's undergraduate commencement exercises in May 1964. In a speech he entitled "Lessons from the Past," Glueck used the opportunity to share some of the insights he had gained from his experience as an archaeologist:

The lesson of the past, as portrayed by Biblical literature, is that there is meaning and order in life, and that man is blessed with a mind to discover not only the rules of nature but the laws of God's moral order, transcending man made codes that do not conform to it. "I have set before you life and good and death and evil; therefore choose life," is God's command.

There was a second lesson:

> All knowledge and all skills are useless and worse unless these lessons are learned and pondered on and remembered — that there is no permanent ownership of material goods, only qualified stewardship; no unrestricted privileges of physical power or position for long, only unrestricted rights and obligations of humanity forever.[26]

The relationship between the two institutions, sustained by the congruence of purpose that energized their presidents, would develop positively. Soon after HUC's California campus was opened, it became the center for Jewish studies for all USC students, providing courses in the Holocaust, Jewish history, and Jewish philosophy and religion. During these same years, Glueck also proved quite successful in soliciting large donations for HUC-JIR's first endowed chairs.[27]

*

The ordination weekend of June 2 to 4, 1967 featured the usual service of consecration for the Cincinnati graduating class Friday evening at the Rockdale Avenue Temple and Saturday morning's ordination at the beautiful Plum Street Temple downtown. A luncheon and group reception followed, and there were other individual events that Glueck needed to attend. But early Monday morning word reached him that Israel had been attacked by its Arab neighbors. The Six Day War had begun. The American State Department placed an immediate embargo on American citizens traveling to Israel. However, with his many connections in the U.S. and in Israel, Glueck had little trouble making arrangements — though he could not depart until he had attended the ordination exercises at the New York school as well.[28]

He arrived in Israel on the following Monday evening, June 12, after an overnight flight from New York. On Tuesday, along with William Dever and Ezra Spicehandler, he then drove over to the captured Old City

Charles, Barbara, Helen, and Nelson Glueck, 1967, at the Cincinnati celebration of Glueck's 20th anniversary as HUC president. (*American Jewish Archives*)

Glueck with his colleague and mentor W. F. Albright, 1967. (*American Jewish Archives*)

and talked his way through various Israeli military checkpoints before he could reach the American School, which had once been in his charge. Glueck's colleague G. Ernest Wright had asked him to take charge of the school once again until its newly-appointed director, Father William Casey, could arrive on the scene. Glueck found everything in good shape at ASOR; the only damage was to some of the glass cases in the room he had used as a study twenty years earlier.[29] He was particularly pleased to find his old friend and the School's major domo, Omar Jibrin, waiting for him. The two had not seen each other in twenty years.

*

In his diary, Glueck proposed his solution to the vexing question — How could Jews and Arabs live together in peace? "I would like to see the part of Palestine occupied largely by Arabs made into a separate Arab canton, with largely self-governing powers, contained within the State of Israel."[30] Glueck also recorded in his diary his musings about the benefits of peace. He argued that if peace could be achieved, a golden era would ensue for everyone in the Middle East. The greatest benefit, to his mind, would accrue to the Egyptians and the rest of the Arab nations. He also referred to the creation of wonderful opportunities for archaeologists and explorers to examine whole regions, heedless of boundaries, following ancient trade routes to their destinations.[31]

By the end of June, Glueck had decided that — surprisingly — it would be possible to begin the summer excavation program at Gezer, which had been postponed due to the outbreak of fighting. He recognized that thousands of people who had come to Israel to help out during the war had completed the tasks they had volunteered for and would be ready to work on a dig.[32] He also decided to hold the annual Summer Institute on Near Eastern Civilizations, begun with such success four years earlier. In this respect, at least, the disruption caused by the war had been minimal.

When Glueck's fears regarding possible damage to Hebrew Union College, the American Schools, or the Rockefeller Museum had been allayed, he found time to attend an extraordinary event that took place on Mt. Scopus, the original home of the Hebrew University. Historian Martin Gilbert described the occasion:

On June 28, 1967, several thousand Jews returned to the Hebrew University amphitheater on Mt. Scopus . . . cut off from the rest of

Jerusalem since 1948. Among those present at the ceremony were
Nobel Prize winner S. J. Agnon, and the president of the University,
Eliahu Elath, who as Eliahu Epstein had also been present at the
opening ceremony in 1925.[33]

Glueck wrote in his diary that "when General Rabin, the Chief of Staff
of the victorious army, took his place on the platform, a great swell of
emotion and applause swept through the packed audience."[34]

The enthusiasm for Israel and things Israeli in the American Jewish
community in the years following the Six Day War helped bring Glueck's
dream of a Jerusalem center for rabbinical studies closer to fruition. Details were finally worked out so that in the fall of 1970 the entering first
year class, along with the continuing third year students, could make
their way to the HUC Biblical and Archaeological School on King David
Street to begin their studies in the city often described as the "capital of
the Jewish soul." In February 1970, a few months before the first-year
program began, Glueck addressed the quarterly meeting of the HUC-
JIR Board of Governors and spoke to them about the program, whose
on-site director would be Ezra Spicehandler. Glueck noted that thirty-
eight of the third year students enrolled at HUC-JIR campuses in Cincinnati and New York were in residence, plus the wives of the married
students. The archaeological activities at Gezer would continue "under
the guidance of Dr. [William] Dever, but most significantly, the rabbinic
part of our student body there next year will be as large as the entire rabbinic department of HUC-JIR was in America ten years ago." The Board
was then treated to a detailed account of how the *ulpan* to teach Hebrew
over the summer would be upgraded, and what the curriculum would
be for the first academic year.[35]

In March of that year, for the first time in its history, the Central Conference of American Rabbis held its annual convention in Israel. It had
been more than two decades since the State was established, in fire and
blood. Glueck felt a great surge of pride when he addressed the men who
gathered in Jerusalem at Shabbat services in the chapel of the school he
had built:

Blessed be you who come in the name of the Lord. It is fitting that
the Sabbath service marking the first official meeting of the Cen-

tral Conference of American Rabbis in Israel should be held in the synagogue of the Jerusalem center of the Hebrew Union College-Jewish Institute of Religion, from whose American schools nearly every one of you has obtained his *semikhah* [ordination]. The occasion must henceforth be regarded as an historical one.

Four men worked diligently with me to create this School — Herbert A. Bloch, Jr. Chairman of the Board of Governors, Jack Lichter, a member of that board, Moshe Sharett, then Prime Minister of Israel, and Levi Eshkol, then its Finance Minister. They grasped immediately the thrust of my endeavor and supported me with all their might.

Your and my passion for Israel, for the ideas and ideals of Israel, for the land and State and people of Israel, for the concept of *klal yisrael* [the bond connecting Jews everywhere] cannot be divorced from our having studied and been ordained at the Hebrew Union College.[36]

Glueck noted that the rabbis had come to Jerusalem "not as tourists, but as pilgrims to the cradle of our race, as participants in building up the new polity of the Third Commonwealth. Our presence here would be meaningless if we did not assert our faith in the God of our Fathers manifesting Himself in our history." Using a Talmudic expression, Glueck referred to the students who would attend the school as "blossoms of the priesthood," and compared the bringing of these young men to the Jerusalem school as "redolent of the harvest offering in ancient days."[37]

Speaking to the issue that had caused him such grief in trying to build the school, the religious coercion practiced by leaders of the Orthodox in Israel, Glueck stated: "We shall labor quietly but determinedly for complete freedom of religious practice here in Israel in all phases of life and are confident that such freedom will eventually be established for all Jews."[38] Glueck must have cherished the moment when the bridge between Israel and American Reform Jewry, involving scores of rabbinical students each year, was completed. Bringing Israeli academicians to Cincinnati and New York had had an impact on the student body, to be sure, but now Israel itself, in all its powerful and many-hued reality, would transform the learning experience of every Reform rabbi.

15

Intimations of Mortality

We believe that the boundaries of Israel
extend to wherever Jews live.

On May 4, 1970, after days of rioting and the burning of the ROTC building on the campus of Kent State University, Ohio's governor, James Rhodes, called out the National Guard to restore order. Tragically, the Guard fired on a group of demonstrators, killing four students and wounding nine others. Tension in the small college town was so great that the students were sent home without completing the spring term.

Because this violence took place on a college campus in Ohio, Glueck was particularly concerned. He told the Board in June: "The tragic events [at Kent State] exerted, and continue to exert, a powerful impact on all of us. We could not pursue our regular course of study without taking more cognizance than ever before of the problems and disturbances of our society and our world."[1] At the same Board meeting, Glueck announced that he was "going back to Jerusalem in a couple of weeks to have the dedication exercises of a new building and a small amphitheater on our campus there. The dedication occurs on October 13. I hereby most warmly invite you to attend."

Glueck celebrated his seventieth birthday on June 4, exactly a month after the Kent State uprising. He had thereby achieved what Jewish tradition had long suggested was the normal span of a human life —"three score and ten, or even by reason of strength, four-score years" (Psalm 90:10). He had already initiated plans for his retirement at HUC-BAS in Jerusalem, and like Morgenstern before him, had given considerable thought to the appointment of his successor.[2] His choice was Alfred Gottschalk, the dean of the California School. A 1957 ordinee of the College-Institute and an acknowledged expert on the Jewish essayist and writer Ahad Ha-Am,[3] Gottschalk had proven his administrative capacity at HUC-Los Angeles, just as Glueck had done at ASOR before becoming president of HUC.

After announcing that Gottschalk had been elected by acclamation to assume the position, Glueck said:

I am supremely happy with this choice, and feel very deeply that the future of our beloved College couldn't have been placed in better hands. . . . How grateful I am to the God of our Fathers that one of the most brilliant and beloved and successful of our students, whom I ordained some thirteen years ago, has been chosen to carry on, beginning July 1972, in my place![4]

He told his successor: "It is a heavy responsibility which will be entrusted to you, Fred, some two years from now,[5] but I know that with God's help you will nobly measure up to it." Glueck then acknowledged with deep pleasure his election to the new and essentially honorary office of chancellor of the HUC-JIR, to commence in July 1972 and continue until July, 1975, which would carry him through the Centennial Year of the school.[6] He also basked in the glory of his election as the executive director of the Jerusalem School for life (unless disabled), with the right to live in his apartment there for as long he and his wife wished.[7] Glueck seemed in the best of spirits and fully in command.

*

In the late summer of 1970 a *Festschrift* celebrating his seventieth birthday had appeared. Entitled *Near Eastern Archaeology in the Twentieth Century,* it was edited by James Sanders,[8] who wrote in the foreword about Glueck's life-work:

> As a boy growing up in Cincinnati, Glueck developed a love for his Jewish heritage that emerged less from a mediating Orthodox tradition than from the young student's boundless curiosity about history and nature. Glueck's emotional loyalty to the miracle of nascent Judaism was inherited from his parents. That was a given.
>
> But as a true son of liberal Judaism, Glueck could not merely accept from the past the "genius of this people." He had to make it his own; he had literally to "dig for it"; so he searched the ground for a background.
>
> Neither the Orthodox nor the secularist fully appreciate the genuine religious liberal like Glueck, who feels that objective investigation is the best *mitzvah* [divine obligation] he can perform.[9]

The book quickly found its way to the desks and libraries of Glueck's archaeological colleagues and many of his friends and supporters. The president of the University of Cincinnati, Dr. Walter C. Langsam, acknowledging receipt of the volume, wrote to Glueck: "Certainly few scholars are as deserving of a *Festschrift* as are you. The book will occupy one of the most valued places in my library."[10]

*

Glueck's visit to Jerusalem in October for the dedication of the Residence Hall of the Jerusalem School would be his last trip abroad, but no one could have asked for a "last hurrah" more meaningful or fulfilling than that occasion. The building had been financed by Rosaline Feinstein; the architect was Ruth Melamede, who had helped complete the initial building and stayed on as the architect of record.[11] Glueck was thrilled that his goal of having all first-year students attend the Jerusalem school had been achieved. He told those attending the event: "I have always maintained that there is nothing which concerns the people, land and State of Israel that doesn't concern Jewry in America. . . . We believe that the boundaries of Israel extend to wherever Jews live."[12]

Prime Minister Golda Meir was on hand that day to receive the honorary degree of Doctor of Humane Letters. She delivered a message confirming the importance of the linkage between HUC-BAS and the state of Israel:

> I want to thank Dr. Glueck and his colleagues and the Hebrew Union College, not only because they come here with their students so that they might learn something about our country and our youth. I venture to suggest that this encounter will be good also for our own young people.
>
> I am always a little afraid that precisely here, where it is so good and so easy to be a Jew, where one can view oneself and our own generation as a natural link to the Jewish past without any need to argue or to prove the point, there lurks a potential danger for the continued strength of our uniqueness.
>
> I am sometimes frightened that this Jewish awareness in Israel might become too natural, too unreflective, and that they might lose the sense of wonderment at the miracle of Jewish survival. And

if this were to happen, something very basic would be missing in the souls of our young people.

That same evening, a gala dinner honoring Mrs. Feinstein was held at the elegant King David Hotel, where Glueck always stayed when in Jerusalem after 1948. On that occasion the president of the Hebrew University, Dr. Avraham Harman, brought greetings. Back in Cincinnati, Glueck spoke to the Board of Governors:

> The Jerusalem program must strengthen all our endeavors in America. The main emphasis of all our undertakings must be the HUC-JIR in America. Our chief task is to train the rabbis, scholars, cantors, educators, and Jewish communal workers whom we shall graduate in the years to come.
>
> Our future for the overwhelming majority of us is here in America, and it is here that we must continue to place the chief accent of our total program, however closely knit we are and remain with the totality of Israel and with the land and people of Israel.[13]

By the beginning of November 1970, it was clear to at least an inner circle of close friends and associates that Glueck's vaunted vitality and strength were ebbing. Shortly after his return from Israel, a tumor had been found on his neck, and he engaged in various treatments, including cobalt radiation, to try to reduce its size. He described his situation in a letter to Robert Adler, his long-time friend and a tireless supporter of HUC:

> I had a medical checkup prior to my going over to Jerusalem. . . which revealed the presence of a tumor on the upper right side of my neck. It then began to grow very rapidly. Fortunately, exhaustive and exhausting medical examination, including surgery, convinced the physicians that it was a benign tumor and would yield to cobalt radiation treatment.
>
> I have been having these treatments five days a week and the lymphoma seems to be steadily getting smaller. The physicians are confident that this treatment will remove the lymphoma. As a result, however, I am confined to Cincinnati for the next month or so.[14]

Adler sent a note to Helen in response, to which was attached a cartoon with the inscription: "Marry an archaeologist. He'll love you even more when you're old," and commented, "I couldn't help but think of you when I saw this, even though I know from years of observation that you need not be old to be loved a lot — and I'm certain you are loved a lot — and not only by Nelson."[15]

A poignant note regarding Glueck's health arrived in mid-January 1971 from Chanan Brichto in Israel, addressed to "Dear Chief":

> Esther Lee [the secretary of HUC-BAS] read your letter to unbelieving ears this afternoon, and now as midnight draws near I still find it hard to accept. First your decision to retire, now this. As Milly [Brichto's wife] put it — it's hard enough to think of an HUC not bossed by Nelson Glueck; an ailing Nelson Glueck is even harder to accept. I suppose we can believe anything except what we most deeply don't want to believe.
>
> And how we grasp at your optimistic prognosis! Pray God that it will be borne out. Frankly, we are counting as much on your will to life and health as on the treatment. We do look forward to your promised visit — to seeing that boyish twinkle in your eyes undimmed. As we do to many more years in the pleasure of your company.[16]

His former HUC teacher and friend of more than five decades, Rabbi Solomon B. Freehof, had shared with Glueck a glowing tribute a few months earlier:

> I feel that a great deal of my own life has been paralleled by your presidency of the College. I prepared you to enter the College and I watched with pride your growth and achievement. It was a fine College when you took over; it has become a great College under your hands. . . . I thank you as an alumnus, and I am proud of you as a colleague.[17]

Glueck remained optimistic till the end. He replied to a Uniongram from the Sisterhood of the Baltimore Hebrew Congregation "speeding collective wishes for his good health," saying, on February 2, "I am delighted to be able to report to you that the treatment I am getting is speeding me along the road to recovery and that within several weeks or so I hope to be as good or as bad as I ever was."[18] On February 5 he wrote to Hugo Dalsheimer, a prominent Reform Jewish leader, "I am making good progress, I think, with the elimination of the tumor. I sometimes think that the curing and its after-effects are worse than the cause."[19]

Meanwhile, despite treatments and hospitalizations, Glueck continued, as his strength permitted, to fulfill the obligations of his office. He maintained a level of correspondence not much diminished from its normal volume. Acknowledging his inability to travel, he asked his secretary, Rissa Alex, to send a note to the head of the American Jewish Conference on Soviet Jewry, scheduled to take place in Brussels in February, indicating that he would not be able to attend. At the same time, he asked her to put the dates of the April meeting of the American Philosophical Society on his calendar.

Glueck could no longer attend the regular weekly meetings of the Literary Club of Cincinnati, noting in a letter to an old friend on the faculty of Bowdoin College that "he had not been well on the night of January 11th, and failed to get to the Literary Club meeting to meet the president of Bowdoin. I hope there will be another occasion soon."[20]

In one of his last public appearances, Glueck officiated at the funeral for John Bloch, son of Jean and (the late) Herbert Bloch on January 24. To show her appreciation, Jean sent a check for a hundred dollars to the library of the Jerusalem School. Notice of her gift arrived on Glueck's desk on February 11, 1971, a day before his death. His lymphoma, which was indeed malignant, had progressed rapidly and the treatments became increasingly ineffectual. Despite the many prayers offered on his behalf, despite his own profound desire to complete his term of office and to ordain Sally Priesand, Glueck passed away as the Sabbath was about to enter.[21]

The funeral was held on February 14 in the HUC Cincinnati Chapel, where Glueck had worshipped since he first attended classes at the College as a teenager. The service began with the recitation of Psalm 121: "I shall lift up mine eyes unto the hills; from whence does my help come." The reader, Paul Steinberg, continued: "Reverently we shall hallow his memory. Help us to go our way bravely even though alone, and do our tasks faithfully day by day. May his memory live on through us, for with Thee is the fountain of light, and in Thy light shall we see light." Then Alfred

Gottschalk arose to speak of his illustrious predecessor:

> Dear Friends: Hayyim Nahman Bialik begins a poem "There was a
> man — he is no more. No more — but there was one more song he
> had to sing."[22] That song, for Nelson Glueck, is forever muted; for
> our beloved president that one song was *Yerushalayim shel zahav.*
> He rediscovered at each moment the Jerusalem of Gold. And he
> was indeed its *kinor*, its harp. Upon him it played its timeless song
> of *kedushah*, of holiness. Israel restored was part of his mystic vision.
> The great journey he wished to take, the life that he and Helen
> wanted to live, *nasi be-yisra'el*, a prince amidst our people, now lies
> silent before us.
>
> I am distressed over thee, my friend Nelson. Very pleasant hast
> thou been to me, wonderful is thy love for me.[23] These ancient
> words ruminate in our hearts in this respectful and sad hour. In the
> midst of this large and close family in this chapel which he loved
> and where he prayed, we seek solace and comfort in our bereave-
> ment. We have lost much.
>
> The Jewish world has lost a commanding figure who personified
> the spirit of an unfettered faith. This profoundly mystical and often
> brooding man brought together in his being the faith of our fathers
> of which he spoke so much, and the free rein of the intellect through
> which he charted our people's history and brought the past with full
> force into the burning present. The people and land of Israel have
> lost a fierce champion for Jewish dignity and Jewish survival. Nelson
> Glueck was, above all else, a son of Jerusalem.
>
> How he delighted in the observation that while he was a native of
> Cincinnati, his very being rested in the heart of our homeland, Jeru-
> salem, in *eretz Yisrael.* The land of our fathers, he often observed,
> drew him as if by an irresistible magnet as he and Helen looked
> forward to the remaining years of fruitful work in Jerusalem. For
> the air of that sacred city awakened him: its life and brilliant hues,
> its old winding streets felt the pounding of his footsteps. He redis-
> covered at each moment the Jerusalem of Gold.
>
> And how the Israelis responded to him. "The Professor," as Glueck
> was always called, was the intimate of the great and the humble alike.[24]

There had been but a few sentences addressed to Helen or Charles during the forty-five minute service, and even less attention paid to Glueck's roots in Cincinnati or to his siblings. The College, it seemed, was saying farewell to its own; family members would have to wend their way through their grief without much public acknowledgment. The Chapel service over, Helen and Charles and those of Glueck's brothers and sisters able to attend, along with the scores of students, faculty, colleagues and friends who had been present at the service, walked slowly to their cars and made their way from the College through the familiar streets of Clifton, South Avondale, and Walnut Hills. Glueck was buried in the United Hebrew Cemetery in Walnut Hills, off Montgomery Road, where in time a modest headstone was placed to mark the site.[25]

A Man of Rare Vision

Once he had learned the skill of reading pottery sherds and had determined what he wanted to do with that skill, Nelson Glueck lived the life of an intrepid explorer, working in harsh climates and with little guidance from anyone other than a local Bedouin guide and his ever-present Bible. He became a figure of romance and mystery, more at home on the back of a camel than in a lecture hall, willing to mingle with sworn enemies of the Jewish people and the British authorities as well as leaders of the *yishuv*.

His discoveries, like those of his older colleague Lipa Sukenik and his younger one Yigael Yadin (Sukenik's son), electrified the Jewish popula tion of Palestine/Israel. These discoveries gave the *yishuv* a powerful hold on its historical relationship with the land, and an awareness that what looked like barren desert could in fact be a rich resource, containing copper beneath the sands and phosphates in the Dead Sea. Even the scanty rainwater in the Negev could be harnessed and channeled for irrigation purposes.

Glueck made many friends among Palestinian Jews and, after 1948, among Israelis. He dined with presidents, prime ministers, mayors, and Knesset members. Glueck was a unique sort of American Jew and even more so a unique sort of rabbi, one who came not to tell Israel how to deal with the Arabs, and certainly not — though he was often accused of this — to uproot traditional religion, but rather to help Israeli Jews trace and then embrace their roots in the ancient soil of the homeland and in the vast reaches of the Negev.

Glueck was also at home with American dignitaries. Successive occupants of the White House, beginning with Kennedy, and continuing with Lyndon Johnson and Richard Nixon, were in touch with him from time to time. Governors, senators, and high-ranking judges were his friends and often received copies of his books as they were published. His contacts in the academic and literary world were, of course, also numerous.

Glueck was able to build a bridge between American Jews and the Jewish state. Because of his efforts, hundreds of students, faculty, and staff from HUC-JIR have come to study not just the curriculum of the College-Institute, but the way in which modern Israel and Jewish life in America could meaningfully intersect. They, in turn, have influenced

others. Since 1970–1971, when the mandatory rabbinical student year in
Israel was inaugurated, a whole generation of Reform rabbis — and later
cantors, educators and communal service students — has been imbued
with a sense of the spirit and destiny of Israel. The bridge that Glueck
built has also played a role in encouraging Israelis to know about and
participate in a form of Judaism quite different from what had been
transferred to Israel from Eastern Europe and the Middle East. Eventually a handful, then a dozen, and finally more than a score of Israelis have
trained for the rabbinate through HUC, the institution that Glueck
brought to Jerusalem.

Golda Meir, the woman from Milwaukee who became Israel's Prime
Minister, conveyed a sense of Glueck's powerful impact on her people
when she said:

> Nelson Glueck has done something wonderful for us. He was not
> content with the spirit alone. He wanted to prove that the spirit of
> the Jewish people is rooted in the soil, in the simplest and most
> physical sense of the word. . . . Our bond with this land is not only
> spiritual.[1]

Rachel Yanait Ben-Zvi, widow of Israel's second president, wrote to
Glueck in the late summer of 1967: "I hope you will soon return to Israel,
even if in America you live with an Israeli spirit."[2] Indeed, for Glueck,
spirituality was tied up with the Land of Israel. As Fritz Bamberger noted
with regard to Glueck's first book, *The River Jordan*:

> Glueck called the Jordan "an enigmatic river, a weird stream of
> limitless sanctity, historical importance, and spiritual significance."
> The book is a geographical and archaeological guidebook of a kind,
> but it is also a guide to the sentiments of the man who wrote it. It is
> filled with hints of personal piety and faith, and as one progresses
> in reading it, one realizes that somewhere the author begins speak-
> ing to the river and the land it traverses, and the river and land
> respond in what becomes an almost spiritual dialogue.[3]

Glueck's very personal relationship to the land was also noted by Yigael
Yadin.[4] He said: "Being a veritable trail-blazer in the development of

biblical archaeology, Glueck instilled in students and readers alike a deep love for the ancient land of Israel and its neighbors, and helped to link the people of the book with their cultural heritage." Yadin characterized Glueck as

> a Jewish Victorian type — strange and unique. He was romantic, even a little childish. He was entranced by the magic of his people's past. The moving force in his life was his faith in the God of his fathers and the history of his people. He wandered to and fro in the desert, not like Lawrence, who was blinded by the oriental charm of the Bedouin, but rather like one who viewed the Bedouins as Abraham, Isaac, and Jacob, still wandering about the face of the land.

W. F. Albright, in his tribute, noted that Glueck was the first of his students to master the then obscure art of dating Palestinian pottery by use of its many typological differences as well as by careful analysis of changes of form.[5] Albright admitted that both he and Glueck had been proven wrong in considering Tell el-Kheleifeh as essentially a series of copper refineries inside a protective fortress wall. They were also wrong in dating the typical pottery of the refinery sites in the Wadi Arabah to the tenth century B.C.E. Instead,

> Nelson Glueck's greatest single discovery bearing on biblical history was his identification of the early patriarchal narratives of Genesis featuring Abraham with Middle Bronze dates (late twentieth and early nineteenth centuries B.C.E.). This he pointed out long before I reached the same conclusion in 1961. During the past decade, new material supporting Glueck's discovery has been pouring in at such a rate that any contrary view becomes extremely difficult, if not impossible, to maintain.
>
> Glueck's most important contribution to general history is almost certainly his work on the history of the Nabataeans, and especially the economy and ecology of the most famous North Arab nation of pre-Islamic times.

Rabbi Kenneth Roseman, who served as dean of students at the Cincinnati campus during Glueck's tenure, believed that Glueck's continued dedication to archaeological matters helped him keep College matters in perspective. He also felt that Glueck's sense of humor and ability to forgive those who made mistakes were key to his effectiveness. Glueck was well aware of his own limitations, especially regarding the vocational choice made by most of his ordinees. He once told Roseman: "I would have made a terrible pulpit rabbi." Glueck had learned what he himself could not do well, and decided early on to let others perform those functions.[6]

There is little doubt that Glueck played an enormously important role in the shaping of American Reform Jewry during the third quarter of the twentieth century. After a false start with the UAHC in the early forties, he returned to Cincinnati in 1947 as a conquering hero. Only Maurice Eisendrath seriously challenged Glueck for pre-eminence among Reform's leaders and spokespersons during their decades in positions of responsibility. Glueck's role as an educator and a leader of American Reform Judaism was duly recognized in the citation for a posthumous degree awarded him by Yale University on June 14, 1971. In that capacity, the document stated, Glueck "preserved and promoted the belief in the prophets of old, and in the God of justice and freedom."

Glueck's own comments in Edward R. Murrow's 1952 volume *This I Believe* further defined his personal faith:

> I am convinced that there can be no guarantee of my happiness except that I help evoke and enhance it by the work of my hands and the dictates of my heart and the direction of my striving. I believe that deep faith in God is necessary to keep me and hold mankind uncowed and confident under the vagaries and ordeals of mortal experience, and particularly so in this period of revolutionary storm and travail. If my values receive their sanction and strength from relationship to divine law and acceptance of its ethical imperatives, then nothing can really harm me.[7]

Notes

Chapter 1: From Ponovezh to Cincinnati

1 The Karaites were members of a Jewish sect that emerged in the eighth century. They accepted only the Torah as their legal tradition and ignored the rabbinic literature (the Oral Law) that followed.

2 Nancy Schoenburg and Stuart Schoenburg, *Lithuanian Jewish Communities* (Northvale, New Jersey: Jason Aronson, 1996), 224–25.

3 Jonathan D. Sarna and Nancy Klein, *The Jews of Cincinnati* (Cincinnati: Center for the Study of the American Jewish Experience, 1989), 181.

4 Ellen Norman Stern, *Dreamer in the Desert: A Profile of Nelson Glueck* (Philadelphia: Ktav, 1980), 1.

5 1915 Yearbook, Woodward High School Archives, Cincinnati.

6 Glueck family lore.

7 Cf. the biographical sketch of Glueck by Dr. Reuben Bullard in Gisela Warburg, *The Nelson and Helen Glueck Collection of Cypriot Antiquities, Cincinnati* (Pocket Book 111 in Studies in Mediterranean Archaeology and Literature) (Jonsered, Sweden: Paul Astroms Forlag, 1992), 32.

Chapter 2: Education for the Reform Rabbinate

1 Folder 1/9, Manuscript Collection 160. Jacob R. Marcus Center, AJA, Cincinnati.

2 In *The Hebrew Union College Jubilee Volume, 1875–1925* (Cincinnati: Hebrew Union College Press, 1925), 29–30.

3 Samuel Cohon, "The History of the Hebrew Union College," in *Publications of the American Jewish Historical Society*, September 1950, 38.

4 Ibid.

5 Ibid., 40.

6 Ibid., 46–47.

7 Ibid.

8 Cf. G. A. Dobbert, "The Ordeal of Gotthard Deutsch," in *American Jewish Archives*, 2, 2 (1968): 119–55.

9 The *Monthly* had been reconstituted in 1914 after a ten-year lapse. In total, it would run for 34 volumes. Its first editor was Abba Hillel Silver, who later played a major role in the Reform movement and as a leading spokesperson for Zionism. Michael A. Meyer, "A Centennial History," in *Hebrew Union College-Jewish Institute of Religion at One Hundred Years*, Samuel Karff, ed. (Cincinnati: HUC Press, 1976), 74.

10 Boston: The Stratford Company, 1920. Deutsch was Professor of Jewish History and Literature at the College, and had served briefly as an interim president between Isaac Mayer Wise (d. 1900) and Kaufmann Kohler (inaugurated in 1903).

11 Vol. 7, no. 2 (December, 1920): 5.

12 London: W. Heinemann Company, 1920.

13 Cf. the biography of Zangwill by Joseph Udelson, *Dreamer of the Ghetto: The Life and Works of Israel Zangwill* (Tuscaloosa: University of Alabama Press, 1990).

14 Vol. 8, no. 3 (January, 1922): 88.

15 Ibid. With regard to his attitude toward Jesus, Glueck would take a totally opposite stance when confronted with Maurice Eisendrath's proposal to award Jesus a more favorable treatment. See chap. 9, 141–42.

16 See below, pp. 117–18.

17 More than three-quarters of a century later, in 1997, a nonagenarian Cincinnatian submitted a letter to *The American Israelite* recalling his 1920 confirmation class at the Isaac M. Wise Temple, and referring to Glueck and Julius Mark as student "jewels." *The American Israelite*, 143, 32 (February 20, 1997).

18 *The New York Post,* October 6, 1961, 51.

19 The correspondence was preserved in Miss Lenhoff's Bible and eventually copied for the AJA. Folder 1/7, Box 1, Manuscript Collection 160.

20 Ibid., Glueck to Miss Lenhoff, June 11, 1922.

21 The Rabbis were killed for teaching Torah in public and for ordaining disciples. The liturgy for Yom Kippur contains an extensive section on these martyrs.

22 Page 110.

23 The fellowship was established by the family of Henry Morgenthau, former secretary of the United States Treasury. The initial sum was $15,000, from which an annual income of $900 could be anticipated.

24 Blank joined the HUC faculty in 1927 as Lecturer in Bible and was eventually promoted to Professor of Bible. Rothman served as the HUC Librarian in the 1940s.

Chapter 3: The Lure of a German Doctorate

1 Although its original intent was to serve pure scholarship, the school soon developed principally into a seminary for the training of rabbis and religious school teachers for large segments of German Jewry. It also welcomed students from abroad, as well as Jewish students from various faculties of the Berlin University itself. Some of the great scholars and teachers of the German Jewish community were to be found there. It was the one institution in Europe in which Jewish learning was taught without any questioning of the religious bent of the student.

2 See Bruce Kuklick, *Puritans in Babylon: The Ancient Near East and American Intellectual Life, 1880–1930* (Princeton: Princeton University Press, 1996), 6–7.

3 Marcus had longed for the company of his colleagues. Cf. Randall M. Falk, *Bright Eminence: The Life and Thought of Jacob Rader Marcus* (Malibu, California: Pangloss Press, 1994), 60–61.

4 Glueck to Morgenstern, December 23, 1923. Folder 1/12, MS Collection 160. AJA.

5 Stefan Lorant, *Sieg Heil! An Illustrated History of Germany from Bismarck to Hitler* (New York: Norton, 1974), 150.

6 Remarks at the celebration of Glueck's fifteenth anniversary as head of HUC-JIR, April 10, 1962. Folder 1/9, MS Collection 160, AJA.

7 *Sieg Heil!* 124.

8 Rathenau (1856–1922), a member of a prominent Jewish family, was appointed economic advisor and negotiator on war reparations in 1919 and foreign minister of the Weimar Republic in February 1922. He was assassinated on June 24 of that year by three right-wing assailants.

9 *Sieg Heil!* 131–32.

10 Late the following February, Hitler and nine others came before the Munich People's Court, charged with fomenting and organizing a *putsch* against the government. During the trial he dominated the proceedings, turning the courtroom into a forum for his propaganda. Hitler received an exceptionally mild sentence: five years, with parole eligibility after six months. He served only nine months, during which he wrote *Mein Kampf. Sieg Heil!*, 140 ff.

11 Glueck to Morgenstern, December 23, 1923. Folder 1/12, MS Collection 160, AJA.

12 Norman Bentwich, *For Zion's Sake* (Philadelphia: Jewish Publication Society, 1955), 25–29.

13 Michael A. Meyer, "A Centennial History," in Samuel E. Karff, ed., *Hebrew Union College-Jewish Institute of Religion at One Hundred Years.* Cincinnati: HUC Press, 1976), 274.

14 Glueck to Morgenstern, December 23, 1923.

15 Ibid.

16 Ibid.

17 Glueck to Morgenstern, March 12, 1924, Folder 1/12, Box 1, MSS. 160, AJA.

18 Ibid.

19 Ibid.

20 April 14, 1924. Folder 1/12, MSS 160, AJA.

21 June 4, 1924 (Glueck's birthday). From the family sheaf of letters.

22 Ibid.

23 From the family sheaf of letters. November 12, 1924.

24 Gershom Scholem had studied at the University of Jena in the fall of 1917. About Staerk's lectures, Scholem wrote, "The theologian Willi Staerk read selections from the Psalms to a very small number of students and did quite a good job. He had a sonorous voice, and in his mouth Hebrew sounded better than I have heard it pronounced by other theologians." See Scholem, *From Berlin to Jerusalem: Memories of My Youth* (New York: Schocken, 1980), 96.

25 Glueck to "Everybody," August 29, 1924. Glueck announced: "I hope also to spend one year in Palestine to learn how to speak modern Hebrew and Arabic. I am studying Syriac now, and next year I shall begin on Arabic." From the family sheaf of letters.

26 March 24, 1925. In this letter Glueck suggested to Harry that if he doesn't complete his pre-med studies he should finish the liberal arts course. He adds: "You might want to go to the Hebrew Union College!" From the family sheaf of letters.

27 Giessen, 1927. The work was translated into English forty years later (1967) by Alfred Gottschalk, Glueck's successor as president of the Hebrew Union College (1971–1996). The English edition, *Hesed in the Bible*, was published by the HUC Press. Gottschalk asserts that when the thesis was first published, it was acknowledged as a methodological landmark in the study of the history of biblical ideas. *Das Wort Hesed* was republished in Germany in 1964.

28 It has been argued that Glueck's thesis was planned as the first chapter of a systematic *Ideengeschichte* in which Glueck intended to include the whole gamut of biblical concepts in a "history of ideas." His career, however, took a sharp turn at that point. Instead of becoming an historian of biblical ideas, he became a biblical archaeologist. See Fritz Bamberger, "The Mind of Nelson Glueck," in James A. Sanders, ed., *Near Eastern Archaeology in the Twentieth Century: Essays in Honor of Nelson Glueck* (New York: Doubleday, 1979).

29 Glueck to Morgenstern, February 24, 1927. Folder 1/9, MSS Collection 160, AJA. Bruno Ernst Meissner was a well known Assyriologist.

30 From the family sheaf of letters.

31 Albright had presented a series of lectures at HUC at Morgenstern's request in 1926 and 1927.

32 Glueck to Albright, July 24, 1927. Folder 1/12, Box 1, MSS 160, AJA.

Chapter 4: *The Nascent Archaeologist*

1 Established by Anna Spafford in 1896, the American Colony was a commune that served as a home for expatriate Americans and provided many charitable services to the poorer inhabitants of Jerusalem's Old City. During World War I it opened a soup kitchen and fed thousands of people. Over the years, foreign correspondents and important visitors frequented the hotel it established. See Jonathan Broder, "A Family, a Colony, a Life of Good Works in the Holy City," *Smithsonian* 27, 12 (March, 1997): 128ff.

2 Correspondence between Marcus and Judah L. Magnes, July 18, 1926, reproduced in the *American Jewish Archives* (April, 1988): 1–4.

3 It is likely that he also corresponded with Sheldon Blank, who spent the spring term of 1926 in Palestine.

4 Martin Gilbert, *Jerusalem in the Twentieth Century* (New York: John Wiley & Sons, 1996), ix.

5 Earlocks

6 Long robe-like garments as worn by seventeenth-century Polish nobility

7 Glueck to "Everybody," Sept. 23, 1927. From the family sheaf of letters.

8 *Biblical Archaeologist* 47, 4 (December, 1984): 200.

9 In the September letter he indicated that he hoped to be able to write them a decent letter in Hebrew, and then they could also answer him in Hebrew. Evidently at least Morris Glueck, if not Anna, was conversant in Hebrew as well as Yiddish and English.

10 He told Morgenstern in a letter dated September 18, 1927, that Epstein charged him a dollar an hour, and that he was taking a lesson every day. Folder 1/9, MSS Collection 160, AJA.

11 The anecdote is recorded in a *Ma'ariv* interview, July 31, 1953. Glueck's preference for Hebrew, especially in the company of American tourists who would be impressed by his linguistic attainments, is also attested to by his assistant at HUC-BAS, Gad Granach, who recalled Glueck chastising him for addressing a question to him in English. From then on Granach made a point of addressing Glueck only in Hebrew, even if the conversation was totally pointless. Interview with Jonathan Brown, January, 1995.

12 From the *Ma'ariv* interview.

13 Sir Flinders Petrie (1857–1942) began excavating at Tell el-Hesi in 1890. An excellent summary of his life and work can be found in the *Biblical Archaeologist* 47, 4 (December, 1984): 220–22 and at the Flinders Petrie Museum on the campus of the University of London.

14 James B. Pritchard, *Archaeology and the Old Testament* (Princeton: Princeton University Press, 1958), 82.

15 Cf. Neil Asher Silberman, *Digging for God and Country: Exploration, Archaeology, and the Secret Struggle for the Holy Land 1799–1917* (New York: Knopf, 1982), 148–50.

16 Wellhausen published his theories in 1889, identifying four major documentary sources for the Pentateuch and related literature: the J source, which is identified by the use of the tetragrammaton; the E source, which is identified by the use of the word *Elohim*; the P source, whose author was a priest, and the D source, which comprises most of the book of Deuteronomy.

17 Bruce Kuklick, *Puritans in Babylon* (Princeton: Princeton University Press, 1996), 199.

18 When Albright resigned his position with ASOR in 1932 and returned to Baltimore, he organized Johns Hopkins' doctoral program in archaeology and related subjects around the concept of an "oriental seminary." Of the 57 doctoral students who completed the program under his aegis, 23 received their degrees in Bible. See David Noel Freedman, "W. F. Albright as an Historian," in Gus Van Beek, ed., *The Scholarship of William Foxwell Albright* (Atlanta: Scholars Press, 1989), 35.

19 Glueck correspondence, Harvard Semitics Museum.

20 H. V. F. Winstone, *Woolley of Ur* (London: Secker and Warburg, 1990). Woolley's excavations at Ur were presented in book form as *Ur of the Chaldees*, Benn, 1929.

21 Winstone, ibid., 150.

22 Philip J. King, *American Archaeology in the Mideast* (Philadelphia: ASOR, 1983), 91.

23 For example, M. Parker's expedition (1909–1911) dug up the area of the Gihon spring. The southern end of the City of David was investigated by the Weill expedition (1913/4, 1923/4). R.A.S. Macalister and J.G. Duncan (1923–1925)

excavated a considerable area in the north of Jerusalem, and the J. W. Crowfoot and G. M. Fitzgerald expedition (1927–1928) dug close to the same area. *Encyclopedia Judaica*, vol. 8, cols. 1521–1522 (1971).

24 December 26, 1927. Folder 9/16. MSS Collection 5, AJA.

25 January 28, 1928. From the family sheaf of letters.

26 May 31, 1928. Glueck estimated that he would return to Cincinnati around October 1.

27 BASOR 29, 1,2. Quoted in L. G. Running and David Noel Freedman, *William Foxwell Albright* (New York: Two Continents Morgan Press, 1975), 145.

28 That is, since the time of the destruction of the first Temple.

29 Running and Freedman, 149.

30 The Samaritans tried to preserve the ancient Jewish sacrificial system as recorded in the Torah. There are only a few hundred remaining adherents to this sect, which cut its ties with normative Judaism centuries ago.

31 April 11, 1928 to the family. From the family sheaf of letters.

32 Jews living in Israel only observe the first day of holidays like Sukkot, Pesah, and Shavuot because the additional day had only been necessary in the Diaspora, too far from ancient Israel to be sure of knowing of the new moon's arrival in time.

33 May 20, 1928.

34 Interview with Jonathan Brown, Jerusalem, July 24, 1996. A similar comment had been made a generation earlier about Sir Flinders Petrie.

35 In a speech presented at Glueck's 20th anniversary celebration as HUC president, Albright recalled: "Besides ever-menacing desert and sometimes threatening men, there were hostile beasts, though mostly quite small, yet scorpions can inflict painful and even dangerous wounds, lice carry typhus, and fleas can be the most unpleasant pests of all. Though old hoboes like me are disdained by fleas — possibly because my first twelve years were spent in a Latin American country [Chile] where fleas are perhaps even more numerous than in the Near East, there are many archaeologists on whom fleas leap with enthusiasm. Nelson belongs to this category."

36 Ellen Norman Stern, *Dreamer in the Desert* (N.Y.: Ktav, 1980), 35–36.

37 From *Pirkei Avot* 5:4. Quoted in *A Modern Commentary on Jewish Ethics*, ed. and trans. Leonard Kravitz and Kerry Olitzky (New York: UAHC Press, 1993), 58–59.

38 Cf. Sheldon Blank's chapter entitled "Bible" in Samuel Karff, ed., *Hebrew Union College-Jewish Institute of Religion at One Hundred Years* (Cincinnati: HUC Press, 1976), 287–89 and *passim*.

39 Ibid., 289.

40 Ibid., 291.

41 Wise had founded the Jewish Institute of Religion in New York in 1922. For a fuller discussion, see Michael A. Meyer, "A Centennial History," in Karff, ed., *HUC-JIR at One Hundred Years*, 137–69.

42 Ibid., 293.

43 Ibid., 297–99.

44 Ibid., and confirmed in conversation of Jonathan Brown with Rabbi David Wice, one of Glueck's students.

45 Quoted in Stern, *Dreamer*, 41.

46 That is, dating from the second century B.C.E.

47 Glueck correspondence, 1931–1932, American Jewish Archives. MS 160.

48 Philadelphia: Westminster Press, 1959.

49 Running and Freedman, *William Foxwell Albright*, 149.

50 *CCAR Yearbook* 39: 265ff.

51 Ibid. In a footnote, Glueck refers to work being undertaken at Gath, Gezer, Beth-Shemesh, Jerusalem, Shechem, Samaria, Megiddo, Ta'anach, Beth-She'an, and Jericho.

52 Ibid.

53 Located southwest of Jerusalem, it was the site of the devastating conclusion to the second revolt against Rome that began in 132 C.E. Bar Kochba, the leader of that rebellion, and thousands of his followers died there in 135 C.E.

54 *CCAR Yearbook*, 39:295. One may well wonder what Blank meant when he said that Beitar would be dug "only by Jews." Presumably he believed that since there was no Christian interest in the place, it would have to be the Jews who excavated it. The same might be said of Gamla in the Golan Heights and of many other sites.

55 Ibid., 295.

56 Ibid., 298–99.

57 *Wissenschaft des Judentums*, the scholarly study of the Jewish religion and people, emerged in the second decade of the nineteenth century among young Jewish intellectuals, having studied in German universities and been exposed to the ideal of an impartial approach to the past. See Michael A. Meyer, *Response to Modernity* (New York, Oxford: Oxford University Press, 1988), 76–99. See chap. 3, n. 1.

58 *CCAR Yearbook*, 265.

59 Ibid., 265–66.

60 Stern, *Dreamer*, 38.

61 Charles was her younger brother, Josephine (Jo) her younger sister.

62 Helen Glueck's mother was also named "Helen" and was sometimes referred to as "big Helen," while her daughter was "little Helen."

63 Oko (1883–1944) served as librarian at HUC from 1906 until 1933 and supervised the construction of the new Library building on the Cincinnati campus. He was an expert on Baruch Spinoza and a close friend of the Iglauers, sharing their cultural and intellectual interests.

64 Glueck, for his part, had made a solemn vow in front of Albright during the previous summer's dig at Tell Beit Mirsim to "marry the first girl he met after returning to Cincinnati."

65 Interview with Jane Meilich, on the staff of the *Cincinnati Post and Times-Star*, 1973. Helen's sister Jo confirmed that their mother was also active with the Cincin-

nati Chapter of Hadassah, which was not the type of organization that upper middle class assimilated German Jewish women would normally join. Perhaps the affiliation was post-1948 when Israel had become a state.

66 Meilich interview.

67 *Discovery*, a publication of the University of Cincinnati Medical Center, Fall/Winter, 1990, 22.

68 Jerry Ransohoff, Helen's cousin, attended the wedding and remembered Harry, Hillel, and Esther being there.

69 It seems that Helen accompanied her grandmother on a tour of Russia while Glueck returned to Palestine.

70 May 1, 1931. In another section of the letter, Glueck expressed his anger at a porter who stuck his suitcase four cars away from where Glueck was seated. "If I ever see that porter again," he wrote, "I'll murder him."

71 Ruth Cohen, who served as public relations person and student liaison at the College from 1960 to 1964, once asked Glueck: If he could live his life over again, what would he have changed about it? He said without hesitation, "I would have married Helen sooner." Conversation with Jonathan Brown, July 23, 1995.

72 Pass-a-Grille was the name of the beach in St. Petersburg just south of the site of the Don Ce-Sar Hotel.

Chapter 5: Head of the American Schools

1 Although the site could be traced to the early Bronze Age, its most impressive period was set in the Maccabean era (164 B.C.E.–37 B.C.E.). Glueck played a major role at the excavations of Beth Zur, with Ovid Sellers of the seminary faculty as his supervisor.

2 His opinion of those who failed to consider its importance was rendered in an article that Albright published in the *Bulletin of the American Schools* in 1933, where he wrote: "This topological research has attracted untrained men to the field, some of whom have unhappily published their results, none of which are of the slightest value."

3 Nelson Glueck, *The Other Side of the Jordan* (New Haven: ASOR, 1940), 52.

4 *The Letters of Gertrude Bell* (New York: Boni and Liveright, 1927).

5 *Other Side of the Jordan*, 61.

6 Moses sent messengers to the king of Edom requesting permission to pass through his territory on this road: "We will not pass through fields or vineyards, and we will not drink water from wells. We will follow the king's highway, turning off neither to the right nor to the left, until we have crossed your territory" (Numbers 20:17).

7 The Hyksos were a Semitic group that invaded Egypt and ruled it during the seventeenth and eighteenth centuries B.C.E. and may have been responsible for the destruction of both Edom and Moab.

8 *Other Side of the Jordan*, 8.

9 May 4, 1931.

10 Interview with Helen taped by Gloria London in Cincinnati, May 1988. Accessed through the Marcus Center, AJA. The next two paragraphs of the text are also quoted from that interview.

11 Her sister Josephine spoke of such an occurrence having taken place in 1936.

12 Letter to Sam and Helen Iglauer, July 1, 1937. From the family sheaf. ·

13 Founded by violinist Bronislaw Huberman, the Israel Philharmonic, then known as the Palestine Orchestra, played its first concert under the leadership of famed conductor Arturo Toscanini on December 26, 1936.

14 Harry Iliffe was then head of the Palestine Archaeological Institute.

15 Dr. Yassky, a brilliant physician and administrator for the Hadassah-Rothschild hospital, was one of 76 staff members who were ambushed and murdered by an Arab mob at Sheikh Jarrah, an Arab village on the only road between Jerusalem and Mt. Scopus. The incident occurred on April 13, 1948, just a month before the Mandate ended. It inflamed the Jewish residents of Palestine against the British, who made no effective efforts to prevent the slaughter, though the firing lasted for several hours and the hospital convoy was clearly marked.

16 Glueck frequently used the term when referring to his own offspring as well as other children.

17 Glueck to Sam and Helen Iglauer, March 12, 1939. From the family sheaf.

18 *The American Israelite* 54/39 (Spring 1935): 1–2.

19 In response to British policies of restricting Jewish immigration to Palestine and Jewish land purchase in Mandatory Palestine, philanthropist Felix Warburg proposed the resettlement of Arab *fellaheen* (Palestinian agricultural laborers) in Transjordan because "its soil, for agricultural purposes is, if anything better than Palestine's, and its water conditions are said to be better than Palestine's as well." Felix M. Warburg, "Transjordan, Part of Palestine," *New Palestine* 19 (November 7, 1930). Quoted in *The American Jewish Archives* 54, 1 (2002):11.

20 The mufti had considerable influence among the Palestinian Arabs and later offered his services to Hitler when he learned of Hitler's intention to exterminate the Jews.

21 In Glueck's ASOR *Newsletter* No. 10, dated August 18, 1939, he offered his opinion that "the show of increased independence which England has granted Transjordan was a wise political move. For once the British government has demonstrated that it does not always reward its enemies; sometimes it deals kindly with its friends. I hope that the reward for good behavior so ostentatiously given in Transjordan will have its proper effect upon Palestine."

22 From *Dateline Jerusalem: A Diary* (Cincinnati, 1968), 35.

23 Ibid., 25.

24 September 1, 1938. From the family sheaf of letters.

25 October 27, 1938. From the family sheaf of letters.

26 *Dateline Jerusalem*, 175.

27 Harding helped Glueck whenever his official duties permitted. Additional

members of Glueck's field staff included Carl Pape, draughtsman, S. J. Schweig, photographer, I. H. Wood, fellow at ASOR, and Clarence Fisher, Professor of Archaeology at the American Schools.

28 Cf. Don Belt, "Petra: Ancient City of Stone," in *National Geographic*, Dec. 1998: 116–33. Also David S. Boyer, "Rose-red Citadel of Biblical Edom," in *National Geographic*, Dec. 1955: 853–70. A Swiss explorer, John Lewis Burkhardt, had stumbled on Petra in 1812. He was the first European to see this wonder of the ancient world.

29 Glueck had located several sanctuaries prior to reaching Khirbet et-Tannur, among them Khirbet Derith, Dhair Ras, Qasr Rabbah, Khirbet Mesheirfeh, Kerak, Mahay-Ma'im, Khirbet Brak, and Dhiban. Cf. Glueck, *Deities and Dolphins: The Story of the Nabataeans* (New York: Farrar, Strauss, and Giroux, 1964), 44ff.

30 Ibid.

31 Much of the credit for *Deities* has been ascribed to Eleanor Vogel, Glueck's archaeological assistant at the time.

32 Page 15. Dov Peretz Elkins, a prominent American Conservative rabbi, had a problem with the book's title. He argued that "the dolphins are deities, and as such, are part of the Nabataean pantheon; therefore the title is misleading."

33 Page 16.

34 In this discussion, we are indebted to the work of Gary Pratico, *Nelson Glueck's 1938–1940 Excavations at Tell el-Kheleifeh: A Reappraisal* (Atlanta: Scholars Press, 1994). Helen Glueck helped finance the book's publication.

35 *Zeitschrift des Deutschen Palästina Vereins* 57 (1934): 208–78. Frank had undertaken an extensive exploration of the Arabah, lasting for many weeks. He traveled mostly on foot with Bedouin guides, just as Glueck had done. Frank is known as the first modern explorer of the Arabah.

36 Glueck, *Rivers in the Desert: A History of the Negev* (Philadelphia: JPS, 1959), 161.

37 Gordon's description of the impact of their arrival at the tell is much more prosaic: "It was a very exciting time in my life. Nelson was fearless in his approach during the survey. There was no problem he wouldn't encounter head on. We were the only trained Orientalists in the group. We managed to cover over five hundred sites, a little too hastily," For more information on Gordon, see his autobiographical essay, *A Scholar's Odyssey: Biblical Scholarship in North America* (Atlanta: SBL, 2000).

38 Glueck argued that that the water's edge might well have receded as much as five hundred meters since Solomon's time, thus refuting Gordon's argument.

39 See N. Glueck, *BASOR* 71 (1938): 3–18; *BASOR* 72 (1938): 2–13; *BASOR* 75 (1939): 8–22; *BASOR* 79 (1940): 1–18; *BASOR* 80 (1940): 3–10; *BASOR* 82 (1941): 3–11; idem., *AASOR* 15 (1935): 26–37; 42–45;47–48; 138–39.

40 Glueck identified Timnah (Mene'iyeh) as one of Solomon's mines. He assumed that the mine at Timnah was active in the Iron II (Solomonic) period. In the 1960s the State of Israel again began extracting copper from the Timnah mines, but eventually abandoned the project when the world price for copper dropped

below the costs of its production. Timnah is some forty kilometers from the Red Sea coast.

41 *Rivers*, 164.

42 Glueck, *The Other Side of the Jordan*, 118–19.

43 Shishak's campaign ravaged the southern sites of Tell Batash (Timnah), Gezer (in the *Shefelah* — the low country southwest of Jerusalem), Tell Ma'an Tell el-Hamash, and Tell el-Saidiye.

44 Unpublished field diary from the Glueck materials in the Semitic Museum at the Harvard Divinity School, Cambridge, Massachusetts. Cf. *The Other Side of the Jordan*, 132–34.

45 The response to the publication of these articles was quite intense. Scholars were very interested in the travel and research potential of his journeys.

46 *Other Side of the Jordan*, 5.

47 From the family sheaf of letters.

48 Letter to Helen, September 8, 1939. From the family sheaf of letters.

49 Letter to Helen, September 10, 1939. From the family sheaf of letters.

50 Ibid.

51 Letter to Helen, September 14, 1939. From the family sheaf of letters.

52 Unpublished field diary from the Glueck materials in the Semitic Museum at the Harvard Divinity School, Cambridge, Massachusetts.

53 Glueck's later exploration of Nabataean sites in the Negev provided a great deal of information about the spice trade from south Arabia through the Arabah valley and on to the Mediterranean basin.

54 (Philadelphia, 1961), 112. Bentwich had volunteered for the (British) Palestine campaign in the Great War. After the British victory over the Turks, he joined the Mandatory government as its Attorney General.

55 *Hebrew Union College Monthly* (December 1940): 6.

Chapter 6: Opportunities at Home and Abroad

1 *The American Hebrew*, February 6, 1942. One of the projects that Glueck had envisioned for the UAHC was the issuing of a periodical about Reform Judaism. He considered it "an extremely important venture" and was determined that it be "first-class" from the beginning.

2 Murray Friedman, ed. *Philadelphia Jewish Life, 1940–2000*, (Philadelphia: Temple University Press, 2003), 82.

3 Bergson, working in the United States, had established a Committee for a Jewish Army just three days before the Pearl Harbor attack. He rapidly acquired influential support from politicians, artists, and non-Jewish theologians. When word of the massacre of European Jewry reached America in 1943, the Committee was transformed into the Emergency Committee to Save the Jewish People of Europe and had much influence on the decision to establish a War Refugee Board the following year. Cf. *The Jerusalem Post*, May 7, 1999, 22.

4 Followers of Ze'ev Jabotinsky.

5 *CCAR Yearbook* 52 (1942): 169–70.

6 Glueck to Freehof, March 26, 1942, posted in Miami Beach. Glueck and his family were visiting Helen's sister Josephine (Jo) and her husband David in their cottage at the time. *CCAR* Anti-Zionism Collection 1/1, MSS 435.

7 Freehof to Glueck, March 27, 1942. Ibid.

8 The phrase was originally used in 1841 by Gustavus Poznanski, the cantor of Congregation Beth Elohim in Charleston, South Carolina.

9 The correspondence quoted below is cited in Floyd Fierman's article "Nelson Glueck and the OSS during World War II," in *The Journal of Reform Judaism*, vol. 32, no. 3 (Summer, 1985): 1–20.

10 The office of Coordinator of Information had recently been established by President Roosevelt as part of the effort to get an American Secret Service up and running. When the Secret Service was moved from the president's jurisdiction to that of the military chiefs of staffs, the name was changed to OSS, the Office of Special Services. Later it became the Office of Strategic Services. The story of the COI/OSS is told in Anthony Cave Brown, *The Last Hero: Wild Bill Donovan, the Biography and Political Experience of Major General William J. Donovan, Founder of the OSS and "Father" of the CIA* (New York: Vintage Books, 1982).

11 Two of Glueck's younger brothers, Sam and Hillel, were already serving in the armed forces. Hillel had been assigned to a supply depot and Sam to the 37th Signal Corps. Reported in Nathan Revel's family newsletter, vol. 1, no. 1 (December, 1941).

12 See Beatrice L. Magnes. *Episodes: A Memoir* (Berkeley: Judah L. Magnes Museum, 1977), 98.

13 From *The Hinge of Fate*, the fourth volume of Churchill's history of the Second World War (Boston: Houghton Mifflin Company, 1950), 603.

14 Vol. 3, no. 2 (October/November, 1943): 5.

15 November 12, 1945. *Ginzei Am Olam*, Hebrew University (Givat Ram), Jerusalem.

16 See Robert St. John, *Eban* (New York: Doubleday), 1971.

17 St. John, *Eban*, 111. Unofficially, he performed "a thousand strange jobs" in connection with the training of Palmach parachutists and saboteurs.

18 Abba Eban, *An Autobiography* (New York: Random House, 1977), 54.

19 Letter to Helen, February 23, 1944, from the family sheaf of letters.

20 Ibid.

21 Letter to Helen, February 26, 1944, from the family sheaf of letters.

22 Fierman, "Nelson Glueck and the OSS," 9.

23 Ibid., 15.

24 An early associate of Donovan's in the OIC/OSS; later he become the executive vice-president of the Chase Manhattan Bank.

25 James Phinney Baxter III, at the time president of Amherst College in Massachusetts.

26 Fierman, 15.

27 Fierman, 16.

28 *BASOR*, April 1971, 6.

29 John Bagot Glubb (1897–1986), an Englishman with extensive experience in the Middle East and known as Glubb Pasha, took over the Jordanian Arab Legion in 1939 and turned it into a formidable fighting force. His Arab Legion was responsible for the conquest of the Jewish quarter of Jerusalem's Old City in 1948.

30 Fierman, 17.

31 Ibid.

32 Letter to an official of the JDC, August 4, 1946. Folder 2512 in the Magnes collection, *Ginzei Am Olam*, Jerusalem.

33 Fierman, 19.

34 The suspicion about archaeologists serving as spies persisted into the era of the Cold War. In 1986, Reuben Bullard, professor at the Cincinnati Bible Seminary and the University of Cincinnati, signed on as a member of an American expedition to search for Noah's ark on Mount Ararat. The team was denied permission to enter the country by the Turkish government, and Bullard suspects it was because the presence of Americans in those mountains would make the Soviets edgy. "The Secret Life of Nelson Glueck: Author, Scholar, Rabbi, and Spy." *Tristate Magazine*, Sunday, January 11, 1987, 5.

35 Philip J. King, *American Archaeology in the Middle East* (Philadelphia: ASOR, 1983) 103, n. 19.

36 According to Alfred Gottschalk, Glueck's successor as president of HUC-JIR, Philip King's comments about Glueck were politically motivated — Glueck had tried to incorporate ASOR into his plans to build a school of archaeology in Jerusalem, and many of the "old-timers," some anti-Zionist and some perhaps even antisemitic, objected. It was this takeover plan that brought on the negative comments about Glueck. Conversation with Jonathan Brown in Cincinnati, February 26, 1997.

37 Alex Joffe, professor of archaeology at Penn State University, noted that any number of American archaeologists offered their services or were recruited by the OSS, including Carlton Coon, Henry Field, and Gordon Loud. From comments submitted to the authors on January 22, 1996 at a seminar on Glueck held at Penn State.

38 From the family sheaf of letters.

39 A. J. Sherman, *Mandate Days: British Lives in Palestine 1918–1948* (N.Y.: Thames and Hudson, 1998), 182–84.

40 Norman Bentwich, *My Seventy-Seven Years* (Philadelphia: JPS, 1961) 112.

41 Correspondence with Jonathan Brown, May, 1996.

42 Ibid.

43 Published by Westminster Press for the Jewish Publication Society of America, Philadelphia, 1946.

Chapter 7: A New Career Beckons

1 Michael A. Meyer, "A Centennial History," in Karff, *HUC-JIR at One Hundred Years* (Cincinnati: HUC Press, 1976), 135–36.

2 The story of the Jewish Institute of Religion is detailed in Michael A. Meyer, "Kelal Yisrael: The Jewish Institute of Religion," in Karff, op. cit., 37–69. Stephen S. Wise was born in Budapest in 1874 and came to a America as a young child. He graduated from Columbia University in 1892 and considered coming to HUC to train for the rabbinate but was reluctant to leave the East Coast. He was eventually ordained privately and made a significant impact on the spiritual and organizational Jewish life of New York. He helped found both the American Jewish Congress and the World Jewish Congress. In the early 1920s, he founded the Jewish Institute of Religion as a non-Orthodox alternative for those who found HUC "too Reform."

3 Family sheaf of letters.

4 Meyer, "A Centennial History," 172.

5 Conversation with Jonathan Brown, January 1995.

6 Prominent Reform rabbi (Cleveland), Zionist leader, spokesperson for American Jewry. Ordained at HUC in 1915.

7 Prominent Reform rabbi (Pittsburgh), profound scholar and great speaker. Ordained at HUC in 1915.

8 Prominent Reform rabbi (Boston), effective preacher, and thoughtful writer. Ordained at HUC in 1930. He served as rabbi of Temple Israel in Boston for 18 years, before his untimely death in 1948.

9 Rabbi, intellectual, and gifted administrator. Ordained at HUC in 1926.

10 Meyer, "A Centennial History," 175.

11 Snyder's letter, which was "not to be released from the [American Jewish] Archives during the lifetime of Nelson or Helen Glueck," contains the following information: "The Alumni [Association] Executive Committee met in the college dormitory the day before the meeting of the HUC Board of Governors at which a new President would be elected. The alumni devoted several hours to analyzing the needs of the college and its future, and seeking someone who would be a recognized leader among Jews. Many names were submitted and posted on the blackboard, including those of Jacob R. Marcus, Abba Hillel Silver, Solomon Freehof, Joshua Loth Liebman, Abram Sachar, and Nelson Glueck. Several closed ballots were held. At this point Abraham Feldman, president of the Alumni Association, interrupted the session with the following statement: 'Mrs. Sulzberger has selected the next president, and tomorrow the Board of Governors will elect him. There was no need for us to meet.' The alumni were shocked. None of the candidates had received fewer votes than Nelson Glueck." Miscellaneous file, small collection 3981, JRM center, AJA.

12 Meyer, "A Centennial History," 175–76.

13 Irving Aaron Mandel, Class of 1947. Letter to Jonathan Brown, July 22, 1999.

14 *American Israelite* 94, 6 (March 11, 1948): 14.

15 ASOR *Newsletter*, January 19, 1947.

16 Isaac Mayer Wise was president from 1875–1900; Moses Mielziner was appointed interim president from 1900–1903, Kaufmann Kohler presided from

1903–1921, and Julian Morgenstern from 1921–1947.

17 Woolf was mistaken about Morgenstern, who did not have a beard and certainly didn't look patriarchal.

18 From the article by S. J. Woolf in the *New York Times*, May 9, 1947, 51.

19 Eleanor Bisbee was professor of philosophy at Robert College and the American College for Girls in Istanbul. She wrote a book called *The New Turks: Pioneers of the Republic* (Philadelphia: Greenwood Press, 1951) She had arrived in Turkey in 1936. July 25, 1947. Box A1a 1947/8. AJA.

20 A letter to Magnes on Feb. 2, 1947 tells of a poignant reunion between the exhausted Glueck and his young son, who was yearning for paternal attention: "I got home on the morning of Jan. 24th and was met at our suburban station of Winton Place by Helen and Charles and Mrs. I [glauer — Helen's mother]. It was wonderful getting back to my family again. I was desperately tired and so when Charles asked me to wrestle with him, I asked to be excused. He began to cry, saying that he had waited for months for me to come home and wrestle with him. I saw Helen urging me with a look to go ahead and wrestle so I said that I would love to wrestle. He had a grand time, and I let him get me down, which made him feel wonderful. Since then I have had to box or wrestle with him every night." From the family sheaf of letters.

21 Ibid., August 3, 1947.

22 Ibid., September 26, 1947. Scholem's letter, dated September, 6, had begun: "They told me yesterday — it would seem that I am living 'outside this world' — about your elevation to the presidency of the Hebrew Union College."

23 *American Israelite*, March 11, 1948, 3.

24 Morris Schulzinger, *The Tale of a Litvak* (New York: Philosophical Library, 1985), 332–33.

25 Statistical information provided by Alan Silverstein in: *Alternatives to Assimilation: the Response of Reform Judaism to American Culture, 1840–1930* (Hanover, New Hampshire: University Press of New England, 1994), 158.

26 Daniel Syme, "The Growth of the Hebrew Union College-Jewish Institute of Religion in the United States and Abroad," unpublished rabbinical thesis (HUC-JIR, Cincinnati), 1972, 83.

27 Ibid.

28 October 12, 1947. Box A1A 1947/8, Glueck: General Correspondence, AJA.

29 E-mail from Rabbi Sanford Rosen, July 14, 1999.

30 Richard Scheuer, long-time HUC Board member and great friend of the Gluecks, said that these fellowships were a crucial feature of Glueck's presidency, as they enabled Christians to learn in a Jewish environment, and then teach at Christian seminaries all over the United States. Glueck's appearance on Bishop Pike's radio program (1956) and participation in a Forum on Judeo-Christian Concepts at the Cooper Union (1961) are but a few of the many ways in which he expressed his deep concern for interfaith relations.

31 The weekend began on Friday morning with a service in the HUC Chapel,

followed by a symposium on the topic "The Future of Torah in America," chaired by Jacob Marcus. An afternoon symposium dealt with "The Preservation of American Judaism: Can the Synagogue meet the crisis?"

32 K. K. Bene Israel, founded in 1824, which had played a significant role in the history of Cincinnati's Reform Jewry.

33 Liebman did not live out the year. Glueck preached a Rosh Hashanah sermon in his memory that year at Liebman's Temple in Boston.

34 *Hebrew Union College Inauguration Volume* (March 1948), 108.

35 Ibid., 135.

36 Ibid., 126.

37 Ibid., 128.

38 A group of scholars working over a period of some thousand years (ca. 500 C.E.–1500 C. E.), whose responsibility was the proper vocalization of the Hebrew text of the Torah. Cf. *The Oxford Dictionary of the Jewish Religion* (New York / Oxford, 1997), 445.

39 *Inauguration Volume*, 129.

40 Ibid.

41 Ibid., 130.

42 Ibid., 132–33.

43 Ibid., 141.

44 Conversation between Rabbi Albert Plotkin and Jonathan Brown, Pittsburgh, Pennsylvania, May 23, 1999.

Chapter 8: Academic Growth and Institutional Challenges 1947–1952

1 Among those whom he had initially approached to become president of JIR were Rabbi Emil G. Hirsch of Chicago, Israel Abrahams, a renowned scholar from England, and Rabbi Mordecai Kaplan, who, as a New York rabbi, would not have had to relocate as would the others. They all declined. In the 1940s none of the scores of Institute alumni were interested either. Wise would be the only president an independent JIR would ever have.

2 The details of a variety of efforts to cooperate, or even consolidate the two institutions can be found in Meyer, "A Centennial History," in Karff, ed. *HUC-JIR at One Hundred Years* (Cincinnati: HUC Press, 1976), 164–68.

3 By the 1930s many in the Reform movement were deeply sympathetic to Zionism, but Cincinnati was still the center of classical Reform, to which Zionism was anathema.

4 May 16, 1947.

5 HUC-JIR "Statement of Purpose." February 1, 1948. Box 159, JRM Center, AJA, Cincinnati. Quoted in Meyer, *A Centennial History*, 168.

6 The HUC Board of Governors meeting of May 1949 noted the passing of the man who had contributed so much to the diversity of the American rabbinate and personally to the well-being of Jews around the world.

7 Memo from Marcus to Glueck, Dec. 28, 1955. Folder 1/8, MSS. 160, AJA.

8 Cf. Michael A. Meyer, "From Cincinnati to New York: A Symbolic Move," in *The Jewish Condition: Essays on Contemporary Judaism Honoring Rabbi Alexander M. Schindler,* Aron Hirt-Manheimer, ed. (New York: UAHC Press, 1995), 302–13.

9 Ibid., 305.

10 Ibid., 310.

11 Ibid.

12 Ibid., 310–11.

13 *Liberal Judaism,* October, 1948: 40. Quoted in Avi M. Schulman, *Like a Raging Fire: A Biography of Maurice N. Eisendrath* (New York: UAHC Press, 1993), 36.

14 *The Jewish Condition,* 306.

15 "The Future of American Judaism," a lecture given in Lexington, Kentucky in 1952. American Jewish Archives Tape No. 495. Quoted in Daniel Syme, "The Growth of HUC-JIR in the U.S. and Abroad," 106.

16 Ben Gurion, Yigael Yadin, Moshe Dayan, Golda Meir, and many others.

17 Daniel Syme, The "Growth," 108.

18 Dated September 1, 1950. Glueck Correspondence Ala 11, 1950, MSS 160, AJA.

19 New York: Schocken Books, 1948.

20 The address is quoted in Wolfgang Hamburger, "Teacher in Berlin and Cincinnati," in *Leo Baeck Institute Year Book* 2 (1957): 32–33. The students were grateful for Baeck's presence among them and for his guidance; upon his return to London in the summer of 1952 they elected him honorary president of the student association.

21 Meyer, *A Centennial History,* 221.

22 As he wrote to a friend and generous supporter of HUC, Edmund Kaufman, vacationing in Lake Placid, "It will be a very large and scientific and deadly dull double volume." Kaufman may have thought otherwise, for the very next year he donated $5,000 to the College. Sept. 16, 1949. Glueck correspondence, Folder Ala 10 (1949) Box 160, AJA.

Chapter 9: Glueck and Eisendrath: Enmity in Velvet Gloves

1 Avi M. Schulman, *Like a Raging Fire: A Biography of Maurice N. Eisendrath* (N.Y.: UAHC Press) 19–20.

2 Ibid., 31.

3 Judah L. Magnes Collection, Folder 223, Ginzei Am Olam, Jerusalem.

4 August 1, 1929. Maurice Eisendrath Collection, 5/4, MSS 167, AJA.

5 From the Proceedings of the Union of American Hebrew Congregations, Seventy-seventh through Eightieth Annual Reports, edited by Rabbi Louis Egelson, 510.

6 Ibid., 163.

7 Schulman, *Like a Raging Fire,* 46.

8 Michael A. Meyer, "A Centennial History," in Karff, ed., *HUC-JIR at One Hundred Years* (Cincinnati: HUC Press, 1976), 201–2.

9 Ibid.

10 Vorspan, a layman, was one of the primary movers in establishing the Religious

Action Center in Washington, DC, and the co-author of several textbooks designed to bring the prophetic mandate of *tikkun olam*, "repairing the world," into the synagogues, homes, and lives of Reform Jews.

11 *Like a Raging Fire*, ii.

12 Ibid., 84.

13 Ibid., 47.

14 Ibid., 48.

15 June 4, 1964. From Appendix M to the HUC-JIR Board of Governors minutes of June 4, 1964, Manuscript Collection #30, Section B, AJA, Cincinnati.

16 January 30, 1964. Ibid., Appendix C.

17 Maurice Eisendrath Collection, 5/4, MSS 167, AJA.

18 A few years later, Barnett's son Rabbi Balfour Brickner initiated an inquiry as to why Nelson Glueck was chosen to give the Inaugural benediction for John F. Kennedy rather than Eisendrath. The respondent did not believe that Eisendrath was considered, but "perhaps he should have been." Letter from Myer Feldman, Deputy Special Counsel to the President to Rabbi Brickner, January 24, 1961. Glueck Correspondence, JRM Center, AJA, Cincinnati.

19 Quoted in *Like a Raging Fire*, 48.

20 Glueck to Eisendrath, September 12, 1958 Maurice Eisendrath Collection, 5/4, MSS 167, AJA.

21 Glueck to Eisendrath, ibid., October 5, 1961.

22 Glueck to Eisendrath, ibid., June 6, 1962.

23 Eisendrath to Glueck, ibid., June 7, 1962.

24 Eisendrath to Glueck, ibid., July 10, 1963.

25 Eisendrath to Glueck, June 28, 1963. Glueck correspondence 1/1m A-K (General) MSS 160, AJA.

26 *Like a Raging Fire*, 63.

27 Ibid., 64.

28 All the quotations are excerpted from a letter written by Glueck to Rabbi Hillel Cohn on January 23, 1964. In the possession of Jonathan Brown.

29 November 29, 1963, p. 51, quoted in *Like a Raging Fire*, 64.

30 Cincinnati: Hebrew Union College Press, 1968.

31 *Like a Raging Fire*, 49.

32 Schulman calls their rivalry "a mixed blessing for the Reform movement. . . . Although Glueck and Eisendrath's bitter struggle for supremacy polarized and demoralized the lay leadership, their intense institutional competition spurred the growth of their respective institutions." Ibid., 49.

Chapter 10: Surveying the Negev

1 After the turmoil in Palestine between 1936 and 1939, Glueck could no longer consider such a suggestion practical. And after 1947 his attention was focused on the much more realizable dream of obtaining the Negev as part of the Jewish state.

2 In fact, Glueck never did return to either site. Nearly sixty years after he began his excavations at Khirbet et-Tannur, an Israeli Ph.D. student in archaeology, Deborah Hershman, journeyed there with photographer Tal Glick and wrote an article for the Israeli journal *Masa Aḥer* (June 1998) about Glueck's original visit to the site. Laurence Kutler attempted in July 1999 to visit Tell el-Kheleifeh, which is guarded by Jordanian military authorities, but he was not successful.

3 Glueck, *Rivers in the Desert: The History of the Negev* (New York: Jewish Publication Society, 1959), 15. In a review in *The Christian World,* George Landes suggested that the subtitle was "overreaching." In the absence of literary records and chronologies, no "history" can be written. However, if the term was meant to convey a narrative stemming from careful analysis of archaeological and epigraphic material, with the purpose of fitting the Negev in its place against the background of general Palestinian history — such a history was now possible.

4 Sde Boker is the kibbutz to which Ben-Gurion and his wife Paula retired. Later, it became a center of research focusing upon the development of arid areas.

5 At the time, a small Israeli outpost on the northern shore of the Gulf of Aqaba.

6 *Rivers in the Desert,* 22.

7 Ibid., xiii.

8 From *Orḥim be-yisrael* (Guests in Israel), *Ma'ariv,* July 31, 1953.

9 Also cited by Michael A. Meyer, "A Centennial History," in Karff, ed., *HUC-JIR at One Hundred Years* (Cincinnati: HUC Press, 1976), 279–80, n. 97.

10 New York: Putnam, 1961.

11 p. 16.

12 Gordon's statement is based on Morris, *Masters,* 384–87.

13 Lowdermilk's book *Palestine: Land of Promise,* was immediately accepted as impressive proof of the viability of the Negev for the substantial settlement of immigrants. Even then U.S. Vice-President Henry Wallace read Lowdermilk's original report and noted, in a speech given on October 31, 1940: "In reading Dr. Lowdermilk's report I was convinced that the material foundations of Zion were very real and deep indeed" (quoted on the book's dust jacket).

14 Ibid., 195.

15 London: no publisher listed, 1915. The report was sponsored by the Palestine Exploration Fund.

16 Lowdermilk, *Land of Promise,* 197–98.

17 The IES was founded as the Jewish Palestine Exploration Society in 1914.

18 Glueck's remarks are taken from *Eilat: The Eighteenth Archaeological Convention, October, 1962* [Hebrew] (Jerusalem: Israel Exploration Society, 1963), 7–20. The English translation is by Laurence Kutler.

   Glueck noted that the Brook of Egypt (Wadi el-Arish) is definitely listed in the Bible as the southwestern-most boundary of Judah; cf. Joshua 15:4, 47, and Numbers 34:4, 5.

19 The information in the preceding paragraphs can be found in Michael Feige, "Identity, Ritual and Pilgrimage: The Meetings of the Israel Exploration Society,"

in Deborah Dash Moore and S. Ilan Troen, eds., *Divergent Jewish Culture: Israel and America* (New Haven and London: Yale University Press, 2001), 87–106.

20 For ultra-Orthodox Jews the re-establishment of a sovereign Jewish state was a messianic task, not to be undertaken by human hands alone. The resident Jewish population in Palestine in the nineteenth century was primarily composed of these ultra-Orthodox families living in the four holy cities of Jerusalem, Safed, Tiberias, and Hebron, with the men studying Talmud and their families sustained by charity from abroad. The system was called *halukah*, and was funded by messengers who traveled on behalf of the communities of scholars, raising money for their own expenses, and sending the remainder back to Palestine. It was predicated on the idea that constant study, of itself, would hasten the advent of the Messiah.

21 David Ben-Gurion, *Memoirs* (Cleveland: World Publishing Company, 1970), 121.

22 Ibid., 131.

23 Rothenberg met Glueck in the early 1950s and served as photographer on Glueck's Negev excursions. For details of his archaeological conflict with Glueck, see chap. 11.

24 *Rivers in the Desert*, 23.

25 From the story of Sinuhe and Egyptian Execration texts.

26 *River in the Desert*, 105–9.

27 C. R. Conder and H. H. Kitchener, 1881.

28 *Eretz-Israel: Archaeological, Historical and Geographical Studies* (Nelson Glueck Memorial Volume) (Jerusalem: Israel Exploration Society, 1975) x.

29 Presumably he meant as a gift to one of his benefactors in return for a large contribution to the College-Institute.

30 Anecdote related to Jonathan Brown via e-mail from Sanford Ragins in July 1998.

31 Conversation with Laurence Kutler in Jerusalem, November, 1995.

32 Gitin was ordained at HUC Cincinnati in 1961, earned his Ph.D. in Syro-Palestinian Archaeology at HUC Cincinnati in 1980, and was appointed head of the American Schools (now the Albright Institute) that same year. He distinguished himself during his work at Gezer and more recently at Tel Miqne (biblical Ekron), one of the cities of the Philistine pentapolis along with Ashkelon, Gath, Gaza, and Ashdod.

33 Gitin studied archaeology with Glueck in 1968–1969 and with Bill Dever in 1969–1970, during the Gezer excavations sponsored by HUC-BAS. Glueck offered him the following advice: "If you want to be an archaeologist, you must either be born rich or marry rich." Conversation with Laurence Kutler in Jerusalem, July, 1999.

Chapter 11: *Tell el-Kheleifeh Refined 1952–1963*

1 See the comments of Yigael Yadin, "Nelson Glueck: A Memorial Address" in *Eretz Yisrael*, vol. 12 (Jerusalem: Israel Exploration Society, 1975).

2 The authors have in their possession a letter from the German philosopher and

social critic Theodor Adorno, written to Gershom Scholem of the Hebrew University, dated April 4, 1960, flatly denying that Beno Rothenberg ever completed the requirements for a German Ph.D., as Rothenberg had claimed.

3 For a thorough discussion of these matters, see "Edomites Advance into Judah" in *Biblical Archaeology Review,* 22, 6 (November/December, 1986): 35. The author, Itzhaq Beit-Arieh, suggests that if the structure at Tell el-Kheleifeh was a fortress, it might have been part of a Judaean fortress system. The purpose of the system would have been to provide protection against Edomite raids during a period when the Edomite kingdom was expanding toward Judaean territory. See also G. Pratico, "A Reappraisal of Nelson Glueck's Excavations at Tell el-Kheleifeh," *ASOR Newsletter* 6, 6–11 (1983) and his monograph *Nelson Glueck's 1938–1940 Excavations at Tell-el Kheleifeh* (Philadelphia: Scholar's Press [ASOR Archaeological Reports no. 3], 1983).

4 N. Glueck, *Explorations in Eastern Palestine* II, 42 ff.

5 See N. Glueck, "The Third Season of Excavation at Tell el-Kheleifeh," *BASOR* 79, 2–18. See also Beno Rothenberg, *The Egyptian Mining Temple at Timna* (London: Institute for Archaeo-Metallurgical Studies, 1988), 7 ff.

6 The discovery of the Ramesside mining temple dedicated to the Egyptian goddess Hathor was a turning point in the history of Arabah research. The identification of the industry as Egyptian, using local inhabitants as workers (Midianites from northwest Arabia and Amalekites from the Negev mountains) led to fundamental changes in the cultural-historical concepts concerning the area adjacent to Elath.

7 Seymour Gitin recalls reading a letter in the Glueck archives in which Albright chides Glueck for giving in to Rothenberg so easily. Conversation with Laurence Kutler in Jerusalem, July 1999.

8 Laurence Kutler conversation with Rothenberg in Tel Aviv, July 1997. In *Dateline Jerusalem: A Diary* (p. 109), Glueck described Perrot as a great prehistoric archaeologist. During the 1960s Perrot was head of the French Archaeological Mission in Israel, prior to reporting to a new assignment as head of the French Mission in Iran.

9 Conversation of Yosef Aviram with Laurence Kutler, July 2003.

10 From a letter in G. Ernest Wright archives at the Harvard Divinity School Library, Cambridge, MA.

11 Letter from Glueck to Gerrish sent on February 19, 1963. G. Ernest Wright Archives.

12 N. Glueck, "Etzion-Geber," *The Biblical Archaeologist* 28, 3 (September 1965): 70–87.

13 Note the editor's comment that introduces the article: "Glueck's new ideas on the matter are extremely important, and they demonstrate a capacity to change cherished convictions gracefully."

14 Abba Eban, *My People: The Story of the Jews* (NY: Behrman House and Random House, 1968), 33.

15 *The Biblical Archaeologist* 22, 4 (1959): 98–100. The first was Albright's work at

Tell Beit Mirsim which was, of course, the place where Glueck first experienced the wonders and the arduous nature of archaeology.

16 Amichai Mazar (son of Binyamin, also an archaeologist of note), a member of the younger generation of Israeli archaeologists found a way to sustain Glueck's original conclusions as late as 1992 in his book *Archaeology and the Land of the Bible: 10,000–586 B.C.E.* (New York: Doubleday and Company, 1992).

Chapter 12: At the Helm 1953–1963

1 Daniel Syme, "The Growth of the Hebrew Union College-Jewish Insitute of Religion in the U.S. and Abroad" (Unpublished rabbinical thesis, 1972), 110. Syme recalled an incident from his years at HUC (Cincinnati), when he had been scheduled to conduct the chapel services but gave up his time to accommodate a guest speaker. Afterwards, Glueck accosted the flustered student, accused him of "dereliction of duty," and required him to conduct services with Glueck as his only congregant that same afternoon.

2 Folder 1/10, MSS. 160. AJA.

3 A fuller account can be found in Meyer, "A Centennial History," in Karff, ed. *HUC-JIR at One Hundred Years* (Cincinnati: HUC Press, 1976), 187–90.

4 In general Glueck reacted very negatively to threats; discussions with student groups were regularly terminated when even an implied threat was uttered, but with regard to the New York School, as determined as Glueck was, he was no match for the equally determined Reform rabbinate of New York City. Despite the solution that had been reached, the New York school remained a step-child. The faculty in New York was allowed to grow only slightly, the number of rabbinical students was deliberately limited, and capital expenditures were approved only for the "utmost necessities." Neither Paul Steinberg, other faculty, nor the students themselves ever felt that the New York School was on a par with Cincinnati. Cf. Meyer, ibid. 190.

5 Polier's letter begins: "Your form letter of February 12th . . . was received by me." Polier to Glueck, Glueck correspondence: Office of the President A1a 98, (1953–1962) MSS 160, AJA.

6 Glueck correspondece, JRM Center, AJA, Cincinnati.

7 Glueck correspondence, JRM Center, AJA, Cincinnati.

8 The faculty for whom Sheldon Blank was responsible numbered twelve full-time members in 1948. By the time Glueck died, in 1971, there were nearly forty full-time teachers at the three American campuses. Most of them were rabbis who had been ordained at the College, and some had received their doctorates there.

9 He was chosen for the position primarily because of his knowledge of American academic life, but his contacts in the scholarly world and his administrative abilities would also prove valuable assets. He served as provost for ten years.

10 *HUC-JIR Bulletin*, vol. 10, no. 1, 6–9.

11 Syme, "Growth," 131.

12 Minutes of the Board meeting of January 22, 1958, Appendix. Quoted in Syme, "Growth," 128.

13 From the family sheaf of letters.

14 Family lore recalled by Jonathan Brown.

15 The staff of the new library was headed by Herbert Zafren (1925–2005). One of Glueck's first initiatives vis-à-vis the library in its new facility was to ask Zafren to co-ordinate the holdings of both HUC and JIR, and to link them in significant ways, so that students in either branch could access books and other materials from either library. Glueck took a serious interest in the library and sent thoughtful memos to Zafren and to his counterpart at the Jewish Institute of Religion, Dr. I. Edward Kiev. In 1966, Zafren was appointed director of libraries, while maintaining responsibility for the Klau facility on the Cincinnati campus.

16 Vol. 1, no. 1 (January, 1961), 3.

17 Glueck: General Correspondence. A1a 98 (1953–1962), MSS 160, AJA.

18 Syme, "Growth," 102–3.

19 The first ordination of Reform rabbis in California took place on May 8, 2002, at the Wilshire Boulevard Temple. Eight students — five women and three men — were ordained under a *huppah* (wedding canopy) created for the occasion.

20 Jonathan Brown conversation with Alfred Gottschalk, February 1996.

21 *HUC-JIR Bulletin* 10, 2 (January, 1958).

22 One of the faculty members whom Glueck had recruited in Jerusalem, and brought back to Cincinnati to tutor the students and to teach Hebrew literature and mysticism, Arie Kahana, committed suicide in the spring of 1963, shortly after his employment was not renewed. Glueck made a special effort to meet with all the students who were close to Dr. Kahana to try to help them understand the circumstances of his death.

23 Nelson Glueck. "Remarks on the Assassination of President John F. Kennedy," Cincinnati, November 22, 1963," JRM Center, AJA, Tape No. 205. Quoted in Syme, "Growth," 147. Kennedy's death created a difficult situation for student rabbi Roger Herst, who learned about the event while en route to his student congregation in Rome, Georgia. Herst scrapped the sermon he had planned, and instead gave a glowing tribute to the martyred president. After services, the congregation's president severely criticized him for eulogizing a man for whom hardly anyone in Rome, Georgia had anything good to say. Herst was asked to take the morning train back to Cincinnati, and not to return to Rome. When Herst reported this situation to Glueck on Monday, Glueck asked for the phone numbers of the leaders of the congregation. The next day he invited Herst back into his study and told him the problem had been resolved; he had simply stated to the president of the congregation that if Herst did not return, HUC would never provide them with a student rabbi again. Herst later published an account of that experience under the title "A Roman Incident" in *Moment* magazine, February, 2000, 41f.

24 Nelson Glueck. Interview with Ruth Lyons on the WLW 50–50 Club. Cincinnati,

December 20, 1963, JRM Center, AJA, Tape No. 495. Quoted in Syme, "Growth," ibid.

25 There was, however, a precedent. On October 15, 1951, Rabbi Louis Finkelstein, head of the Jewish Theological Seminary, appeared on the cover of TIME, looking very much like the rabbi and scholar that he was, and about whom the editors wrote: "Dr. Finkelstein is the leader of perhaps the most influential school of Jewish theology in the United States today." Quoted in Jack Wertheimer, *Tradition Renewed: A History of the Jewish Theological Seminary* (New York: JTS, 1997), vol. 1, 185.

Chapter 13: Establishing a Foothold in Jerusalem: 1948–1963

1 Psalm 118:22

2 According to the 2004 exhibit "Petra: Lost City of Stone" at the Cincinnati Art Museum, these included the Baltimore Hebrew University, the Claremont Graduate School, Duke University, the Garrett Theological Seminary, and the University of Southern California, among others.

3 In the 1990s, for example, more than fifty major sites were excavated every summer. (Cf. *Biblical Archaeology Review* 26, 10 [January/ February 2000]: 26–43.)

4 While it was theoretically possible for an Orthodox Jew to participate in an archaeological excavation that did not require working on the Sabbath or eating non-kosher food, the Orthodox attitude toward archaeology and archaeologists was decidedly antagonistic. Some of the archaeological findings challenged traditional understanding of the biblical text and even the existence of cherished figures like David and Solomon, and the uncovering of human remains required complex procedures for exhumation and reburial that would have paralyzed any archaeological work for weeks at a time.

5 Sharett had read Glueck's published work and had been quite impressed.

6 Having been invited to the dedication exercises for HUC-BAS in 1963, Ben-Zvi declined to attend, but agreed to host the honorary degree recipients. That was his last public function; he died a few weeks later, within the first year of his third term as president.

7 Tractate B'rachot (blessings) 8a. Ben Zvi further noted that the matter is discussed in related sources identifying dolphins as "fish of the sea, half of which are in human form and half in the form of fish." A1a, Folder B, Glueck correspondence, MSS 160, AJA.

8 Quoted in Daniel Syme, "Growth of the Hebrew Union College-Jewish Institute of Religion in the U.S. and Abroad," (unpublished rabbinical thesis, 1972), 108.

9 Ibid., 113.

10 Ariel Stone, "Im Tirtzu Ein Zo Aggadah: The History of HUC-JIR in Jerusalem" (unpublished manuscript, 1993), 11. A week later, Prime Minister Sharett wrote to Glueck of his "very great satisfaction" in reading of "the establishment of the Jerusalem branch of the Hebrew Union College."

11 Stone, "Im Tirtzu," 13.

12 Ibid., 15.

13 Ibid.

14 Syme, "Growth," 16.

15 Teddy Kollek later claimed that he personally had arranged for the sale of the property, though in fact he had had nothing to do with it. Amos Kollek and Teddy Kollek, *For Jerusalem: A Life* (New York: Behrman House, 1978), 110.

16 Many years later, Alfred Gottschalk noted that Herzl had visited Palestine in 1904 and stayed in a house on Mamilla Street just below the site of HUC-BAS. There, Gottschalk found a photo of "five distinguished gentlemen, each dressed in a tuxedo with white tie, standing on a piece of property strangely similar to the one we are on today, facing the Tower of David. It was a photograph of Theodor Herzl and four other members of the World Zionist Organization . . . . They were looking to the new Jerusalem. As are we." Stone, "Im Tirtzu," 286.

17 Syme, "Growth," 119. The concepts of a resident director and annual professor were no doubt patterned after the arrangements Glueck had experienced at ASOR.

18 Ibid.

19 Quoted in Stone, "Im Tirtzu," 20.

20 Ibid., 26.

21 Ibid., 122.

22 *CCAR Journal* 11,3 (October 1969): 13.

23 Evidently this was not an uncommon tactic for Israeli contractors who had a dispute with those responsible for a project.

24 The pressure which Glueck had to exert to obtain Fefferman was quite extraordinary. But he finally agreed to work with Glueck and later indicated his pleasure at having been involved with the project. Stone, "Im Tirtzu," 61.

25 Melamede's father had served in the Mandatory government and also with the Jewish state as a civil servant. Her uncle was Dr. Epstein, with whom Glueck had studied Hebrew when he first arrived in Palestine in the fall of 1927.

26 Quoted in Stone, "Im Tirtzu," 69.

27 Nelson Glueck, "The Role of the Hebrew Union College in Jerusalem," *CCAR Journal* (October 7, 1963): 10. Quoted in Syme, "Growth," 139–40.

28 Ibid., 12.

29 Ibid.

30 Ibid., 13–14. Quoted in Syme, *"Growth,"* 140–41.

31 Stone, "Im Tirtzu," 69.

32 Ibid., 70. Non-Orthodox rabbis may officiate at Jewish weddings in Israel, but there must be an Orthodox rabbi in attendance to sign the *ketubah* and record the event for the religious authorities. An interfaith ceremony is not permitted, and Israelis wishing to marry in a civil ceremony must go outside the country for such a ceremony.

33 Stone, "Im Tirtzu," 72.

34 HUC-BAS was not a primary sponsor of this excavation, but was invited to participate along with other interested institutions.

35 Quoted in Stone, "Im Tirtzu," 71.

36 A student of Albright in the 1940s, Frank Moore Cross Jr. achieved an international reputation for his expertise in Northwest Semitic languages. Cross served as ASOR president from 1974–1976.

37 Albright had initially been appointed as the first archaeological director of HUC-BAS (1961–1962), but due to the construction delays he could not take the position and spent the year lecturing in Cincinnati instead.

38 Neither Jews nor non-Jews could enter Jordan from Israel if there was an Israeli stamp on their passport.

39 The first book brought out by the group was Albright's *The Biblical Period from Abraham to Ezra* (New York: Harper & Brothers, 1949).

40 London: SCM Press, 1956.

41 In 1959, John Bright published *A History of Israel* (Philadelphia: Westminster Press, 1959).

42 In 1956, Jacob Epstein, the young and energetic founding editor of Anchor Books, had approached Albright about a series of brief introductions to the books of the Bible. It was intended to be a project of interdenominational scope, assigned to scholars who could present to Doubleday works that would be devoid of any religious and theological underpinnings. Each volume in the series would be prefaced by introductory archaeological, theological and philological background on the book. Albright agreed to the project only if David Noel Freedman would do the editorial work. Freedman agreed, but thought it best to use the members of the Colloquium as the authors of the project. See Burke O. Long, *The Planting and Reaping of Albright: Politics, Ideology, and Interpreting the Bible* (University Park, PA: Penn State University Press, 1997), 60.

43 Interview of Freedman by Dr. Laurence Kutler, fall 1999.

44 Burke O. Long, *Planting*, 59.

45 William Dever and H. Darrell Lance, both Harvard graduate students, were in search of an archaeological project. Wright suggested Gezer as a site in need of re-excavation. After the first season, when Wright served as field director, he relinquished the post to Dever, who became director, with Lance as associate director. Under their joint leadership the first phase of the new excavations at Gezer continued through 1971. See Philip J. King, *American Archaeology in the Middle East* (New Haven: ASOR, 1983), 168.

46 A member of the Gezer staff suggested that the fortification may have been erected in response to either Hyksos or Amorite aggression about 1750 B.C.E.–1700 B.C.E.

47 See William Dever, "Excavations at Gezer," in *Biblical Archaeologist* 30, 2 (1967): 53–62 and "Further Excavations at Gezer, 1967–1971 in *The Biblical Archaeologist* 34, 4 (1971: 94–132. See also W. G. Dever, H. Darrell Lance, G. Ernest Wright, *Preliminary Report of the 1964–66 Seasons* (Jerusalem, HUC-BAS, 1970) and W. G. Dever, *Gezer II Report of the 1967–70 Seasons in Fields I and II* (Jerusalem,

HUC-BAS, 1974). Also Seymour Gitin, *Gezer III- A Ceramic Typology of the Late Iron II, Persian and Hellenistic Periods at Tell Gezer* (Jerusalem: HUC/NGSBA, 1990) J. D. Seger, *Gezer V: The Field I Caves* (Jerusalem: HUC/NGSBA, 1988); and W. G. Dever, principal author and ed., *Gezer IV: The 1969–71 Seasons in Field VI, "The Acropolis"* (Jerusalem: NGSBA, 1986).

Chapter 14: Issues and Events 1964–1970

1 Jonathan D. Sarna and Nancy H. Klein, *The Jews of Cincinnati* (Cincinnati: Center for the Study of the Jewish Experience, 1989), 150.
2 Albert J. Slomovitz, *The Fighting Rabbis: Jewish Military Chaplains and American History* (New York and London: New York University Press, 1999), 18.
3 "Escape from Turpitude, in Which a Class Encounters the Chaplaincy." In *variant* 4,3 (1964): 23–30.
4 Daniel Syme, "The Growth of the Hebrew Union College-Jewish Institute of Religion in the United States and Abroad." Unpublished rabbinical thesis (HUC-JIR, Cincinnati, 1972), 44.
5 HUC-JIR Board of Governors Meeting, 1966.
6 Michael A. Meyer, "A Centennial History," in Karff, *HUC-JIR at One Hundred Years* (Cincinnati: Hebrew Union College Press, 1976), 231.
7 Ibid.
8 Syme, "Growth," 149.
9 Addendum, Minutes of the Board of Governor's Meeting, Report of the President, February 2, 1967, 1–3.
10 Meyer, "Centennial History," 282, n. 139.
11 This description of Glueck at Charlevoix, slightly edited, was prepared by Barbara Glueck and submitted to the authors on April 7, 1997.
12 See chap. 7, 115–16.
13 Meyer, "Centennial History," 224.
14 Addendum A, President's Report to the Board of Governors, February 8, 1968, 4.
15 She had only one rabbinical predecessor, Regina Jonas (1902–1944), ordained in Nazi Germany. See Katharina von Kellenbach, "'God Does Not Oppress Any Human Being:' The Life and Thought of Rabbi Regina Jonas." *Leo Baeck Institute Yearbook* 34 (1994): 213–25.
16 See Pamela S. Nadell, *Women Who Would Be Rabbis: A History of Women's Ordination, 1889–1985* (Boston: Beacon Press, 1998).
17 Ibid., 149.
18 Ibid., 165.
19 Letter from Sally Priesand to Jonathan Brown, August 30, 1996.
20 Jonathan Brown, conversation with Helen Glueck, January 1995.
21 In a letter Helen wrote to Priesand after Glueck's death, in response to Priesand's presentation at a memorial service in Cincinnati: "I read with great interest your beautiful talk. You gave a wonderful review of his life and a

wonderful description of his personality. I have already told you how meaningful your ordination would have been for him, and how he would have loved to
have seen that day. And I am sure when I see you ordained, in my mind's eye, it
will be his hands on your shoulders, for no matter whose hands are there, the
meaning will be clear: the continuity of Jewish life and his immortality of spirit."
Letter from Helen Glueck to Sally Priesand, March 19, 1971. Provided to Jonathan Brown by Sally Priesand.

22 Telegram to Rissa Alex, July 26, 1968. Folder A1a, A-B, Box 165, AJA.

23 Syme, "Growth," 141–42.

24 MacGregor had taught a course in theology at the original HUC-California
campus on Appian Way.

25 Jonathan Brown, conversation with Alfred Gottschalk, February 2, 2000. According to Gottschalk, Glueck had to be dragged into the project; he seemed as little
interested in strengthening HUC's presence in Los Angeles as he had initially
been in maintaining the Jewish Institute of Religion's authority to ordain rabbis
in New York City.

26 Quoted from a copy of the speech in Jonathan Brown's possession.

27 Syme, "Growth," 142–43. In 1964 he announced a $500,000 gift from the Regen-
stein family of Chicago for the establishment of the Joseph and Helen Regenstein
Chair in Religion, Ethics, and Human Relations. About a year later, the Nelson
Glueck Chair of Bible was established, as well as the Milton and Hattie Kutz
Chair in American Jewish History.

28 An amusing incident attended his departure from the States. Glueck had told
the dean of the California School, Alfred Gottschalk, about his plans and said
to him: "Fred, I need you in Jerusalem. Come as soon as you can." Gottschalk
dutifully made his plans, and as soon as the State Department embargo on
travel was lifted, took a flight from New York to Jerusalem. He hastened to
Glueck's apartment at HUC-BAS. When he entered, Glueck looked up from his
desk and said: "Why, Fred, what in the world are you doing here?" Conversation with Jonathan Brown in January 1999.

29 Nelson Glueck, *Dateline: Jerusalem. A Diary* (Cincinnati: Hebrew Union College
Press, 1968) 10.

30 Ibid., 15.

31 Ibid., 66.

32 Glueck noted: "There are literally thousands of college men and women from
the USA, South Africa, and England in the country, who would give their eye-
teeth to be given an opportunity to join our dig as volunteers." Ibid., 32.

33 Martin Gilbert, *Jerusalem in the Twentieth Century* (New York: John Wiley,
1996), 296.

34 Glueck, *Dateline,* 42.

35 Addendum A, President's report to the Board of Governors, February 5, 1970.

36 *Central Conference of American Rabbis Yearbook* 80 (1971): 71–74 [Hebrew].

37 Ibid., 73.

38 Ibid.

Chapter 15: Intimations of Mortality

1 Daniel Syme, "The Growth of the Hebrew Union College-Jewish Institute of Religion in the United States and Abroad." Unpublished rabbinical thesis (HUC-JIR, Cincinnati, 1972), 155. Students and faculty participated in five days of general seminars and a week in Washington. The Board was assured that all academic work would be completed by early fall. Ibid., 156. Glueck's positive impression of American college students had been articulated in a *Cincinnati Enquirer* article November 27, 1968: "They are much less interested in personal security than in creating a better world. The restlessness of youth today is basically idealistic and commands respect and admiration. Young people lack experience and judgment frequently, but I feel the values that impel them are good."

2 Glueck's intention to retire was no secret. A note from Norman P. Auburn, President of the University of Akron, thanking Glueck for an inscribed copy of *The Other Side of the Jordan*, contained the comment: "We shall both be entering post-retirement assignments soon, and I know that you too, will always have engrossing plans." Manuscript Collection 20, Box Ala-165, Folder A. AJA To the Vice-President and Provost for Academic Affairs at the University of Cincinnati, Glueck had written in September: "I can assure you mine will be an active retirement. I shall probably never catch up with all the writing that I have to do, although I have during the years, somehow or other, made the time to keep up a good portion of my academic work."

3 Ahad Ha-Am (1856–1927), the pen name of Asher Zvi Ginsberg, means "one of the people." His form of Zionism came to be known as cultural Zionism.

4 Appendix D, President's report to the Board of Governors, HUC-JIR, Cincinnati, Ohio, November 12, 1970, 16.

5 This arrangement was intended to ensure that it would be Glueck who would ordain Sally Priesand.

6 On October 2, Glueck had sent a note to S.L. Kopald, chairman of the Board of Governors, containing a description of the role of chancellor, which was modeled on the arrangement proposed to the Board of Brandeis University by its retiring president, Abram Sachar.

7 Appendix D, 3–4.

8 Garden City, New York: Doubleday & Company, Inc., 1970. Sanders at the time was the Auburn Professor of Biblical Studies at Union Theological Seminary in New York.

9 Sanders, ibid., xiii–xiv.

10 Manuscript collection no. 20, Box ala-168, Folder L AJA.

11 It would prove to be her last commission for HUC-BAS. There were problems with the building and a disagreement between the College and Ms. Melamede about the amount she was entitled to be paid for her services.

12 Syme, "Growth," 156.

13 Appendix D, President's Report to the Board of Governors, HUC-JIR, Cincinnati, Ohio, November 12, 1970. Not long after Glueck's death, efforts were made to acquire an additional twelve dunams of land originally withheld from the

property leased to HUC-JIR in Jerusalem in 1956. The College needed space for a library, an archaeological museum, and an auditorium. Meanwhile, the UAHC also expressed interest in building on the property. They wanted a youth hostel, classrooms, an educational resource center, and office space.

14 JRM Center Manuscript collection no. 20, box ala-165, folder A.

15 Ibid. In a letter to Adler the previous week, Glueck had added: "It probably wouldn't be noticed any more were it not for the swelling by the surgery on my neck to determine whether the tumor was local."

16 JRM Center. Manuscript collection no. 20, box ala-165, folder B.

17 November 27, 1970. JRM Center. Manuscript collection no. 20, box ala-166, folder F.

18 Folder D, Manuscript collection no. 20, box ala-166, JRM Center

19 JRM Center. Manuscript collection no. 20, box ala-165, folder D.

20 JRM Center. Manuscript collection no. 20, box ala-165, folder A.

21 The weekly portion for that Sabbath was *Yitro*, Exodus 18:1–20:23. In this portion, Moses' father-in-law Jethro instructs him in the need to delegate responsibility so that Moses would be able to focus on the most important issues (Exodus 18:13–26).

22 "Aḥarei Moti" (After My Death), *Songs from Bialik: Selected Poems of Hayim Nahman Bialik,* ed. and trans. Atar Hadari (Syracuse: Syracuse University Press, 2000), 59.

23 A reference to David's love for Jonathan, Saul's son, in his lament over Jonathan's death at the hands of the Philistines (II Samuel, 1:26).

24 A written tribute by Gottschalk can be found in the *CCAR Yearbook* 81 (1971): 62–63.

25 Following her death on August 8, 1995, Helen was interred next to her husband.

Conclusion: A Man of Rare Vision

1 Golda Meir. *A Land of Our Own: An Oral Biography* (New York: Putnam and Sons, 1973), 178. Meir also spoke about Yigael Yadin, whom she believed "shared this sense of concreteness of our physical relationship with the soil and atmosphere of the very land of Israel. They and their fellow archeologists here dwell on the natural and blessed link between the Jewish spirit and the concrete facts of our history, our rootedness in the soil of this holy land."

2 August 27, 1967. Glueck correspondence, JRM Center, AJA, Cincinnati.

3 Bamberger was speaking at a memorial service at Temple Emanu-El in New York, March 25, 1971.

4 Nelson Glueck Memorial Volume, ed. B. Mazar (Jerusalem: Israel Exploration Society, 1975), x.

5 BASOR, April 1971: 2–5.

6 Correspondence between Kenneth Roseman and Jonathan Brown, April, 1997.

7 The first volume of Edward R. Murrow, *This I Believe* (New York: Simon and Schuster, 1952), 60.

Bibliography

Primary Sources

Items for which no location is given are in possession of the authors.

American Jewish Archives (Jacob R. Marcus Center), Cincinnati, Ohio

Nelson Glueck Files   Kaufmann Kohler Files

Robert A. Goldman Files   Julian Morgenstern Files

American Schools of Oriental Research *Newsletters* (1932–1947, 1985, 1991).

Blank, Sheldon. Unpublished autobiography, 1988.

Curtis, Sanford. "Family Notes." Part of the 1992 Glueck family reunion volume.

Dever, William. "Report from Jerusalem on the Third Day of Fighting." June 7, 1967.

Ginzei Am Olam (The Archives of the Eternal People), Hebrew University/Givat Ram campus, Jerusalem. Judah Leon Magnes Files.

Family sheaf of letters (supplied by Barbara Glueck). Collected letters from 1923–1946.

Family Tree and Directory, 1992. Part of the 1992 Glueck family reunion volume.

Glueck, Charles and Barbara. "In Anticipation of Maturation," a poem written on the occasion of Glueck's sixtieth birthday.

Glueck, Helen. "My Father the Doctor." Unpublished pamphlet (1946).

Glueck, Nelson. "The Voice of Jerusalem, by Israel Zangwill." *HUC Monthly* 8, no. 2 (December, 1921).

——. "On the Trail of King Solomon's Mines." *The National Geographic Magazine* 85,2 (February, 1944): 233–56.

——. "The Geography of the Jordan." *The National Geographic Magazine* 86, 6 (December, 1944): 719–44.

——. "An Archeologist Looks at Palestine." *The National Geographic Magazine* 92,6 (December, 1947): 739–52.

——. "Explorations in Eastern Palestine." *AASOR* XIV (1934), XV (1935), XVIII–XIX (1939) and XXC–XVIII (1951).

——. "Kilwa." *The Illustrated London News* (June 3, 1933).

——. Dedicatory address at opening of the Hebrew Union College-Biblical Archaeological School in Jerusalem, March 27, 1963. In Hebrew.

——. "Lessons from the Past." Baccalaureate Address at the University of Southern California, 1964. Published in pamphlet form by the University of Southern California, pp. 9–20.

——. "Lion of Judah." Address delivered at a "Memorial Hour" in tribute to Dr. Judah Leon Magnes, 1958.

——. Mimeographed newsletters from Israel: June 28–August 12, 1969; December 12–26, 1969; March 3–19, 1970; July 18–August 24, 1970

——. President's Report to the Board of Governors: February 2, 1967, June 2, 1967, October 24, 1967, February 8, 1968, June 7, 1968, October 31, 1968, February 6, 1969, June 5, 1969, October 23, 1969, February 6, 1970, November 12, 1970. Citations from earlier meetings of the Board are found in Syme, "Growth."

——. Presidential Newsletters dated February 1962, November 1962, March, 1964, September 1964, October 1966.

——. *The Other Side of the Jordan*. New Haven: American Schools of Oriental Research, 1940.

——. *Dateline: Jerusalem. A Diary by Nelson Glueck*. Cincinnati: Hebrew Union College Press, 1968.

——. *Deities and Dolphins: The Story of the Nabataeans*. New York: Farrar, Strauss and Giroux, 1964.

——. *Explorations in Eastern Palestine*, Vols. 1–4. Baltimore: ASOR, 1934–1951.

——. *Ḥesed in the Bible.* Trans. Alfred Gottschalk. Cincinnati: Hebrew Union College Press, 1967.

——. *The River Jordan.* Philadelphia: The Jewish Publication Society of America, 1946.

——. *Rivers in the Desert. A History of the Negev.* Philadelphia: The Jewish Publication Society of America, 1959.

Hebrew Union College Inauguration Volume. Cincinnati: Hebrew Union College Press, March 1948.

Hebrew Union College Jubilee Volume, 1875–1925 (Cincinnati: Hebrew Union College Press), 1925.

Herst, Roger. "A Roman Incident." 6 pages. Typescript. 1999.

Hilton, Robert. Copies of Glueck's presentations at the Cincinnati Literary Club, 1950–1966 on a variety of subjects related to archaeology.

Iglauer, Gene. "A Biography of Nelson Glueck." 8 pages. Typescript. 1995.

Klein, Gary M. "Nelson Glueck: A Leader of Liberal Jewry." Unpublished rabbinical thesis (Cincinnati: HUC-JIR), 1975.

Melamede, Ruth. Personal letters; articles about her father, Yitzhak Melamede, and correspondence relating to the construction of the Feinstein Building on the HUC-BAS campus in Jerusalem.

Perlmutter, Hayyim Goren. Correspondence relating to the proposed change in the name of HUC-JIR. 1957.

Plaut, W. Gunther. Material relating to his arrival in Cincinnati in 1935 with four other rabbinical students from Germany (Wolli Kaelter, Leo Lichtenberg, Herman Schaalman and Alfred Wolf).

Revel, Nathan. Family newsletters, 1941–1944.

Sachs, Miriam Blank. Material from the 15th anniversary celebration of Glueck's presidency of HUC-JIR and a copy of a program performed by HUC students at Rockdale Temple in 1922.

Stone, Ariel. "Im Tirtzu Eyn Zo Aggadah: The story of HUC-JIR in Jerusalem." Unpublished manuscript, 1993.

Syme, Daniel. "The Growth of the Hebrew Union College-Jewish Institute of Religion in the United States and Abroad." Unpublished rabbinical thesis (HUC-JIR, Cincinnati), 1972.

Turner, Rachel Revel. "A Biography of Nelson Glueck." February 1, 1957.

Part of the 1992 Glueck Family reunion papers.

Weiner, Herbert. Correspondence and a newsletter relating to his taking administrative responsibility for HUC-BAS between October, 1962 and March, 1963.

Newspapers

Cincinnati Enquirer

Cincinnati Post and Times-Star

The American Israelite (Cincinnati)

The New York Times

The Jerusalem Post (before 1948: *The Palestine Post*)

Ma'ariv

Other Periodicals

Discovery, University of Cincinnati Medical Center, Fall / Winter, 1990

Hebrew Union College Bulletin (1951, 1955, 1962)

Hebrew Union College Monthly (1916–1923; 1941–1957)

variant: *A Journal of Student Opinion* (1961–1969)

Woodward (Cincinnati) High School *Yearbook*, 1916

University of Cincinnati *Yearbook*, 1920

Yearbook of the Central Conference of American Rabbis (CCAR) (1929, 1941, 1942, 1947, 1970, 1971)

Interviews by Jonathan Brown

ISRAEL

Archaeologists: Yosef Amiram, Avraham Biran, Moshe and Trude Dothan, Israel Finkelstein, Seymour Gitin, Deborah Hershman, Avraham Malamat, Binyamin Mazar, Lawrence Stager, and David Usshishkin.

HUC Jerusalem Faculty and Staff: Michael Chernick, Gad Granach, Esther Lee, Inna Pomerantz.

Others: Teddy Kollek, Hava Magnes, Ruth Melamede, Yosef and Yehudit Shadur, Ilan Troen.

UNITED STATES

HUC-JIR Faculty, Administration, and Staff: Eugene Borowitz, Ruth Cohen, Edward Goldman, Alfred Gottschalk, Samuel Greengus, Robert L. Katz, Jacob R. Marcus, Eugene Mihaly, Philip Miller, Herbert Paper, Ellis Rivkin, Kenneth Roseman, Richard Sarason, Ezra Spicehandler, Paul Steinberg, and Herbert Zafren.

HUC Alumni: Gustav Buchdahl, Stanley Garfein, Wolli Kaelter, Gunther Plaut, Sally Priesand. Additional alumni who offered material via e-mail and written correspondence include Hillel Cohn, David Hachen, Hayyim Goren Perlmutter, and Harold Waintrup.

Family Members: Helen Glueck, Hillel Glueck, Josephine Joseph, Alan Shapiro, Jerry, Regine, and William Ransohoff, Tasia Revel, and Barbara Weinberger Glueck.

Others: Reuben Bullard, William Dever, Frances Magnes, Richard Scheuer, and Audrey Skirball Kenis.

Interviews by Lawrence Kutler

Scholars: Ruth Amiran, William Dever, Trude Dothan, David Noel Freedman, Seymour Gitin, Cyrus Gordon, Burke Long, Eric Meyers, Beno Rothenberg, G. Ernest Wright.

HUC Jerusalem: Inna Pomerantz

Others: Helen Glueck, Ruth Melamede, Omar Jibrin (cook at ASOR)

Cassette Tapes

Interviews with members of the HUC-JIR Board of Governors, recorded by Rabbi Joseph Glaser and Carol Green, 1971.

Funeral of Nelson Glueck, 1971. At the JRM Center, AJA, Cincinnati.

Interview with Dora Aaronsohn by five HUC students, 1961. At the JRM Center, AJA, Cincinnati.

Secondary Sources

ABBREVIATIONS

AASOR *Annual of the American Schools of Oriental Research*

ADAJ *Annual of the Department of Antiquities, Jordan*

BAR *Biblical Archaeological Review*

BASOR *Bulletin of the American Schools of Oriental Research*

PEQ *Palestine Exploration Quarterly*

QDAP *Quarterly, Department of Antiquities*, Palestine

ZDPV *Zeitschrift des deutschen Palästina Vereins*

Aharoni, Yohanan. *The Archaeology of the Land of Israel, from the Prehistoric Beginnings to the End of the First Temple Period.* Philadelphia: The Westminster Press, 1978

Albright, William F. "Excavations and Results at Tell el-Ful (Gibeah of Saul)." *AASOR* 4 (1924)

——. "The Excavation of Tell Beit Mirsim III: The Iron Age." *AASOR* 12 (1943): 21–22.

Archaeological Discoveries in the Holy Land. Compiled by the Archaeological Institute of America. New York: Bonanza Books, 1967.

Bamberger, Fritz. "The Mind of Nelson Glueck." In James A. Sanders, ed. *Near Eastern Archaeology in the Twentieth Century: Essays in Honor of Nelson Glueck.* New York: Doubleday, 1979.

Bell, Gertrude. *The Letters of Gertrude Bell.* New York: Boni and Liveright, 1927.

Belt, Don. "Petra: Ancient City of Stone." *National Geographic Magazine* 194,6 (December, 1998): 116–33.

Ben-Gurion, David. *Memoirs*. New York and Cleveland: The World Publishing Company, 1970.

Bentwich, Norman. *For Zion's Sake: A Biography of Judah L. Magnes, First Chancellor and First President of the Hebrew University of Jerusalem.* Philadelphia: Jewish Publication Society of America, 1954.

——. *My Seventy Seven Years: An Account of My Life and Times.* Philadelphia: Jewish Publication Society, 1961.

——. *The Hebrew University of Jerusalem 1918–1960.* London: Weidenfeld and Nicolson, 1961.

—— and Helen Bentwich. *Mandate Memories 1918–1948.* New York: Schocken Books, 1965.

Brenner, Michael. *The Renaissance of Jewish Culture in Weimar Germany.* New Haven: Yale University Press, 1996.

Daikanai, D. "Orḥim be-Yisrael" (Guests in Israel). *Ma'ariv* (July 31, 1953).

Dever, William. "Excavations at Gezer." *The Biblical Archaeologist* 24, 4 (1971): 94–132.

——. "Gezer Revisited: New Excavations of the Solomonic and Assyrian Period Defenses." *Biblical Archaeologist* 47, 4 (December, 1984): 206–18.

Eban, Abba. *Abba Eban: An Autobiography.* New York: Random House, 1997.

Elkins, Dov Peretz. "The Rediscovery of the Nabataeans." *Judaism* (Spring, 1966): 240–42.

Falk, Randall M. *Bright Eminence: The Life and Thought of Jacob Rader Marcus.* Malibu, CA: Pangloss Press, 1994.

Feige, Michael. "Identity, Ritual and Pilgrimage: The Meetings of the Israel Exploration Society." In *Divergent Jewish Culture: Israel and America*, ed. Deborah Dash Moore and S. Ilan Troen. New Haven and London: Yale University Press, 2001, 87–106.

Fierman, Floyd. "Rabbi Nelson Glueck: An Archaeologist's Secret Life in the Service of the OSS." *BAR* 12, 5 (September/October, 1986):18–22.

Finkelstein, J. J. "A Review of Rivers in the Desert." *Commentary* 27, 4 (April, 1959): 341–50.

Fritz, Volkmar. *The City in Ancient Israel.* Sheffield: Sheffield Academic Press, 1995.

Gilbert, Martin. *Jerusalem in the Twentieth Century.* New York: John Wiley & Sons, 1996.

Hess, R. "Early Israel in Canaan: A Survey of Recent Evidence and Interpretations." *PEQ* 125 (1993): 125–41.

Horsfield, George and Agnes. "Sela-Petra, The Rock of Edom and Nabatene." *QDAP* 7 (1938): 87–115 and 9 (1942): 105–204.

Hebrew Union College-Jewish Institute of Religion at One Hundred Years, ed. Samuel Karff. Cincinnati: Hebrew Union College Press, 1976.

King, Philip J. *American Archaeology in the Mideast.* Philadelphia: ASOR, 1983.

King, Philip J. "ASOR at 85." *Biblical Archaeologist* 47, 4 (December, 1984): 197–205.

Kollek, Amos and Teddy Kollek. *For Jerusalem: A Life.* New York: Behrman House, 1978.

Kuklick, Bruce. *Puritans in Babylon: The Ancient Near East and American Intellectual Life, 1830–1930.* Princeton: Princeton University Press, 1996.

Long, Burke O. "Mythic Trope in the Autobiography of Albright." *Biblical Archaeology* 56, 1 (1993): 36–45.

——. *The Planting and Reaping of Albright: Politics, Ideology and Interpreting the Bible.* University Park: Pennsylvania State University Press, 1997.

Lowdermilk, Walter Clay. *Palestine: Land of Promise.* New York: Harper Brothers, 1944.

Ma'ayeh, Farah. "Recent Archaeological Discoveries in Jordan." *QDAP* 4 and 5 (1960): 114–16 and plate 3.

Magnes, Beatrice L. *Episodes: A Memoir.* Berkeley: Judah L. Magnes Museum, 1977.

Mazar, Amichai. *Archaeology and the Land of the Bible: 10,000–586 B.C.E.* New York: Doubleday and Company, 1992.

Meyer, Michael A. "A Centennial History." In *HUC-JIR at One Hundred Years*, ed. Samuel Karff. Cincinnati: Hebrew Union College Press, 1976.

——. "From Cincinnati to New York: A Symbolic Move." In *The Jewish Condition: Essays on Contemporary Judaism Honoring Rabbi Alexander M. Schindler*, ed. Aron Hirt-Manheimer. New York: UAHC Press, 1995, 302–13.

——. *Response to Modernity: A History of the Reform Movement in Judaism.* New York: Oxford University Press, 1988.

Morgenstern, Julian. "The Next Stage in Jewish Biblical Scholarship." *Hebrew Union College Quarterly* (First Quarter, 1949): 4–7.

Murrow, Edward R. Murrow. *This I Believe.* New York: Simon and Schuster, 1952.

Nadell, Pamela S. *Women Who Would Be Rabbis: A History of Women's Ordination, 1889–1985.* Boston: Beacon Press, 1998.

Near Eastern Archaeology in the Twentieth Century, ed. James Sanders. Garden City, New York: Doubleday, 1970.

O'Donnell, Patrick. *Operatives, Spies, and Saboteurs: The Unknown Story of the Men and Women of World War II's OSS.* New York: Free Press, 2004.

Pratico, Gary. *Nelson Glueck's 1938–1940 Excavations at Tell el-Kheleifeh: A Reappraisal.* Atlanta: Scholars Press, 1994.

——. "Where is Etzion-geber? A Reappraisal of the Site Archaeologist Nelson Glueck Identified as King Solomon's Red Sea Port." *BAR* 12, 5 (September/October 1986): 24–35.

Pritchard, James B. *Archaeology and the Old Testament.* Princeton: Princeton University Press, 1958.

Rothenberg, Beno. *The Egyptian Mining Temple of Timnah.* London: Institute for Archaeo-Metallurgical Studies, 1988.

Rothkoff, Aaron. *Bernard Revel: Builder of American Jewish Orthodoxy.* Philadelphia: Jewish Publication Society of America, 1972.

Running, Leona G., and David Noel Freedman. *William Foxwell Albright.* New York: Two Continents Morgan Press, 1975.

Sanders, James, A., ed. *Near Eastern Archaeology in the Twentieth Century. Essays in Honor of Nelson Glueck.* Garden City, New York: Doubleday & Company, Inc., 1979.

Sarna, Jonathan and Nancy Klein. *The Jews of Cincinnati.* Cincinnati: Center for the Study of the American Jewish Experience, 1989.

Schulman, Avi M. *Like a Raging Fire: A Biography of Maurice N. Eisendrath.* New York: UAHC Press, 1993.

Sherman, A. J. *Mandate Days: British Lives in Palestine 1918–1948.* New York: Thames and Hudson, 1998.

Silberman, Neal Asher. *Digging for God and Country: Exploration, Archaeology, and the Secret Struggle for the Holy Land 1799–1917.* New York: Knopf, 1982.

Silberman, Neil Asher and David B. Small, eds. *The Archaeology of Israel: Constructing the Past, Interpreting the Present.* Sheffield (England): Sheffield University Press, 1997.

Slomovitz, Albert J. *The Fighting Rabbis: Jewish Military Chaplains and American History.* New York and London: New York University Press, 1999.

Stern, Ellen Norman. *Dreamer in the Desert: A Profile of Nelson Glueck.* New York: Ktav, 1980.

Urofsky, Melvin I. *A Voice that Spoke for Justice: The Life and Times of Stephen S. Wise.* Albany: State University of New York Press, 1982.

Van Beek, Gus. *The Scholarship of William Foxwell Albright: An Appraisal.* Semitics Studies 33, Atlanta: Scholars Press, 1989.

Wasserstein, Bernard. *The British in Palestine: The Mandatory Government and the Arab Jewish Conflict 1917–1929.* Oxford: Oxford University Press, 1991.

Winstone, H. V. F. *Woolley of Ur.* London: Secker and Warburg, 1990.

Wright, G. Ernest. "Is Glueck's Aim to Prove that the Bible is True?" *BAR* 22:4 (1996): 101–8.

——. and David Noel Freedman. *The Biblical Archaeological Reader.* New York: Anchor Books, 1961.

Yadin, Yigael. "Nelson Glueck: A Memorial Address." In *Eretz Yisrael*, vol. 12. Jerusalem: Israel Exploration Society, 1975.

Biblical and Ancient Near Eastern Sites and Topographical Features

General Index